T0096582

A Psalter
for Prayer

An Adaptation of the Classic Miles Coverdale
Translation, Augmented by Prayers and
Instructional Material Drawn from Church
Slavonic and Other Orthodox Christian Sources

Pocket Edition

Compiled, arranged, and edited by
David Mitchell James

HOLY TRINITY PUBLICATIONS
The Printshop of St. Job of Pochaev
Holy Trinity Monastery
Jordanville, New York

Printed with the blessing of
His Eminence, Metropolitan Hilarion,
First Hierarch of the Russian Orthodox Church
Outside of Russia,
and of His Grace, the Right Reverend Jerome,
Chairman of the Synodal Translation Committee.

Text © David Mitchell James 2011
Pocket edition © 2016 Holy Trinity Monastery
Second Printing of the Pocket Edition 2019

PRINTSHOP OF
SAINT JOB OF POCHAEV

An imprint of

HOLY TRINITY PUBLICATIONS
Holy Trinity Monastery
Jordanville, New York 13361-0036
www.holytrinitypublications.com

ISBN: 978-0-88465-418-6 (Pocket edition)
ISBN: 978-0-88465-474-2 (Hardback 7 inch x 10 inch)
ISBN: 978-0-88465-188-8 (Hardback 8.5 inch x 11 inch)
ISBN: 978-0-88465-198-7 (ePub)
ISBN: 978-0-88465-234-2 (Mobipocket)

Library of Congress Control Number 2010917032

Contents

How the Psalter Is to Be Said Throughout the Whole Year

¶ From the Sunday after Pascha, which is called Thomas Sunday, until the apodosis of the Exaltation of the Precious and Life-Giving Cross, we undertake to recite the Psalter thusly:

On the Saturday of Bright Week at Vespers, we say the 1st kathisma, *Blessed is the man;* on Sunday at Matins, the 2nd and 3rd kathismata, but the 17th kathisma is not said, since the Polyeleos is sung. On other Sundays, when the Polyeleos is not sung, at Matins we also say the 17th kathisma, with its troparia.

But if a Sunday should coincide with a feast of the Lord, or of the Theotokos, or of a commemorated saint, after the two kathismata is the Polyeleos, and after the Megalynarion, having not sung *Glory, both now* or *Alleluia,* we sing the troparia, *The assembly of angels;* and after the litany, the sessional hymn of the feast, or of the saint.

On Sunday at Vespers throughout the whole year the Psalter is never read, except, if a feast should occur, then we sing, *Blessed is the man,* the first antiphon.

On Monday at Matins, the 4th and 5th kathismata. At Vespers, the 6th kathisma. On Tuesday

at Matins, the 7th and 8th kathismata. At Vespers,
the 9th kathisma. On Wednesday at Matins, the
10th and 11th kathismata. At Vespers, the 12th
kathisma. On Thursday at Matins, the 13th and
14th kathismata. At Vespers, the 15th kathisma.
On Friday at Matins, the 19th and 20th kathismata. At Vespers, the 18th kathisma. On Saturday
at Matins, the 16th and 17th kathismata. But at the
Midnight Office, on Monday, Tuesday, Wednesday,
Thursday, and Friday throughout the whole year,
we say the 17th kathisma, *Blessed are the blameless in the way;* but on Saturday at the Midnight
Office, we always say the 9th kathisma, *Unto Thee,
O God, belongeth praise in Zion.*

¶ After the apodosis of the feast of the Exaltation
   of the Precious and Life-Giving Cross, from the
   22nd day of the month of September, until the
   20th day of the month of December, we undertake to say the Psalter as here set forth:

On Saturday at Vespers, the 1st kathisma,
Blessed is the man. On Sunday at Matins, the 2nd
and 3rd kathismata, to which we add the Polyeleos
(meaning, "greatly merciful"), i.e., Psalm 134, *O
praise ye the Name of the Lord,* and Psalm 135, *O
give thanks unto the Lord,* and immediately the
troparia, *The assembly of angels,* and the Hypakoe
of the tone.

But if a feast of the Lord, or of the Theotokos, or
a commemorated saint, should fall on a Sunday,

then after the psalms *O praise ye the Name of the Lord,* and *O give thanks unto the Lord,* the megalynarion of the feast, and the selected psalm, and the troparia, *The assembly of angels,* and the sessional hymn of the feast. On Monday after the Exaltation, at Matins, the 4th, 5th, and 6th kathismata; but at Vespers throughout the whole week we say the 18th kathisma. On Tuesday at Matins, the 7th, 8th, and 9th kathismata. On Wednesday at Matins, the 10th, 11th, and 12th kathismata. On Thursday at Matins, the 13th, 14th, and 15th kathismata. On Friday at Matins, the 19th and 20th kathismata. On Saturday at Matins, the 16th and 17th kathismata. But if a feast should coincide with a day on which three kathismata are appointed at Matins, then we say the first two kathismata at Matins, and the 3rd follows at Vespers.

As generally in the rubrics, from the 22nd day of the month of September, three kathismata are appointed at Matins. Even if the day before or after the 20th should be a Sunday, without exception from Monday we begin the recitation of three kathismata.

¶ From the 20th day of the month of December, until the 14th day of the month of January, which is the apodosis of the feast of Holy Theophany.

We again recite the Psalter, as on the Sunday after Pascha, which is Thomas Sunday, with two kathismata at Matins, and the third in order at Vespers.

From the 15th day of the month of January, until the Saturday before the Sunday of the Prodigal Son, we again recite the Psalter at Matins with three kathismata, and at Vespers the 18th kathisma, *When I was in trouble I called upon the Lord.*

But on the two Sundays, Meatfare and Cheesefare, we say two kathismata at Matins, and at Vespers a third in sequence, because the brethren have little rest. But on the Sunday of the Prodigal, and on Meatfare, and on Cheesefare, at Matins, after the psalms *O praise ye the Name of the Lord,* and *O give thanks unto the Lord,* we sing also a third, Psalm 136, *By the waters of Babylon,* with the beautiful *Alleluia,* followed by the troparia, *The assembly of angels,* and the Hypakoe of the tone.

Let it be known how, from Cheesefare Sunday even until the Exaltation of the Precious Cross, the Polyeleos is celebrated; it is sung only at vigils of feasts of the Lord. But after the apodosis of the Exaltation of the Precious and Life-Giving Cross of the Lord, even until Cheesefare Sunday, except during the forefeasts and afterfeasts of the Nativity of Christ and of Theophany, in cathedrals and in other large churches, on Sundays at Matins the Polyeleos is sung, and likewise in larger monastic communities.

¶ The rule for how the Psalter is to be recited during the Holy and Great Fast.

In the 1st, 2nd, 3rd, 4th, and 6th weeks, so that each kathisma will be read according to its time, and that no kathisma be omitted:

On Saturday at Vespers, the 1st kathisma, *Blessed is the man;* on Sunday at Matins, the 2nd, 3rd, and 17th kathismata. On Monday at Matins, the 4th, 5th, and 6th kathismata. At the 1st Hour there is no kathisma. At the Hours, the 7th, 8th, and 9th kathismata. At Vespers on all these weekdays we say the 18th kathisma, *When I was in trouble I called upon the Lord.* On Tuesday at Matins, kathismata 10, 11, 12. At the 1st Hour, kathisma 13. At the Hours, kathismata 14, 15, 16. On Wednesday at Matins, kathismata 19, 20, 1. At the 1st Hour, the 2nd kathisma. At the Hours, the 3rd, 4th, and 5th kathismata. On Thursday at Matins, the 6th, 7th, and 8th kathismata. At the 1st Hour, kathisma 9. At the Hours, kathismata 10, 11, 12. On Friday at Matins, kathismata 13, 14, 15. At the 1st Hour there is no kathisma. At the Hours, kathismata 19, 20. At the 9th Hour there is no kathisma. On Saturday at Matins, kathismata 16, 17. And thus is the rule of the Psalter carried out.

¶ The decree concerning how to say the kathismata during the fifth week of the Holy Great Fast.

On Saturday at Vespers, the 1st kathisma. On Sunday at Matins, the 2nd, 3rd, and 17th kathismata, but at Vespers there is no kathisma. On Monday at Matins, the 4th, 5th, and 6th kathismata. At the 1st Hour there is no kathisma. At the Hours, the 7th, 8th, and 9th kathismata. At Vespers, the 10th kathisma. On Tuesday at Matins, the 11th, 12th, and 13th kathismata. At the 1st Hour, the 14th kathisma. At the Hours, the 15th, 16th, and 18th kathismata. At Vespers, the 19th kathisma. On Wednesday at Matins, the 20th, 1st, and 2nd kathismata. At the 1st Hour, the 3rd kathisma. At the Hours, the 4th, 5th, and 6th kathismata. At Vespers, the 7th kathisma. On Thursday at Matins, the 8th kathisma. At the 1st Hour there is no kathisma. At the Hours, the 9th, 10th, and 11th kathismata. At Vespers, the 12th kathisma. On Friday at Matins, the 13th, 14th, and 15th kathismata. At the 1st Hour there is no kathisma. At the Hours, the 19th and 20th kathismata. At the 9th Hour there is no kathisma. At Vespers, the 18th kathisma. And so is the rule of the Psalter carried out.

¶ It is fitting to know how to say the Psalter during the Holy and Great Heptad of Passion Week. Let it also be known that, during this holy Great Week, we recite the Psalter only in church. It is recited in this manner:

On Lazarus Saturday at Vespers, the 1st kathisma. On Palm Sunday at Matins, the 2nd and

3rd kathismata. On Monday at Matins, the 4th, 5th, and 6th kathismata. At the 1st Hour there is no kathisma. At the Hours, the 7th and 8th kathismata. At the 9th Hour there is no kathisma. At Vespers, the 18th kathisma. On Tuesday at Matins, the 9th, 10th, and 11th kathismata. At the 1st Hour there is no kathisma. At the Hours, the 12th and 13th kathismata. At the 9th Hour there is no kathisma. At Vespers, the 18th kathisma. On Great Wednesday at Matins, the 14th, 15th, and 16th kathismata. At the 1st Hour there is no kathisma. At the Hours, the 19th and 20th kathismata. On this same Wednesday at Vespers, the 18th kathisma, without bows. And then we lay aside the Psalter until the eve of Thomas Sunday at Vespers.

The Seven-Bow Beginning

The Prayer of the Publican

God be merciful to me a sinner. Bow.

Thou hast created me, O Lord; have mercy upon me. Bow.

I have sinned immeasurably; Lord, have mercy and forgive me, a sinner. Bow.

IT is truly meet to bless thee, O Theotokos, ever-blessed and most pure, and the Mother of our God. More honorable than the Cherubim, and incomparably more glorious than the Seraphim; who without corruption gavest birth to God the Word, the very Theotokos, thee do we magnify. And a prostration, always.

Glory be to the Father, and to the Son, and to the Holy Spirit. Bow.

Both now, and ever, and unto the ages of ages. Amen. Bow

Lord, have mercy. Thrice.

LORD Jesus Christ, Son of God, through the prayers of Thy most pure Mother, by the power of the precious and life-giving Cross, by the prayers of my holy guardian angel, and of all the Saints, have mercy upon me and save me a sinner, for Thou art good and lovest mankind. Amen. And a bow to the ground (without crossing oneself, if there is a priest present).

¶ All bows are made to the ground, except on Saturdays and Sundays, and on feast days; and likewise for all of the fifty days from Pascha to Pentecost, and on the twelve days of Christmas, make bows from the waist. But after **It is truly meet**, a great bow to the ground. However, on Glory ..., both now ..., it is common, outside of fasting periods, to make the bows from the waist, but after the dismissal, a bow to the ground.

These bows are made upon entering a church, or when beginning a rule of prayer, and again upon the completion of a rule of prayer, or when departing from a church, the same bows are made.

Prayers Before Reading the Psalter

Let it be with understanding that one sings the Psalter, in particular.

If there is a priest, he says:

Blessed is our God, always; now, and ever, and unto the ages of ages. Amen.

If not, say with compunction:

Through the prayers of our holy fathers, O Lord Jesus Christ our God, have mercy upon us. *Amen.*

HEAVENLY King, the Comforter, the Spirit of Truth, Who art everywhere present and fillest all things, Treasury of blessings and Giver of life: Come and abide in us, and cleanse us of every impurity, and save our souls, O Good One. Bow.

¶ From Pascha until the Feast of the Ascension, instead of the prayer, O heavenly King, the troparion for Holy Pascha, Christ is risen, is said, thrice. And from Ascension Day until Pentecost, begin with the Trisagion.

The Trisagion

Holy God, Holy Mighty, Holy Immortal, have mercy upon us. Thrice, with bows.

Glory be to the Father, and to the Son, and to the Holy Spirit; Both now, and ever, and unto the ages of ages. Amen. Bow.

O Most Holy Trinity, have mercy upon us. O Lord, wash away our sins. O Master, pardon our transgressions. O Holy One, visit and heal our infirmities for Thy Name's sake.

Lord, have mercy. Thrice.

Glory be to the Father, and to the Son, and to the Holy Spirit; Both now, and ever, and unto the ages of ages. Amen. Bow.

The Lord's Prayer

OUR Father, Who art in heaven, hallowed be Thy Name. Thy kingdom come. Thy will be done, on earth as it is in heaven. Give us this day our daily bread. And forgive us our debts, as we forgive our debtors. And lead us not into temptation; but deliver us from the evil one.

If there is a priest, he says:

For Thine is the kingdom, the power, and the glory: of the Father, and of the Son, and of the Holy Spirit; Now, and ever, and unto the ages of ages. Amen.

If not, say:

O Lord Jesus Christ, Son of God, have mercy upon us. Amen.

And these troparia, in Tone VI:

Have mercy upon us, O Lord, have mercy upon us; for at a loss for any defense, this prayer do we sinners offer unto Thee, as Master: have mercy upon us!

Glory be to the Father, and to the Son, and to the Holy Spirit;

The Church hath shown forth the honored feast of Thy prophet, O Lord, to be as heaven, for thereon the angels join chorus with men. Through his prayers, O Christ God, guide our life in peace, that we may sing unto Thee: Alleluia!

Both now, and ever, and unto the ages of ages. Amen.

Many are the multitudes of my sins, O Theotokos; unto thee have I fled, imploring salvation, O most pure one. Do thou visit my feeble soul, and entreat thy Son and our God to grant me pardon for the evil I have done, O thou only blessed one.

¶ Lord, have mercy [40]. And we make as many prostrations as we are able. Then this prayer to the holy and life-creating Trinity:

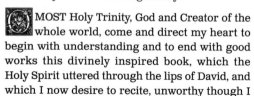 MOST Holy Trinity, God and Creator of the whole world, come and direct my heart to begin with understanding and to end with good works this divinely inspired book, which the Holy Spirit uttered through the lips of David, and which I now desire to recite, unworthy though I

am. Knowing well mine own ignorance, I fall down before Thee and pray, begging Thy help, O Lord, direct my mind, and make my heart steadfast, that I grow not weary because of the words which my lips read, but that I be gladdened with the understanding of what is read and myself prepared for the doing of the good works which I learn; and I say, Enlightened by good deeds, may I become a citizen of the land which is at Thy right hand, with all of Thine elect. And now, O Master, bless me, that, having sighed from my heart, I may sing with my tongue, saying,

O come, let us worship God, our King. Bow.

O come, let us worship and fall down before Christ, our King and God. Bow.

O come, let us worship and fall down before Christ Himself, our King and God. Bow.

¶ Stand a while, until all the senses are calm. Then begin, not rapidly, nor yet too slowly, but earnestly and with a contrite heart, saying Psalm 1, Blessed is the man, quietly, with understanding, and attentively, so that the mind may grasp what is being said.

СТЫЙ ПРРОКЪ И ѰАЛМОПѢВЕЦЪ ЦРЬ ДАВІДЪ

The Holy Prophet and Psalmist, King David

The Song of David
the Prophet and King

The First Kathisma

Psalm 1. *Beatus vir, qui non abiit &c.*
A Psalm of David. Without superscription in the
Hebrew.

BLESSED is the man that hath not walked in the counsel of the ungodly, nor stood in the way of sinners, and hath not sat in the seat of the scornful.

2 But his delight is in the Law of the Lord, and in His Law will he exercise himself day and night.

3 And he shall be like a tree planted by the waterside, that will bring forth his fruit in due season; his leaf also shall not fall, and all whatsoever he doeth, it shall prosper.

4 Not so are the ungodly, not so; but they are like the dust, which the wind scattereth away from the face of the earth.

5 Therefore the ungodly shall not rise at the

judgment, neither the sinners in the council of the righteous.

⁶ For the Lord knoweth the way of the righteous, and the way of the ungodly shall perish.

Psalm 2. *Quare fremuerunt gentes?*
A Psalm of David.

 HY have the heathen raged, and the peoples imagined vain things?

² The kings of the earth stood up, and the rulers gathered together, against the Lord, and against His Christ:

³ Let us break their bonds asunder, and cast away their cords from us.

⁴ He that dwelleth in heaven shall laugh them to scorn; the Lord shall have them in derision.

⁵ Then shall He speak unto them in His wrath, and vex them in His sore displeasure.

⁶ Yet I am set up as King by Him upon His holy hill of Zion,

⁷ Preaching the Lord's commandment. The Lord said unto Me, Thou art My Son, this day have I begotten Thee.

⁸ Desire of Me, and I shall give Thee the nations for Thine inheritance, and the utmost parts of the earth for Thy possession.

⁹ Thou shalt herd them with a rod of iron, and break them in pieces like a potter's vessel.

¹⁰ Be wise now therefore, O ye kings; be instructed, all ye that are judges of the earth.

¹¹ Serve the Lord in fear, and rejoice unto Him with trembling.

¹² Choose chastening, lest the Lord be angry, and so ye perish from the right way, when His wrath be suddenly kindled; blessed are all they that put their trust in Him.

Psalm 3. *Domine, quid multiplicati?*
A Psalm of David, when he fled from
Absalom his son.

ORD, why are they increased that trouble me? Many are they that rise against me.

³ Many one there be that say of my soul, There is no salvation for him in his God.

⁴ But Thou, O Lord, art my helper, my glory, and the lifter up of my head.

⁵ I did call upon the Lord with my voice, and He heard me out of His holy hill.

⁶ I laid me down and slept, and rose up again, for the Lord will sustain me.

⁷ I will not be afraid for ten thousands of the people that have set themselves against me round about.

⁸ Arise, O Lord; save me, O my God, for Thou hast smitten all who without cause are mine enemy; Thou hast broken the teeth of sinners.

⁹ Salvation is of the Lord, and Thy blessing is upon Thy people.

Glory be to the Father, and to the Son, and to the

Holy Spirit; both now, and ever, and unto the ages of ages. Amen.

Alleluia, alleluia, alleluia. Glory be to Thee, O God. Thrice.

Lord, have mercy. Thrice.

Glory be to the Father, and to the Son, and to the Holy Spirit; both now, and ever, and unto the ages of ages. Amen.

Second Stasis

Psalm 4. *Cum invocarem.*
Unto the end, in verses, a Psalm of David.

WHEN I called, the God of my righteousness heard me; Thou hast set me at liberty when I was in trouble. Be gracious unto me, and hearken unto my prayer.

³ O ye sons of men, how long will ye be heavy-hearted; why do ye take such pleasure in vanity, and seek after falsehood?

⁴ Know ye also, that the Lord hath made His holy one wonderful; when I call upon Him, the Lord will hear me.

⁵ Be angry, and sin not; for what ye say in your hearts, be sorry upon your beds.

⁶ Offer the sacrifice of righteousness, and put your trust in the Lord.

⁷ There be many that say, Who will show us any good? The light of Thy countenance hath been signed upon us, O Lord.

⁸ Thou hast put gladness in my heart; from the fruit of their wheat, and wine, and oil are they increased.

⁹ I will lay me down in peace, and also take my rest, for it is Thou, Lord, only, who hast made me to dwell in hope.

Psalm 5. *Verba mea auribus.*
Unto the end, for her that obtaineth the inheritance, a Psalm of David.

EAR my words, O Lord; consider my cry.
³ Attend unto the voice of my supplication, my King, and my God, for unto Thee will I pray, O Lord.

⁴ Early in the morning shalt Thou hear my voice; early in the morning will I stand before Thee, and Thou shalt watch over me.

⁵ For Thou art a God that hast no pleasure in wickedness; the evil-doer shall not dwell nigh Thee.

⁶ Such as be lawless shall not stand in Thy sight, for Thou hatest all them that work iniquity.

⁷ Thou shalt destroy all them that speak lies; the Lord will abhor the blood-thirsty and deceitful man.

⁸ But as for me, by the multitude of Thy mercy I will come into Thine house; in Thy fear will I worship toward Thy holy temple.

⁹ Lead me, O Lord, in Thy righteousness;

because of mine enemies, make my way plain before Thee.

¹⁰ For there is no truth in their mouth; their heart is vain; their throat is an open sepulcher; they flatter with their tongue.

¹¹ Judge them, O God; let them fall through their own imaginations; cast them out according to the multitude of their ungodliness; for they have embittered Thee, O Lord.

¹² And let all them that put their trust in Thee be glad; they shall ever rejoice; and Thou shalt dwell in them and they that love Thy Name shall be joyful in Thee.

¹³ For Thou wilt bless the righteous, O Lord, for with the shield of Thy favorable kindness hast Thou crowned us.

Psalm 6. *Domine, ne in furore.*
Unto the end, in verses, a Psalm of David, among the hymns for the octave.

 LORD, rebuke me not in Thine anger, neither chasten me in Thy wrath.

³ Have mercy upon me, O Lord, for I am weak; O Lord, heal me, for my bones are vexed.

⁴ My soul also is sore troubled; but Thou, O Lord, how long?

⁵ Turn Thee, O Lord, and deliver my soul; O save me, for Thy mercy's sake.

⁶ For in death no man remembereth Thee, and who will give Thee thanks in hell?

⁷ I am worn out with my groaning; every night wash I my bed, and water my couch with my tears.

⁸ Mine eye is clouded with anger; I have grown old among all mine enemies.

⁹ Away from me, all ye that work iniquity, for the Lord hath heard the voice of my weeping.

¹⁰ The Lord hath heard my petition; the Lord will receive my prayer.

¹¹ Let all mine enemies be confounded and sore vexed; let them be turned back, and put to shame suddenly.

Glory be to the Father, and to the Son, and to the Holy Spirit; both now, and ever, and unto the ages of ages. Amen.

Alleluia, alleluia, alleluia. Glory be to Thee, O God. Thrice.

Lord, have mercy. Thrice.

Glory be to the Father, and to the Son, and to the Holy Spirit; both now, and ever, and unto the ages of ages. Amen.

Third Stasis

Psalm 7. *Domine, Deus meus.*
The Psalm of David, which he sang unto the Lord,
  concerning the words of Cush the Benjamite.

 LORD my God, in Thee have I put my trust;
save me from all them that persecute me,
and deliver me;

3 Lest they seize my soul like a lion, and tear it in
pieces, while there is none to deliver, nor to save.

4 O Lord my God, if I have done any such thing,
if there be unrighteousness in my hands;

5 If I have repaid evil unto him that dealt
unfriendly with me, may I then fall back empty
before my enemies.

6 Then let the enemy persecute my soul; yea, let
him take and trample my life into the dirt, and lay
mine honor in the dust.

7 Arise, O Lord, in Thy wrath, exalt Thyself in the
borders of mine enemies, and rise up, O Lord my
God, by the injunction that Thou hast enjoined,

8 And a congregation of the peoples shall gather
round Thee; and for their sakes return Thou on
high.

9 The Lord shall judge the peoples; give sentence
with me, O Lord, according to my righteousness,
and according to the innocency that is in me.

10 O let the wickedness of sinners come to an
end, and guide Thou the righteous, O God, who
triest the very hearts and reins.

¹¹ My help is from God, who saveth them that are true of heart.

¹² God is a righteous Judge, strong, and patient, and inflicteth not vengeance every day.

¹³ Except ye be converted, He will whet His sword; He hath bent His bow, and made it ready.

¹⁴ He hath fitted it with the instruments of death; He hath forged his arrows in the fire.

¹⁵ Behold, he hath travailed with unrighteousness, he hath conceived sorrow, and brought forth iniquity.

¹⁶ He hath graven a pit, and digged it up, and is fallen himself into the hole he made,

¹⁷ For his travail shall come upon his own head, and his unrighteousness shall fall on his own pate.

¹⁸ I will give thanks unto the Lord, according to His righteousness, and I will praise the Name of the Lord Most High.

Psalm 8. *Domine, Dominus noster.*
Unto the end, on the presses, a Psalm of David.

LORD, our Lord, how wonderful is Thy Name in all the world; for Thy majesty is lifted high above the heavens!

³ Out of the mouth of babes and sucklings hast Thou perfected praise, because of Thine enemies, to destroy the enemy, and the avenger.

⁴ For I will consider the heavens, even the works

of Thy fingers, the moon and the stars which Thou hast ordained.

⁵ What is man, that Thou art mindful of him? Or the son of man, that Thou visitest him?

⁶ Thou hast made him little lower than the angels; Thou hast crowned him with glory and honor,

⁷ And hast set him over the works of Thy hands; Thou hast put all things in subjection under his feet;

⁸ All sheep and oxen, yea, and the beasts of the field;

⁹ The fowls of the air, and the fishes of the sea, and whatsoever walketh through the paths of the seas.

¹⁰ O Lord, our Lord, how wonderful is Thy Name in all the world!

Glory be to the Father, and to the Son, and to the Holy Spirit; both now, and ever, and unto the ages of ages. Amen.

Alleluia, alleluia, alleluia. Glory be to Thee, O God. Thrice.

¶ After the First Kathisma, the Trisagion Prayers, and these troparia, in Tone I:

Conceived in iniquities, prodigal that I am, I dare not gaze upon the heights of heaven; yet, confident of Thy love for mankind, I cry: O God, cleanse me and save me, a sinner!

If the righteous man can hardly be saved, where shall I, a sinner, find myself? I have not borne the burdens and heat of the day; yet, number me among them that were hired at the eleventh hour, O God, and save me!

Glory be to the Father, and to the Son, and to the Holy Spirit.

Make haste to open unto me Thy Fatherly embrace, for as the Prodigal I have wasted my life. In the unfailing wealth of Thy mercy, O Saviour, reject not my heart in its poverty, for with compunction I cry unto Thee, O Lord: Father, I have sinned against heaven and before Thee.

Both now, and ever, and unto the ages of ages. Amen.

O most holy Virgin, hope of Christians, with the heavenly hosts unceasingly entreat God, to Whom thou gavest birth in manner past understanding and recounting, that He grant remission of sins and amendment of life unto all of us who with faith and love ever honor thee.

Lord, have mercy [40]. And this Prayer:

MASTER, Almighty, Unapproachable, Origin of light, and Power beyond comprehension, Who art the Father of the hypostatic Word, and from Whom came forth the Spirit Who is one with Thee in power; Who, for the sake of the mercy of Thy loving-kindness and Thine ineffable goodness, hast not scorned human nature, which is held fast in the darkness of sin, but hast illumined the world with the divine beacons of Thy sacred teachings, the Law and the Prophets; Who in latter times wast well pleased for Thine only-begotten Son to shine forth upon us in the flesh and guide us to the effulgence of Thy glorious light, may Thine ears be attentive unto the voice of our supplication; and grant, O Lord, that we may pass the whole night of this present life with a vigilant and watchful heart, awaiting the coming of Thy Son and our God, the Judge of all. And may we, without having lain down to sleep, but keeping vigil and upright, enter together into His joy, where the voice is unending of them that behold the ineffable beauty of Thy face. For Thou art a good God and the Lover of mankind, and unto Thee do we ascribe glory, to the Father, and to the Son, and to the Holy Spirit; both now, and ever, and unto the ages of ages. Amen.

The Second Kathisma

Psalm 9. *Confitebor tibi.*
Unto the end, on the hidden things of the Son,
a Psalm of David.

I WILL give thanks unto Thee, O Lord, with my whole heart; I will speak of all Thy marvelous works.

³ I will be glad and rejoice in Thee; yea, I will sing unto Thy Name, O Thou Most Highest.

⁴ When mine enemies are driven back, they shall falter and perish at Thy presence,

⁵ For Thou hast maintained my judgment and my cause; Thou hast sat on the throne, Who rightly dividest the truth.

⁶ Thou hast rebuked the heathen, and the impious one hath perished; Thou hast wiped out his name for ever and ever.

⁷ The swords of the enemy are utterly broken, and Thou hast destroyed his cities; with a clamor is his memory wiped out,

⁸ But the Lord endureth for ever; He hath prepared His throne for judgment,

⁹ And He shall judge the whole world unto truth; He shall minister judgment unto the people in righteousness.

¹⁰ The Lord is become also a refuge for the poor, a helper in due time of trouble.

¹¹ And let them that know Thy Name put their trust in Thee, for Thou, Lord, hast never forsaken them that seek Thee.

¹² O praise the Lord which dwelleth in Zion; proclaim His doings among the nations.

¹³ As the blood-avenger doth He remember them; He forgetteth not the complaint of the poor.

¹⁴ Have mercy upon me, O Lord; see how mine enemies humiliate me, Thou that liftest me up from the gates of death,

¹⁵ That I may show all Thy praises within the gates of the daughter of Zion; we will rejoice in Thy salvation.

¹⁶ The heathen are sunk down in the ruin that they made; in the same net which they hid privily is their foot taken.

¹⁷ The Lord is known by the judgments He dealeth; the sinner is trapped in the work of his own hands.

¹⁸ Let the sinners be turned into hell, all the nations that forget God.

¹⁹ For the lowly shall not always be forgotten; the patient abiding of the poor shall not perish for ever.

²⁰ Arise, O Lord, and let not man have the upper hand; let the heathen be judged before Thee.

²¹ Set a law-giver over them, O Lord, that the heathen may know themselves to be but men.

²² Why standest Thou so far off, O Lord, and disdainest us in the needful time of trouble?

²³ When the ungodly man vaunteth himself, the poor man flareth up; they are taken in the crafty wiliness that they have imagined.

²⁴ For in the lusts of his soul the sinner commendeth himself, and he that offendeth counteth himself blessed.

²⁵ The sinner hath provoked the Lord; he is so wrathful, that he careth not; God is not before him.

²⁶ His ways are always defiled; Thy judgments are far above out of his sight; he shall have power over all his enemies.

²⁷ For he hath said in his heart, I shall never be cast down; from generation unto generation shall no harm happen unto me.

²⁸ His mouth is full of cursing, bitterness, and deceit; under his tongue is toil and misery.

²⁹ With the rich he sitteth thievishly in lurking dens, to murder the innocent; his eyes are set against the poor.

³⁰ He lurketh in secret as a lion in his den, that he may ravish the poor; to ravish the poor, when he getteth him into his net.

³¹ He humbleth himself; he croucheth and falleth, that the poor may fall into his hands.

³² For he hath said in his heart, God hath forgotten; He hath turned away His face, that He may never see.

³³ Arise, O Lord my God, let Thy hand be lifted up; forget not Thy poor before the end.

³⁴ Wherefore hath the wicked man blasphemed God? Because he hath said in his heart, He will not look into it.

³⁵ Thou seest, for Thou beholdest misery and anger, that Thou mayest take the matter into Thy hand. The poor man is abandoned unto Thee; Thou art the helper of the orphan.

³⁶ Break Thou the arm of the sinner and the evil man; his sin shall be sought, and shall not be found.

³⁷ The Lord is King for ever, and for ever and ever; ye heathen shall perish out of His land.

³⁸ Thou hast heard the desire of the poor, O Lord; Thine ear hearkeneth unto the disposition of their hearts.

³⁹ O judge for the fatherless and humble, that no man on earth may continue to boast.

Psalm 10. *In Domino confido.*
Unto the end, a Psalm of David.

I N the Lord have I put my trust; how say ye then to my soul, Flee as a bird unto the hills?

² For lo, the sinners have bent their bow, they have made ready their arrows within the quiver, that they may in darkness shoot at them which are true of heart.

³ For they have cast down what Thou hast built, but what hath the righteous done? The Lord is in His holy temple.

⁴ The Lord's throne is in heaven; His eyes consider the poor, and His eye-lids try the children of men.

⁵ The Lord trieth the righteous and the ungodly, but he that delighteth in wickedness hateth his own soul.

⁶ Upon sinners He shall rain down snares; fire and brimstone, and the stormy wind, shall be the portion of their cup.

⁷ For the Lord is righteous and loveth righteousness; His countenance hath beheld just things.

Glory be to the Father, and to the Son, and to the Holy Spirit; both now, and ever, and unto the ages of ages. Amen.

Alleluia, alleluia, alleluia. Glory be to Thee, O God. Thrice.

Lord, have mercy. Thrice.

Glory be to the Father, and to the Son, and to the Holy Spirit; both now, and ever, and unto the ages of ages. Amen.

Second Stasis

Psalm 11. *Salvum me fac.*
Unto the end, on the octave, a Psalm of David.

AVE me, Lord, for there is not one godly man left, for truth is minished from among the children of men.

³ They have talked of vanities every one with his neighbor; they do but flatter with their lips, and dissemble in their double heart.

⁴ The Lord shall destroy all lying lips, and the tongue that speaketh proud things;

⁵ Which have said, Our tongue will we magnify, our lips are our own; who is lord over us?

⁶ For the comfortless troubles' sake of the needy, and because of the deep sighing of the poor, Now will I arise, saith the Lord; I will set myself unto salvation; I will do it for all to see.

⁷ The words of the Lord are pure words, even as the silver, which from the earth is tried, and purified seven times in the fire.

⁸ Thou shalt keep us, O Lord, and shalt preserve us from this generation and for ever.

⁹ The ungodly walk on every side; according unto Thy height hast Thou increased the children of men.

Psalm 12. *Usque quo, Domine?*
Unto the end, a Psalm of David.

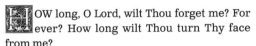OW long, O Lord, wilt Thou forget me? For ever? How long wilt Thou turn Thy face from me?

³ How long shall I seek counsel in my soul, with anguish in my heart day and night? How long shall mine enemies triumph over me?

⁴ Look upon me, hear me, O Lord my God; lighten mine eyes, that I sleep not in death.

⁵ Lest mine enemy say, I have prevailed against him.

⁶ They that trouble me will rejoice, if I be cast down.

⁷ But I have put my trust in Thy mercy. My heart shall rejoice in Thy salvation; I will sing unto the Lord Who hath dealt so lovingly with me, and I will chant unto the Name of the Lord Most High.

Psalm 13. *Dixit insipiens.*
Unto the end, a Psalm of David.

HE fool hath said in his heart, There is no God. They are corrupt, and become abominable in their doings; there is none that doeth good, no not one.

² The Lord looked down from heaven upon the children of men, to see if there were any that would understand, or seek after God.

³ They are all gone astray, they are altogether

become unprofitable; there is none that doeth good, no not one.

⁴ Shall all they that are such workers of mischief never learn, that eat up my people as it were bread? They called not upon the Lord.

⁵ There did they tremble for fear, even where no fear was; for the Lord is in the generation of the righteous.

⁶ Ye have made a mock at the counsel of the poor, but the Lord is his hope.

⁷ O who shall give the salvation of Israel out of Zion?

⁸ When the Lord turneth the captivity of His people, then shall Jacob rejoice, and Israel shall be glad.

Glory be to the Father, and to the Son, and to the Holy Spirit; both now, and ever, and unto the ages of ages. Amen.

Alleluia, alleluia, alleluia. Glory be to Thee, O God. Thrice.

Lord, have mercy. Thrice.

Glory be to the Father, and to the Son, and to the Holy Spirit; both now, and ever, and unto the ages of ages. Amen.

Third Stasis

Psalm 14. *Domine, quis habitabit?*
A Psalm of David.

ORD, who shall dwell in Thy tabernacle, or who shall rest upon Thy holy hill?

² Even he that walketh blameless, and doeth the thing which is right, that speaketh the truth in his heart.

³ He that hath used no deceit in his tongue, nor done evil to his neighbor, and hath not reproached his friend.

⁴ He that setteth not by the evil-doer, and maketh much of them that fear the Lord; he that sweareth unto his neighbor, and disappointeth him not.

⁵ He that hath not given his money upon usury, nor taken a bribe against the innocent; whoso doeth these things shall never fall.

Psalm 15. *Conserva me, Domine.*
A pillar inscription of David.

RESERVE me, O Lord, for in Thee have I put my trust.

² I said unto the Lord, Thou art my Lord, my goods are nothing unto Thee.

³ Unto the saints that are in His land hath the Lord made wonderful all His desires in them.

⁴ Their infirmities increased, whereupon they made haste; I will not convene their assemblies of

blood, neither make mention of their names with my lips.

⁵ The Lord is the portion of mine inheritance, and of my cup; it is Thou who restorest mine inheritance unto me.

⁶ The best portions are fallen unto me; for I have a goodly inheritance.

⁷ I will bless the Lord, Who hath given me wisdom; yea, even until night have my reins corrected me.

⁸ I foresaw the Lord always before me, for He is on my right hand, that I should not be moved.

⁹ Therefore did my heart rejoice, and my tongue was glad; moreover, my flesh also shall rest in hope,

¹⁰ Because Thou shalt not leave my soul in hell, neither shalt Thou suffer Thine Holy One to see corruption.

¹¹ Thou hast made known to me the paths of life; Thou shalt make me full of gladness with Thy countenance, and beauty is in Thy right hand for evermore.

Psalm 16. *Exaudi, Domine.*
A Prayer of David.

HEAR my just cause, O Lord; attend unto my supplication. Hearken unto my prayer, that goeth not out of flattering lips.

² From Thy presence shall my judgment come

forth; let mine eyes look upon the things that are right.

³ Thou hast proved my heart; Thou hast visited in the night. Thou hast tried me, and unrighteousness hath not been found within me.

⁴ That my mouth shall not speak of men's works, for the sake of the words of Thy lips I have kept hard ways.

⁵ O hold Thou up my goings in Thy paths, that my footsteps slip not.

⁶ I called, for Thou hast heard me, O God; incline Thine ear to me, and hearken unto my words.

⁷ Make Thy mercies marvelous, Thou that art the Saviour of them which put their trust in Thee, from such as resist Thy right hand.

⁸ Keep me, O Lord, as the apple of Thine eye; hide me under the shelter of Thy wings,

⁹ From the presence of the ungodly that trouble me; mine enemies compass my soul round about.

¹⁰ They are enclosed in their own fat, and their mouth speaketh proud things.

¹¹ They that cast me out have now surrounded me; they have turned their eyes down to the ground,

¹² Like as a lion that is greedy of his prey, and as it were a lion's whelp, lurking in secret places.

¹³ Arise, O Lord, disappoint them, and trip them up; deliver my soul from the ungodly, Thy sword from the enemies of Thy hand.

¹⁴ O Lord, divide them in their life from the

few of the earth; yea, from Thy hid treasure hath their belly been filled. They had children at their desire, and left the rest of their substance for their babes.

¹⁵ But as for me, in righteousness shall I appear before Thy face; when Thy glory is revealed, I shall be satisfied.

Glory be to the Father, and to the Son, and to the Holy Spirit; both now, and ever, and unto the ages of ages. Amen.

Alleluia, alleluia, alleluia. Glory be to Thee, O God. Thrice.

¶ After the Second Kathisma, the Trisagion Prayers, and these troparia, in Tone II:

As I am a tree barren of fruit, O Lord, I am utterly devoid of the fruit of contrition; I fear lest I be cut down, and am afraid of the unquenchable fire. Wherefore, I pray Thee, before these are necessary, do Thou convert and save me!

Like the waves of the sea have mine iniquities risen up against me; like a sailor alone upon the deep am I buffeted by the storm of my sins. Yet do Thou guide me by repentance into the calm haven, O Lord, and save me!

Glory be to the Father, and to the Son, and to the Holy Spirit.

Have mercy upon me, said David; and I cry out

to Thee, I have sinned, O Saviour! Having cleansed me by repentance, save me!

Both now, and ever, and unto the ages of ages. Amen.

O Theotokos, fervent intercessor for Christians, beseech thy Son, that by thy supplications He deliver us from all the malice and cruelty of the foe and grant us forgiveness of the sins we have committed, for the sake of the loving-kindness of His mercy, O Virgin Mother.

Lord, have mercy [40]. And this Prayer:

ALMIGHTY Master, Father of our Lord Jesus Christ, Thine only-begotten Son, grant me a body undefiled, a pure heart, a vigilant mind, an intellect not given to prodigality, and that the Holy Spirit may come upon me, unto the acquisition and sufficiency of truth in Thy Christ, with Whom glory, honor and worship is due unto Thee, with the Holy Spirit; now, and ever, and unto the ages of ages. Amen.

The Third Kathisma

Psalm 17. *Diligam te, Domine.*
Unto the end, by David, the servant of the Lord,
who spake unto the Lord the words of this song
in the day that the Lord delivered him from
the hand of all his enemies, and from the hand
of Saul. And he said,

I WILL love Thee, O Lord, my strength.

³ The Lord is my firm foundation, and my fortress, and my deliverer; my God is my helper, and I will trust in him, my defender, the horn also of my salvation, and my protector.

⁴ Giving praise, I will call upon the Lord, and so shall I be safe from mine enemies.

⁵ The pains of death surrounded me, and the overflowings of ungodliness made me afraid.

⁶ The pains of hell encircled me; the snares of death overtook me.

⁷ And in my trouble I called upon the Lord, and cried unto my God; so He heard my voice out of

His holy temple, and my cry before Him shall enter even into His ears.

8 The earth trembled and quaked; the very foundations also of the hills were troubled, and shook, because God was angry with them.

9 There went up smoke in His wrath, and fire flared forth from His face; coals were kindled at it.

10 He bowed the heavens also, and came down, and thick darkness was under His feet.

11 He mounted upon the Cherubim, and did fly; He came flying upon the wings of the wind.

12 He made darkness His hiding-place, His tabernacle round about Him, dark water in the clouds of the air.

13 At the brightness that was before Him the clouds removed; hailstones and coals of fire.

14 The Lord also thundered out of heaven, and the Highest gave His voice.

15 He sent out His arrows, and scattered them; He multiplied lightnings, and troubled them.

16 And the springs of waters were seen, and the foundations of the world were uncovered, at Thy chiding, O Lord, at the blasting of the breath of Thy displeasure.

17 He sent down from on high to fetch me; He took me out of many waters.

18 He shall deliver me from my strong enemies, and from them which hate me, for they are too mighty for me.

¹⁹They came upon me in the day of my trouble, and the Lord was my upholder.

²⁰ He brought me forth also into a place of liberty; He will deliver me, because He had a favor unto me.

²¹The Lord also shall reward me after my righteous dealing, and according to the cleanness of my hands shall He recompense me,

²²Because I have kept the ways of the Lord, and have not forsaken my God.

²³For all His judgments are before me, and His statutes have not departed from me,

²⁴And I will be blameless with Him, and shall keep myself from mine own wickedness.

²⁵And the Lord shall reward me after my righteous dealing, and according unto the cleanness of my hands in His eye-sight.

²⁶With the holy Thou shalt be holy, and with an innocent man Thou shalt be innocent.

²⁷With the elect Thou shalt be elect, and with the froward Thou shalt be froward.

²⁸ For Thou shalt save the humble, and shalt bring down the high looks of the proud.

²⁹For Thou shalt light my lamp, O Lord my God; Thou shalt make my darkness to be light.

³⁰ For by Thee am I delivered from temptation, and by my God I shall leap over a wall.

³¹As for my God, His way is undefiled; the words of the Lord also are tried in the fire; He is the defender of all them that put their trust in Him.

³² For who is God, but the Lord, or who is God, except our God?

³³ It is God that hath girded me with strength, and made my way perfect,

³⁴ That maketh my feet like harts' feet, and setteth me up on high,

³⁵ That teacheth mine hands to fight, and hath made mine arms like a bow of copper.

³⁶ Thou hast given me also the shield of salvation, and Thy right hand shall hold me up, and Thy chastening shall utterly correct me; and it is Thy chastening that shall teach me.

³⁷ Thou hast stretched my foot-steps under me, and my feet did not get tired.

³⁸ I will pursue mine enemies, and overtake them, neither will I turn back, until they are dead.

³⁹ I will smite them, and they shall not be able to stand; they shall fall under my feet.

⁴⁰ For Thou hast girded me with strength unto the battle; Thou hast crushed under me them that rose up against me.

⁴¹ Thou hast made mine enemies also to turn their backs upon me, and Thou hast utterly destroyed them that hated me.

⁴² They cried, but there was none to save them; even unto the Lord, and He did not hear them.

⁴³ I will grind them down as the dust before the face of the wind; I will trample them as the mud in the streets.

⁴⁴ Thou shalt deliver me from the strife of the

people, and Thou shalt make me the head of the nations; a people whom I have not known have served me.

⁴⁵ As soon as they heard, they obeyed me; the strange children dissembled with me.

⁴⁶ The strange children have grown old, and tottered out of their way.

⁴⁷ The Lord liveth, and blessed be God, and praised be the God of my salvation.

⁴⁸ It is God that avengeth me, and subdueth the peoples unto me;

⁴⁹ My deliverer from my belligerent enemies, that lifteth me up above them that rise up against me; Thou shalt rid me from the wicked man.

⁵⁰ For this cause will I give thanks unto Thee among the nations, O Lord, and sing praises unto Thy Name,

⁵¹ Who extolleth the salvation of the king, and worketh mercy unto David His anointed, and unto his seed for evermore.

Glory be to the Father, and to the Son, and to the Holy Spirit; both now, and ever, and unto the ages of ages. Amen.

Alleluia, alleluia, alleluia. Glory be to Thee, O God. Thrice.

Lord, have mercy. Thrice.

Glory be to the Father, and to the Son, and to the Holy Spirit; both now, and ever, and unto the ages of ages. Amen.

Second Stasis

Psalm 18. *Cœli enarrant.*
Unto the end, a Psalm of David.

 HE heavens declare the glory of God, and the firmament showeth His handy-work.

³ Day unto day uttereth speech, and night unto night showeth knowledge.

⁴ There is neither speech nor language, in which their voices are not heard.

⁵ Their sound is gone out into all the earth, and their words unto the ends of the world. He hath set His tabernacle in the sun,

⁶ And, coming forth as a bridegroom out of His chamber, He rejoiceth as a giant to run His course.

⁷ His going forth is from the uttermost part of heaven, and His circuit even unto the end of it again, and there is no one who can hide from the heat thereof.

⁸ The Law of the Lord is pure, converting the soul; the testimony of the Lord is sure, giving wisdom unto the simple.

⁹ The statutes of the Lord are right, gladdening the heart; the commandment of the Lord is bright, giving light unto the eyes.

¹⁰ The fear of the Lord is clean, enduring for ever and ever; the judgments of the Lord are true, and righteous altogether.

¹¹ More to be desired are they than gold and

much precious stone; sweeter also than honey, and the honey-comb.

¹² Therefore Thy servant keepeth them, and in keeping of them there is great reward.

¹³ Who can understand his fallings into sin? O cleanse Thou me from my secret faults,

¹⁴ And from strangers spare Thy servant; if they get not the dominion over me, then shall I be undefiled, and I shall be cleansed of great sin.

¹⁵ And the words of my mouth, and the meditation of my heart shall be always acceptable before Thee, O Lord, my helper, and my deliverer.

Psalm 19. *Exaudiat te Dominus.*
Unto the end, a Psalm of David.

 HE Lord hear thee in the day of trouble; the Name of the God of Jacob defend thee;

³ Send thee help from the sanctuary, and strengthen thee out of Zion;

⁴ Remember all thy sacrifices, and make acceptable thy whole-burnt offering.

⁵ The Lord grant thee according to thy heart, and fulfill all thy counsel.

⁶ We will rejoice in thy salvation, and triumph in the Name of the Lord our God; the Lord perform all thy petitions.

⁷ Now know I, that the Lord hath saved His Christ; He will hear Him from His holy heaven; the salvation of His right hand cometh with sovereignty.

⁸ Some put their trust in chariots, and some in horses, but we will call upon the Name of the Lord our God.

⁹ They are overthrown, and fallen, but we are risen, and stand upright.

¹⁰ O Lord, save the king, and hear us in the day when we call upon Thee.

Psalm 20. *Domine, in virtute tua.*
Unto the end, a Psalm of David.

LORD, the King shall be glad in Thy strength, and in Thy salvation shall he greatly rejoice.

³ Thou hast given him his heart's desire, and hast not denied him the requests of his lips.

⁴ For Thou hast gone before him with the blessings of goodness; Thou hast set a crown of precious stone upon his head.

⁵ He asked life of Thee, and Thou gavest him a long life, even for ever and ever.

⁶ Great is his glory in Thy salvation; glory and majesty shalt Thou lay upon him.

⁷ For Thou shalt give him everlasting felicity; Thou shalt make him glad with the joy of Thy countenance,

⁸ Because the King putteth his trust in the Lord, and in the mercy of the Most Highest he shall not be provoked.

⁹ Let all Thine enemies feel Thy hand; let Thy right hand find out them that hate Thee.

¹⁰ For Thou shalt make them like a fiery oven in time of Thy presence; the Lord shall trouble them in His displeasure, and the fire shall consume them.

¹¹ Their fruit shalt Thou root out of the earth, and their seed from among the children of men.

¹² For they intended mischief against Thee, and imagined such counsels as they are not able to perform.

¹³ For Thou shalt make them to turn their back; among them that are Thy remnant Thou shalt prepare their face.

¹⁴ Rise up, O Lord, by Thy power; we will chant and sing of Thy power.

Glory be to the Father, and to the Son, and to the Holy Spirit; both now, and ever, and unto the ages of ages. Amen.

Alleluia, alleluia, alleluia. Glory be to Thee, O God. Thrice.

Lord, have mercy. Thrice.

Glory be to the Father, and to the Son, and to the Holy Spirit; both now, and ever, and unto the ages of ages. Amen.

Third Stasis

Psalm 21. *Deus, Deus meus.*
Unto the end, a Psalm of David,
concerning help that cometh in the morning.

 GOD, my God, hear me; why hast Thou forsaken me? Far from my salvation are the words of my fallings into sin.

³ O my God, I cry in the day-time, and Thou hearest not; and in the night-season, and it is not foolishness unto me,

⁴ For Thou dwellest in the holy place, O Thou praise of Israel.

⁵ Our fathers hoped in Thee; they trusted, and Thou didst deliver them.

⁶ They called upon Thee, and were saved; they put their trust in Thee, and were not confounded.

⁷ But as for me, I am a worm, and no man; a very scorn of men, and the out-cast of the people.

⁸ All they that saw me laughed me to scorn; they whispered with their lips, and wagged their heads, saying,

⁹ He trusted in God, that He would deliver him; let Him save him, seeing He careth for him.

¹⁰ For Thou art He that took me out of the belly; my hope, when I hanged yet upon my mother's breast.

¹¹ From the womb was I promised unto Thee; Thou art my God, even from my mother's belly.

¹² O go not from me, for trouble is hard at hand, and there is none to help me.

¹³ Many oxen are come about me; fat bulls have closed me in on every side.

¹⁴ They gape upon me with their mouths, as it were a ramping and a roaring lion.

¹⁵ I am poured out like water, and all my bones are out of joint; my heart also in the midst of my body is even like melting wax.

¹⁶ My strength is dried up like a potsherd, and my tongue hath cleaved to the back of my throat, and Thou hast brought me down into the dust of death.

¹⁷ For many dogs are come about me, and a throng of the wicked layeth siege against me; they pierced my hands and my feet.

¹⁸ They have counted all my bones; they gazed and stared upon me.

¹⁹ They parted my garments among them, and cast lots upon my vesture.

²⁰ But Thou, O Lord, withdraw not Thy help from me; attend unto my defense.

²¹ Deliver my soul from the sword, and my only-begotten from the hand of the dog.

²² Save me from the lion's mouth, and my lowliness also from the horns of the unicorns.

²³ I will declare Thy Name unto my brethren; in the midst of the church will I sing of Thee.

²⁴ O praise Him, ye that fear the Lord; glorify

Him, all ye of the seed of Jacob. Let all the seed of Israel fear Him.

25 For He hath not despised, nor abhorred, the prayers of the poor; He hath not hid His face from me, and when I called unto Him, He heard me.

26 My praise is of Thee; in the great church will I give thanks unto Thee; my vows will I perform in the sight of them that fear Him.

27 The poor shall eat, and be satisfied, and they that seek after the Lord shall praise Him; their hearts shall live for ever and ever.

28 All the ends of the world shall remember themselves, and be turned unto the Lord, and all the kindreds of the nations shall worship before Him.

29 For the kingdom is the Lord's, and He is the Governor among the nations.

30 All such as be fat upon earth have eaten, and worshipped; all they that go down into the dust shall kneel before Him, and my soul liveth for Him.

31 Yea, my seed shall serve Him; a generation to come shall tell of the Lord,

32 And they shall declare His righteousness unto a people that shall be born, whom the Lord hath made.

Psalm 22. *Dominus regit me.*
A Psalm of David.

HE Lord is my shepherd; therefore can I lack nothing.

² He maketh me to lie down in a green pasture; He leadeth me beside the still water.

³ He hath converted my soul; He hath set me on the paths of righteousness, for His Name's sake.

⁴ Yea, though I walk through the valley of the shadow of death, I will fear no evil, for Thou art with me; Thy rod and Thy staff, they have comforted me.

⁵ Thou hast prepared a table before me against them that trouble me; Thou hast anointed my head with oil, and Thy cup that inebriateth me, how strong it is!

⁶ And Thy mercy shall follow me all the days of my life, and I will dwell in the house of the Lord unto length of days.

Psalm 23. *Domini est terra.*
A Psalm of David, on the first day of the week.

HE earth is the Lord's, and the fullness thereof; the compass of the world, and all that dwell therein.

² He hath founded it upon the seas, and prepared it upon the floods.

³ Who shall ascend into the hill of the Lord, or who shall stand in His holy place?

⁴ Even he that hath clean hands, and a pure heart, who doth not take his soul in vain, nor swear falsely to his neighbor.

⁵ He shall receive a blessing from the Lord, and mercy from God his Saviour.

⁶ This is the generation of them that seek the Lord, even of them that seek the face of the God of Jacob.

⁷ Lift up your gates, O ye princes, and be ye lift up, ye everlasting doors, and the King of glory shall come in.

⁸ Who is this King of glory? It is the Lord strong and mighty, even the Lord mighty in battle.

⁹ Lift up your gates, O ye princes, and be ye lift up, ye everlasting doors, and the King of glory shall come in.

¹⁰ Who is this King of glory? Even the Lord of hosts, He is the King of glory.

Glory be to the Father, and to the Son, and to the Holy Spirit; both now, and ever, and unto the ages of ages. Amen.

Alleluia, alleluia, alleluia. Glory be to Thee, O God. Thrice.

¶ After the Third Kathisma, the Trisagion Prayers, and these troparia, in Tone III:

Repent, O my soul, whilst thou yet livest on earth, for dust doth not sing in the grave, nor doth it deliver from transgression; but cry aloud unto

Christ God, I have sinned, O Thou Who knowest men's hearts! Before Thou condemnest me, have mercy upon me!

How long, O my soul, shalt thou remain in transgressions? How long before thou wilt accept the suggestion of repentance? Bear in mind the coming judgment, and cry out to the Lord, I have sinned, O Thou Who knowest men's hearts! Before Thou condemnest me, have mercy upon me!

Glory be to the Father, and to the Son, and to the Holy Spirit.

At the dread tribunal I shall be convicted without accusers; without witnesses shall I be condemned. For the books of men's consciences will be opened, and their hidden deeds disclosed. Before Thou dost try us at that universal spectacle, cleanse me of the sins I have committed, and save me, O God!

Both now, and ever, and unto the ages of ages. Amen.

Incomprehensible and unapproachable is the awesome mystery wrought in thee, O Lady full of the grace of God; for, having conceived Him Who cannot be encompassed, thou gavest birth unto Him in the flesh, clad in thy pure blood. Entreat Him as thy Son, O pure one, that He save all that praise thee.

Lord, have mercy [40]. And this Prayer:

ALMIGHTY and all-perfect Word of the unoriginate Father, Jesus Christ, Who of Thy loving-kindness never departest from Thy servants, but ever abidest with them, O most holy King, forsake me not, but grant me, Thine unworthy servant, the joy of Thy salvation, and illumine my mind with the light of the knowledge of Thy Gospel; enfold my soul in the love of Thy Cross, and adorn my body with Thy dispassion; calm my thoughts, keep my feet from sliding, and destroy me not with mine iniquities, O good Lord, but test me, O God, and admonish my heart. Try me, and know my steps, and see if there be the path of unrighteousness within me, and turn me away therefrom, and guide me to the everlasting way. For Thou art the way, the truth and the life, and unto Thee do we send up glory, with Thine unoriginate Father, and Thy most holy, good and life-creating Spirit; now, and ever, and unto the ages of ages. Amen.

The Fourth Kathisma

Psalm 24. *Ad te, Domine, levavi.*
A Psalm of David.

Unto Thee, O Lord, have I lifted up my soul; my God, I have put my trust in Thee: O let me never be confounded, neither let mine enemies laugh me to scorn.

2 For all they that wait on Thee shall not be ashamed.

3 Let them be ashamed such as transgress without a cause.

4 Tell me Thy ways, O Lord, and teach me Thy paths.

5 Lead me forth unto Thy truth, and teach me, for Thou art God my Saviour, and upon Thee have I waited all the day long.

6 Remember Thy loving-kindnesses, O Lord, and Thy mercies, which are from everlasting.

7 O remember not the sins of my youth, and of mine ignorance; according to Thy mercy think Thou upon me, O Lord, for Thy goodness' sake.

⁸ Gracious and righteous is the Lord, therefore will He give a Law to sinners in the way.

⁹ He will guide the meek unto judgment, He shall teach the meek His ways.

¹⁰ All the paths of the Lord are mercy and truth unto such as keep His covenant, and His testimonies.

¹¹ For Thy Name's sake, O Lord, be merciful unto my sin, for it is great.

¹² What man is he, that feareth the Lord? To him shall He give a Law in the way which He hath chosen.

¹³ His soul shall dwell at ease, and his seed shall inherit the land.

¹⁴ The Lord is the strength of them that fear Him, and He will show them His covenant.

¹⁵ Mine eyes are ever toward the Lord, for He shall pluck my feet out of the net.

¹⁶ Be charitable unto me, and have mercy on me, for I am only-begotten and poor.

¹⁷ The sorrows of my heart are enlarged; O bring Thou me out of my troubles.

¹⁸ Look upon my humbleness and my hardship, and forgive all my sins.

¹⁹ Consider mine enemies, how many they are, and they bear a tyrannous hate against me.

²⁰ O keep my soul, and deliver me; let me not be confounded, for I have put my trust in Thee.

²¹ The innocent and the upright have cleaved unto me, for I waited upon Thee, O Lord.

²² Deliver Israel, O God, out of all his troubles.

Psalm 25. *Judica me, Domine.*
A Psalm of David.

BE Thou my Judge, O Lord, for I have walked innocently and, trusting in the Lord, I shall not falter.

² Examine me, O Lord, and prove me; try out my reins and my heart.

³ For Thy mercy is ever before mine eyes, and I have behaved well in Thy truth.

⁴ I have not sat with the company of the vainglorious, neither will I have fellowship with wrong-doers.

⁵ I have hated the congregation of the wicked, and will not sit among the ungodly.

⁶ I will wash my hands in innocency, O Lord, and so will I go round about Thine altar;

⁷ That I may hear the voice of Thy praise, and tell of all Thy wondrous works.

⁸ Lord, I have loved the beauty of Thy house, and the dwelling-place of Thy glory.

⁹ O destroy not my soul with the ungodly, nor my life with the blood-thirsty;

¹⁰ In whose hand is wickedness, and their right hand is full of bribes.

¹¹ But as for me, I have walked innocently; deliver me, O Lord, and have mercy upon me.

¹² My foot hath stood on the right; I will bless Thee, O Lord, in the churches.

Psalm 26. *Dominus illuminatio.*
A Psalm of David, before he was anointed.

HE Lord is my light, and my Saviour; whom then shall I fear? The Lord is the defender of my life; of whom then shall I be afraid?

² When they that had enmity against me, even mine enemies, and my foes, came nigh to eat up my flesh, they faltered and fell.

³ Though a legion were laid against me, yet shall not my heart be afraid; and though there rise up war against me, yet will I put my trust in Him.

⁴ One thing have I desired of the Lord, which I will require; even that I may dwell in the house of the Lord all the days of my life, to behold the fair beauty of the Lord, and to visit His holy temple.

⁵ For in the day of my trouble He hath hidden me in His tabernacle; yea, in the secret place of His dwelling did He shelter me, and set me up upon a rock.

⁶ And now, behold, He hath lifted up mine head above mine enemies; therefore have I gone round about and offered in His dwelling a sacrifice of praise and jubilation; I will sing and chant unto the Lord.

⁷ Hearken, O Lord, unto my voice, with which I have cried, Have mercy upon me, and hear me.

⁸ My heart hath said unto Thee, I will seek the Lord; my face hath sought Thee; Thy face, O Lord, will I seek.

⁹ O turn not Thou Thy face from me, nor turn away from Thy servant in displeasure; be Thou my helper; reject me not, neither forsake me, O God, my Saviour.

¹⁰ For my father and my mother have forsaken me, but the Lord taketh me up.

¹¹ Teach me a law, O Lord, in Thy way, and set me on the right path, because of mine enemies.

¹² Deliver me not over to the souls of them that afflict me, for false witnesses are risen up against me, and iniquity hath lied to itself.

¹³ I believe that I shall see the goodness of the Lord in the land of the living.

¹⁴ Wait thou on the Lord; be of good courage, and let thine heart stand firm, and wait thou on the Lord.

Glory be to the Father, and to the Son, and to the Holy Spirit; both now, and ever, and unto the ages of ages. Amen.

Alleluia, alleluia, alleluia. Glory be to Thee, O God. Thrice.

Lord, have mercy. Thrice.

Glory be to the Father, and to the Son, and to the Holy Spirit; both now, and ever, and unto the ages of ages. Amen.

Second Stasis

Psalm 27. *Ad te, Domine.*
A Psalm of David.

NTO Thee, O Lord, will I cry; O my God, be not silent unto me, lest, if Thou keep silence unto me, I become like them that go down into the pit.

² Hear, O Lord, the voice of my humble petition when I pray unto Thee, when I hold up my hands toward Thy holy temple.

³ O pluck me not away with the sinners, neither destroy me with the wrong-doers, which speak peace to their neighbors, but imagine mischief in their hearts.

⁴ Reward them, O Lord, according to their deeds, and according to the wickedness of their own inventions; recompense them after the work of their hands; pay them that they have deserved.

⁵ For they understood not the works of the Lord, nor the operation of His hands; therefore shalt Thou break them down, and not build them up.

⁶ Blessed be the Lord, for He hath heard the voice of my humble petition.

⁷ The Lord is my helper, and my protector; my heart hath trusted in Him, and I am helped; even

my flesh hath revived, and gladly will I praise Him.

⁸ The Lord is the strength of His people, and He is the defender of the salvation of His anointed.

⁹ Save Thy people, and bless Thine inheritance; and be their shepherd, and carry them for ever.

Psalm 28. *Afferte Domino.*
A Psalm of David, of the going forth of the Tabernacle.

BRING unto the Lord, O ye sons of God, bring young rams unto the Lord; bring unto the Lord glory and honor.

² Bring unto the Lord the glory due unto His Name; worship the Lord in His holy court.

³ The voice of the Lord is upon the waters; the God of glory hath thundered. The Lord is upon many waters.

⁴ The voice of the Lord in power; the voice of the Lord in majesty,

⁵ The voice of the Lord Who breaketh the cedar-trees; yea, the Lord will break the cedars of Lebanon.

⁶ He will break them in pieces like the calf, Lebanon, but the beloved is like a young unicorn.

⁷ The voice of the Lord Who divideth the flame of fire.

⁸ The voice of the Lord Who shaketh the wilderness; yea, the Lord will shake the wilderness of Kadesh.

⁹ The voice of the Lord Who gathereth the hinds, and discovereth the leafy glade, and in His temple doth every man speak glory.

¹⁰ The Lord dwelleth in the water-flood, and the Lord shall sit as King for ever.

¹¹ The Lord shall give strength unto His people; the Lord shall bless His people with peace.

Psalm 29. *Exaltabo te, Domine.*
A Psalm and Song at the dedication of the house of David.

I WILL exalt Thee, O Lord, for Thou hast raised me up, and not made my foes to triumph over me.

³ O Lord my God, I cried unto Thee, and Thou hast healed me.

⁴ O Lord, Thou hast brought my soul out of hell; Thou hast saved me from them that go down to the pit.

⁵ Sing unto the Lord, O ye saints of His, and give thanks at the memory of His holiness.

⁶ For there is wrath in His anger, but in His pleasure is life; tears may endure for a night, but joy cometh in the morning.

⁷ But in my prosperity I said, I shall never be removed.

⁸ Thou, Lord, of Thy favor hast given power to my goodness, but Thou didst turn Thy face from me, and I was troubled.

⁹ Unto Thee, O Lord, will I call, and I will pray unto my God.

¹⁰ What profit is there in my blood, when I go down to corruption? Shall the dust give thanks unto Thee, or shall it declare Thy truth?

¹¹ The Lord heard, and had mercy upon me; the Lord was my helper.

¹² Thou hast turned my tears into joy; Thou hast put off my sackcloth, and girded me with gladness,

¹³ That my glory may sing unto Thee, and I shall not be sorry; O Lord my God, I will give thanks unto Thee for ever.

Glory be to the Father, and to the Son, and to the Holy Spirit; both now, and ever, and unto the ages of ages. Amen.

Alleluia, alleluia, alleluia. Glory be to Thee, O God. Thrice.

Lord, have mercy. Thrice.

Glory be to the Father, and to the Son, and to the Holy Spirit; both now, and ever, and unto the ages of ages. Amen.

Third Stasis

Psalm 30. *In te, Domine, speravi.*
Unto the end, a Psalm of David, of rapture.

IN Thee, O Lord, have I put my trust; let me never be confounded, but rescue me in Thy righteousness, and deliver me.

3 Bow down Thine ear to me; make haste to deliver me, and be Thou unto me a defending God, and a house of refuge to save me.

4 For Thou art my strength, and my safe haven; be Thou also my guide, and my provider, for Thy Name's sake.

5 Thou shalt draw me out of this net that they laid privily for me; for Thou art my protector, O Lord.

6 Into Thy hands will I commend my spirit, for Thou hast redeemed me, O Lord, Thou God of truth.

7 Thou hast hated them that hold of superstitious vanities, but my hope hath been in the Lord.

8 I will be glad, and rejoice in Thy mercy, for Thou hast considered my lowliness, and hast saved my soul from adversity.

9 And Thou hast not shut me up into the hand of the enemy, but hast set my feet in a place of liberty.

10 Have mercy upon me, O Lord, for I am in trouble; mine eye is troubled with anger; yea, my soul and my body.

¹¹ For my life hath been used up in suffering, and my years in sighing; my strength failed me, because of my poverty, and my bones were troubled.

¹² I became a reproof among all mine enemies, but especially among my neighbors, and they of mine acquaintance were afraid of me; and they that did see me without fled from me.

¹³ I am clean forgotten, as a dead man out of mind; I am become like a broken vessel.

¹⁴ For I have heard the blasphemy of the multitude who dwell on every side, while they conspired together against me, and took their counsel to take away my life.

¹⁵ But I have put my trust in Thee, O Lord; I said, Thou art my God,

¹⁶ My lots are in Thy hand; deliver me from the hand of mine enemies, and from them that persecute me.

¹⁷ Show Thy servant the light of Thy countenance, and save me for Thy mercy's sake.

¹⁸ Let me not be confounded, O Lord, for I have called upon Thee; let the ungodly be put to confusion, and be brought down into hell.

¹⁹ Let the lying lips be put to silence which disdainfully, and scornfully, speak iniquity against the righteous.

²⁰ O Lord, how plentiful is the abundance of Thy goodness, which Thou hast laid up for them that fear Thee, and that Thou hast prepared for

them that put their trust in Thee, before the sons of men!

²¹ Thou shalt hide them in the secret place of Thy presence from the provoking of all men; Thou shalt shelter them from the strife of tongues.

²² Blessed be the Lord, for He hath marvelously showed His mercy in a strong city.

²³ But in my confusion, I said, I am cast out of the sight of Thine eyes; therefore, Thou heardest the voice of my prayer when I cried unto Thee.

²⁴ O love the Lord, all ye His saints, for the Lord requireth truth, and plenteously rewardeth the proud doer.

²⁵ Be of good courage and let your heart stand firm, all ye that put your trust in the Lord.

Psalm 31. *Beati, quorum.*
A Psalm of David, of understanding.

BLESSED are they whose iniquities are forgiven, and whose sins are covered.

² Blessed is the man unto whom the Lord imputeth no sin, and in whose lips there is no guile.

³ Because I was silent, my bones consumed away, whereupon I called the whole day long.

⁴ For Thy hand was heavy upon me day and night; I was brought to misery by a piercing thorn.

⁵ I have acknowledged my transgression and my sin have I not hid; I said, Against myself will I confess my transgression unto the Lord, and so Thou forgavest the irreverence of my heart.

⁶ For this shall every one that is godly make his prayer unto Thee in a seasonable time; therefore in the great water-floods the waves shall not come nigh him.

⁷ Thou art my refuge from the afflictions that overwhelm me; my Joy, deliver me from them that circle me round about.

⁸ I will teach thee, and set thee on the way wherein thou shalt go; Mine eyes shall watch over thee.

⁹ Be ye not like to horse and mule, which have no understanding, whose jaws must be bound by bit and bridle, if they be skittish unto thee.

¹⁰ Many are the wounds of the ungodly, but whoso putteth his trust in the Lord, mercy embraceth him on every side.

¹¹ Be glad in the Lord, and rejoice, O ye righteous, and sing praises, all ye that are true of heart.

Glory be to the Father, and to the Son, and to the Holy Spirit; both now, and ever, and unto the ages of ages. Amen.

Alleluia, alleluia, alleluia. Glory be to Thee, O God. Thrice.

¶ After the Fourth Kathisma, the Trisagion Prayers, and these troparia, in Tone VII:

O Lord, visit Thou my lowly soul which hath squandered its whole life in sins. As Thou didst receive the harlot, receive me also, and save me.

Sailing the sea of this present life, I think of the ocean of my many offenses; and, not having a pilot for my thoughts, I call to Thee with the cry of Peter, Save me, O Christ! Save me, O God! For Thou art the Lover of mankind.

Glory be to the Father, and to the Son, and to the Holy Spirit.

Soon shall we all go in together unto Christ the Bridegroom. May we all hear the blessed voice of Christ our God: Come, ye that love the glory of heaven, who have become partakers with the wise virgins and made your lamps radiant with faith!

Both now, and ever, and unto the ages of ages. Amen.

O my soul, repent before thy departure, for the judgment of sinners is impartial and unbearable; but cry out to the Lord in contrition of heart: I have sinned against Thee in knowledge and in ignorance, O Compassionate One; take pity on me through the prayers of the Theotokos, and save me!

Lord, have mercy [40]. And this Prayer:

NTO Thee, O Lord, Who alone art good and not mindful of the evils I have committed, do I confess my sins. I have sinned, O Lord; I have sinned, and am not worthy to lift up mine eyes to the heights of heaven because of the multitude of my unjust deeds. But, O Lord, my Lord, grant me tears of contrition, O Thou Who alone art good and merciful, that therewith I may entreat Thee, that I be cleansed of every sin before the end. For frightening and terrible is the place to which I shall go when my soul is separated from the body, and a dark and inhuman horde of demons shall meet me, and I shall have no companion to help and deliver me. Wherefore, I fall down before Thy goodness and cry, Betray me not unto them that oppress me, neither let mine enemies triumph over me, O good Lord, nor let them say, Thou hast come into our hands and hast been betrayed unto us! Nay, O Lord, forget not Thy loving-kindness, and reward me not according to mine iniquities, and turn not Thy face from me; but do Thou, O Lord, chastise me, albeit with mercy and compassion. And let not mine enemy rejoice over me, but put an end to his threats against me. Abolish all of his activity, and grant me a straight path unto Thee, O good Lord; for, though I have sinned, yet have I not had recourse unto any other physician, nor have I stretched out my hands toward any strange god. Reject not, therefore, my supplication, but hearken unto me in Thy goodness, and establish my heart in the fear of Thee; and may Thy grace be upon me, O Lord, as a fire which utterly consumeth the impure thoughts within me. For Thou, O Lord, art Light transcending all light, Joy surpassing all joy, Peace beyond all peace, and true Life and Salvation which abidest unto the ages of ages. Amen.

The Fifth Kathisma

Psalm 32. *Exultate, justi.*
A Psalm of David. Without superscription in the
Hebrew.

EJOICE in the Lord, O ye righteous, for praise becometh well the upright.

² Give thanks unto the Lord with harp, sing unto Him with the ten-stringed psaltery.

³ Sing unto Him a new song, sing praises lustily unto Him with jubilation.

⁴ For the word of the Lord is true, and all His works are faithful.

⁵ The Lord loveth alms-giving and justice; the earth is full of the mercy of the Lord.

⁶ By the Word of the Lord were the heavens made, and all the hosts of them by the Breath of His mouth,

⁷ Who gathereth the waters of the sea together, as it were in a wine-skin, Who layeth up the deeps, as in a treasure-house.

⁸ Let all the earth fear the Lord; be shaken of Him, all ye that dwell in the world.

⁹ For He spake, and they came to be; He commanded, and they were created.

¹⁰ The Lord bringeth the counsel of the heathen to naught, He maketh the thoughts of the people to be of none effect, and casteth out the counsels of princes.

¹¹ But the counsel of the Lord endureth for ever, and the thoughts of His heart from generation to generation.

¹² Blessed are the people, whose God is the Lord, the folk, that He hath chosen to be an inheritance unto Him.

¹³ The Lord looked down from heaven, and beheld all the children of men;

¹⁴ From His prepared habitation, He considereth all them that dwell on the earth,

¹⁵ Having made the hearts of every one of them, and understanding all their works.

¹⁶ A king is not saved by many armies, and a giant is not saved by his great strength.

¹⁷ Vain is the horse for salvation, neither shall he deliver any man by his great power.

¹⁸ Behold, the eyes of the Lord are upon them that fear Him, and upon them that put their trust in His mercy;

¹⁹ To deliver their souls from death, and to feed them in the time of dearth.

²⁰ But our soul shall patiently wait upon the Lord, for He is our helper and defender.

²¹ For our heart shall rejoice in Him, and we have hoped in His holy Name.

²² Let Thy mercy, O Lord, be upon us, according as we have put our trust in Thee.

Psalm 33. *Benedicam Domino.*
A Psalm of David, when he changed his behavior before Abimelech; who drove him away, and he departed.

 will bless the Lord at all times, His praise is ever in my mouth.

³ In the Lord shall my soul be praised; let the meek hear, and be glad.

⁴ O magnify the Lord with me, and we shall exalt His Name together.

⁵ I sought the Lord and He heard me, yea, He delivered me out of all my troubles.

⁶ Come unto Him, and be enlightened, and your faces shall not be ashamed.

⁷ This poor man cried and the Lord heard him, and saved him out of all his troubles.

⁸ The angel of the Lord tarrieth round about them that fear Him, and delivereth them.

⁹ O taste, and see, that the Lord is good; blessed is the man that trusteth in Him.

¹⁰ O fear the Lord, all ye that are His saints, for they that fear Him lack nothing.

¹¹ The rich have lacked, and suffered hunger, but they that seek the Lord shall want no manner of thing that is good.

¹² Come, ye children, and hearken unto me; I will teach you the fear of the Lord.

¹³ What man is he that lusteth to live, and would gladly see good days?

¹⁴ Keep thy tongue from evil, and thy lips, that they speak no guile.

¹⁵ Shun evil, and do good; seek peace, and pursue it.

¹⁶ The eyes of the Lord are over the righteous, and His ears are open unto their prayers.

¹⁷ But the countenance of the Lord is against them that do evil, to root out the remembrance of them from the earth.

¹⁸ The righteous cried, and the Lord heard them, and delivered them out of all their troubles.

¹⁹ The Lord is nigh unto them that are of a contrite heart, and will save such as be of an humble spirit.

²⁰ Many are the troubles of the righteous, but the Lord delivereth them out of all.

²¹ The Lord keepeth all their bones; not one of them shall be broken.

²² The death of sinners is evil, and they that hate the righteous shall sin greatly.

²³ The Lord will deliver the souls of His servants, and all they that put their trust in Him shall do no sin.

Glory be to the Father, and to the Son, and to the Holy Spirit; both now, and ever, and unto the ages of ages. Amen.

Alleluia, alleluia, alleluia. Glory be to Thee, O God. Thrice.

Lord, have mercy. Thrice.

Glory be to the Father, and to the Son, and to the Holy Spirit; both now, and ever, and unto the ages of ages. Amen.

Second Stasis

Psalm 34. *Judica, Domine.*
A Psalm of David.

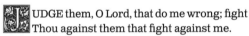 UDGE them, O Lord, that do me wrong; fight Thou against them that fight against me.

[2] Lay hold of shield and buckler, and come to my help.

[3] Draw forth the sword, and stop the way against them that persecute me; say unto my soul, I am thy salvation.

[4] Let them be confounded, and put to shame, that seek after my soul; let them be turned back, and brought to confusion, that imagine mischief for me.

[5] Let them be as the dust before the face of the wind, and the angel of the Lord persecuting them.

⁶ Let their way be dark and slippery, and the angel of the Lord pursuing them.

⁷ For they have privily laid their net to destroy me without a cause; in vain have they reproached my soul.

⁸ Let that net come upon him unawares, and let the snare that he hath laid privily catch himself, that he may fall into his own mischief.

⁹ But my soul shall be joyful in the Lord, it shall rejoice in His salvation.

¹⁰ All my bones shall say, Lord, O Lord, who is like unto Thee, who deliverest the poor from him that is too strong for him, and the poor man, and the needy, from him that despoileth him?

¹¹ False witnesses did rise up against me, they laid to my charge things that I knew not.

¹² They repaid me evil for good, and barrenness to my soul.

¹³ But when they troubled me, I put on sackcloth, and humbled my soul with fasting, and my prayer shall turn into mine own bosom.

¹⁴ As to a neighbor, as to our brother, so I behaved friendly; as one weeping and mourning, so I humbled myself.

¹⁵ But they rejoiced, and gathered themselves together against me; they plotted harm against me, and I was unawares; they were beside themselves and had no mercy.

¹⁶ They tempted me, they mocked at me with busy mockery, they gnashed upon me with their teeth.

¹⁷ Lord, when wilt Thou see? O rescue my soul from their evil-doing, my only-begotten from the lions.

¹⁸ I will give Thee thanks in the great congregation; I will praise thee among much people.

¹⁹ O let not them triumph over me that are mine enemies unjustly, that hate me without a cause and wink with their eyes.

²⁰ For while they spake peaceably unto me, in their anger they imagined lies.

²¹ They gaped upon me with their mouths, and said, Well, well, our eyes have seen.

²² Thou hast seen, O Lord; hold not Thy tongue. O Lord, forsake me not.

²³ Rise up, O Lord, and attend unto my judgment, O my God; even, O my Lord, unto my cause.

²⁴ Judge me, O Lord, according to Thy righteousness, and let them not triumph over me, O Lord my God.

²⁵ Let them not say in their hearts, Good! It doeth our hearts good! Neither let them say, We have swallowed him up.

²⁶ Let them be put to confusion and shame together, that rejoice at my trouble; let them be clothed with rebuke and dishonor, that boast themselves against me.

²⁷ Let them be glad and rejoice, that favor my

righteous dealing; and let them say always, The Lord be praised, who hath pleasure in the peace of His servant.

²⁸ And my tongue shall teach of Thy righteousness, and of Thy praise all day.

Psalm 35. *Dixit injustus.*
Unto the end, a Psalm of David, the servant of the Lord.

THE sinner, that he may sin, saith within himself, There is no fear of God before his eyes.

³ For he hath dissembled before Him, that he may find his wickedness, and learn to hate.

⁴ The words of his mouth are iniquity and deceit; he hath not wished to understand how to do good.

⁵ He hath imagined mischief upon his bed; he hath set himself in no good way, neither doth he abhor any thing that is evil.

⁶ Thy mercy, O Lord, is unto the heavens, and Thy truth unto the clouds.

⁷ Thy justice is as the mountains of God, Thy judgments are as the bottomless deep; man and beast shalt Thou save, O Lord.

⁸ O how hast Thou multiplied Thy mercy, O God; so shall the children of men put their trust in the shelter of Thy wings.

⁹ They shall be drunk from the plenteousness of Thy house, and Thou shalt give them drink of Thy pleasure, as out of a river.

¹⁰ For with Thee is the fountain of life; in Thy light shall we see light.

¹¹ O continue Thy mercy unto them that know Thee, and Thy righteousness unto them that are true of heart.

¹² O let not the foot of pride come against me, and let not the hand of the ungodly provoke me.

¹³ There are they fallen, all them that work wickedness; they are cast down, and shall not be able to stand.

Glory be to the Father, and to the Son, and to the Holy Spirit; both now, and ever, and unto the ages of ages. Amen.

Alleluia, alleluia, alleluia. Glory be to Thee, O God. Thrice.

Lord, have mercy. Thrice.

Glory be to the Father, and to the Son, and to the Holy Spirit; both now, and ever, and unto the ages of ages. Amen.

Third Stasis

Psalm 36. *Noli œmulari.*
A Psalm of David.

Fret not thyself because of the wicked, neither be thou envious against them that do unlawfulness,

² For they shall soon wither like the grass, and quickly fall away even as the green herb.

³ Put thou thy trust in the Lord, and be doing good, and dwell in the land, and thou shalt graze on the riches thereof.

⁴ Delight thou in the Lord, and He shall give thee thy heart's desire.

⁵ Open thy way unto the Lord, and put thy trust in Him, and He shall bring it to pass,

⁶ And He shall make thy righteousness as plain as the light, and thy judgment as the noonday.

⁷ Give thyself up to the Lord, and pray unto Him; fret not thyself at him whose way doth prosper, at the man that doeth after evil counsels.

⁸ Leave off from wrath, and let go displeasure; fret not thyself, else thou do evil,

⁹ For the wicked doers shall be utterly consumed, but they that patiently abide the Lord, those shall inherit the land.

¹⁰ Yet a little while, and the sinner shall be clean gone; yea, thou shalt seek after his place, and wilt not find it,

¹¹ But the meek shall inherit the earth, and shall be refreshed in the multitude of peace.

¹² The sinner shall watch over the just man, and gnash upon him with his teeth,

¹³ But the Lord shall laugh him to scorn, for He seeth that his day is coming.

¹⁴ The sinners have drawn out the sword, they have bent their bow, to cast down the poor and needy, to slay such as are true of heart.

¹⁵ Let their sword pierce their own hearts, and let their bows be broken.

¹⁶ A small thing that the righteous hath, is better than great riches of the ungodly,

¹⁷ For the arms of the sinner shall be broken, but the Lord upholdeth the righteous.

¹⁸ The Lord knoweth the ways of the blameless, and their inheritance shall endure for ever.

¹⁹ They shall not be confounded in the perilous time, and in the days of dearth they shall have enough; as for the sinners, they shall perish.

²⁰ But the enemies of the Lord, as soon as they are honored and exalted, shall vanish away; even as smoke, shall they vanish.

²¹ The sinner borroweth, and payeth not again, but the righteous is merciful, and giveth,

²² For such as bless him shall possess the land, but such as curse him shall be rooted out.

²³ By the Lord are a man's steps directed, and he shall well like His way.

²⁴ Though he fall, he shall not be harmed, for the Lord upholdeth him with His hand.

²⁵ I have been young, and now am old, and yet saw I never the right eous forsaken, nor his seed begging their bread.

²⁶ The righteous is merciful all day, and lendeth, and his seed shall be blessed.

²⁷ Shun evil, and do good, and dwell for evermore,

²⁸ For the Lord loveth justice, and will not forsake His saints; they shall be kept forever, but the unrighteous will be driven out, and the seed of the ungodly shall be utterly consumed.

²⁹ And the righteous shall inherit the land, and dwell therein for ever.

³⁰ The mouth of the righteous is exercised in wisdom, and his tongue will be talking of judgment.

³¹ The Law of his God is in his heart, and his footsteps shall not slide.

³² The sinner seeth the righteous, and seeketh occasion to slay him,

³³ But the Lord will not leave him in his hand, nor condemn him when He judgeth him.

³⁴ Wait thou on the Lord, and keep His way, and He shall promote thee, that thou shalt possess the land; when the sinners perish, thou shalt see it.

³⁵ I have seen the ungodly in great power, and flourishing like the cedars of Lebanon,

³⁶ Then I went by, and lo, he was gone; yea, I sought him, but his place could nowhere be found.

³⁷ Keep innocency, and heed the right, for that shall bring a man peace at the last,

³⁸ But the transgressors shall perish together, and the ungodly shall be rooted out to the last one.

³⁹ But the salvation of the righteous is from the Lord, and He is their defender in time of trouble,

⁴⁰ And the Lord shall help them, and deliver

them; He shall rescue them from the sinner, and shall save them, because they put their trust in Him.

Glory be to the Father, and to the Son, and to the Holy Spirit; both now, and ever, and unto the ages of ages. Amen.

Alleluia, alleluia, alleluia. Glory be to Thee, O God. Thrice.

¶ After the Fifth Kathisma, the Trisagion Prayers, and these troparia, in Tone V:

Awesome is Thy throne, and wicked is my life; and who will then deliver me from want, if Thou dost not have mercy upon me, O Christ God, as Thou only art compassionate and the Lover of mankind?

Glory be to the Father, and to the Son, and to the Holy Spirit.

Concern for life hath driven me from Paradise, and what shall I do, wretch that I am? Wherefore, I knock at the gate and cry, Lord, O Lord, open unto me for repentance, and save me!

Both now, and ever, and unto the ages of ages. Amen.

What shall we call thy temple, O Theotokos? A spiritual haven, or a paradise of the sweetness of heaven which is the means of everlasting life? For as thou possessest all good things, ever pray to Christ, that our souls be saved.

Lord, have mercy [40]. And this Prayer:

 GOD righteous and praised, O God great and mighty, O God Who transcendest time, Hearken unto the entreaty of a sinful man at this hour! Hearken unto me, O Thou Who hast promised to hearken unto them that call upon Thee in truth, and do not loathe me whose lips are unclean and who am held fast in sin, O Thou hope of all the ends of the earth, and of them that wander afar off. Lay hold of shield and buckler, and come to my help; draw forth Thy sword, and stop the way against them that persecute me; fend off the unclean spirits from the face of my mindless folly, and may there be divorced from my thought the spirit of hatred and remembrance of evil, the spirit of jealousy and falsehood, the spirit of fear and despondency, the spirit of pride and of every evil; and may every burning and movement of my flesh brought about by the activity of the Devil be extinguished, and may my soul and my body and spirit be enlightened by the light of the divine knowledge of Thee; that through the multitude of Thy compassions I may attain unto the unity of the faith, unto perfect humanity, unto the measure of my years, and with the angels and all Thy saints I shall glorify Thy most honorable and majestic Name, of the Father, and of the Son, and of the Holy Spirit; now, and ever, and unto the ages of ages. Amen.

The Sixth Kathisma

Psalm 37. *Domine, ne in furore.*
A Psalm of David, for a remembrance of
the Sabbath.

 LORD, rebuke me not in Thine anger, neither chasten me in Thy wrath:

³ For Thine arrows are stuck fast in me, and Thy hand presseth me sore.

⁴ There is no health in my flesh, because of Thy displeasure; neither is there any rest in my bones, by reason of my sin.

⁵ For my wickednesses are gone over my head; like a sore burden have they become too heavy for me.

⁶ My wounds stink, and are corrupt, because of my foolishness.

⁷ I am brought into great torment and misery; I go mourning all the day long.

⁸ For my loins are filled with sores, and there is no healing in my flesh.

⁹ I was bitter, and utterly humbled; I roared for the very groaning of my heart.

¹⁰ Lord, all my desire is before Thee, and my lamentation is not hid from Thee.

¹¹ My heart is troubled; my strength hath failed me, and the light of mine eyes, even that is gone from me.

¹² My friends and my neighbors came right up to me and confronted me,

¹³ While my kinsmen stood afar off, and they that sought my soul clamored for it; and they that wished me evil spake vanity, and imagined deceit all the day long.

¹⁴ But I was like a deaf man, and heard not, and as one that is dumb, who doth not open his mouth.

¹⁵ And I became as a man that heareth not, and in whose mouth are no reproofs.

¹⁶ For in Thee, O Lord, have I put my trust; Thou wilt hear me, O Lord my God.

¹⁷ For I said, Let never mine enemies triumph over me; for when my foot slipped, they boasted against me.

¹⁸ For I am ready for scourges, and my pain is ever before me.

¹⁹ For I will confess my wickedness, and be sorry for my sin.

²⁰ But mine enemies live, and are stronger than I, and they are become many that hate me wrongfully.

²¹ They also that reward me evil for good have

slandered me, because I follow the thing that good is.

²² Forsake me not, O Lord my God, be not far from me.

²³ Attend unto my help, O Lord of my salvation.

Psalm 38. *Dixi, custodiam.*
Unto the end, even to Jeduthun, a Song of David.

I SAID, I will take heed to my ways, that I sin not with my tongue; I kept my mouth as it were with a bridle, when the sinner stood up against me.

³ I was mute and held my peace; I kept silent, even from good words, and my sorrow was renewed.

⁴ My heart grew hot within me, and while I was thus musing, the fire kindled; I spake with my tongue,

⁵ O Lord, tell me mine end, and the number of my days, what it is, that I may know what is wanting to me.

⁶ Behold, Thou hast made my days as it were a span long, and my existence is as nothing before Thee; verily, every man living is altogether vanity.

⁷ Therefore man walketh as a shadow, and disquieteth himself in vain; he heapeth up riches, and knoweth not for whom he gathereth them.

⁸ And now, who is my patient endurance? Is it not the Lord? Even my existence is from Thee.

⁹ From all mine offenses deliver me; Thou hast made me a rebuke unto the foolish.

¹⁰ I became dumb, and opened not my mouth, for it was Thy doing.

¹¹ Take Thy scourges from me, for I have fainted from the vehemence of Thy hand.

¹² With rebukes hast Thou chastened man for sin, and hast brushed his life away like a spider's web; yea, every man is but vanity.

¹³ Hear my prayer, O Lord, and give ear unto my petition; hold not Thy peace at my tears. For I am a sojourner with Thee, and a pilgrim, as all my fathers were.

¹⁴ O spare me, that I may recover my strength, before I go hence, and be no more.

Psalm 39. *Expectans expectavi.*
To the chief Musician, a Psalm of David.

WITH hope did I wait for the Lord, and He heard me, and heeded my prayer.

³ And He brought me up out of the horrible pit, and out of the miry clay, and set my feet upon the rock, and ordered my steps.

⁴ And He hath put a new song in my mouth, even a hymn unto our God. Many shall see it, and fear, and shall put their trust in the Lord.

⁵ Blessed is the man whose hope is in the Name of the Lord, and hath not had regard unto vanities and lying follies.

⁶ O Lord my God, many are the wondrous works

which Thou hast done, and in Thy thoughts there is none that compareth unto Thee. I declared and spake, They are multiplied beyond number.

7 Sacrifice and offering Thou wouldest not, but a body hast Thou made for me; whole-burnt offerings, and sin offerings, hast Thou not required.

8 Then said I, Lo, I come; in the heading of the book it is written of me,

9 That I should long to do Thy will, O my God; yea, Thy Law is within my heart.

10 I have preached righteousness in the great church; lo, I will not refrain my lips; O Lord, Thou knowest.

11 I have not hid Thy righteousness within my heart; I have declared Thy truth and Thy salvation; I have not kept back Thy mercy and truth from the great assembly.

12 And Thou, O Lord, withdraw not Thy lovingkindness from me; let Thy mercy and Thy truth always preserve me.

13 For innumerable troubles are come about me; my sins have taken such hold upon me, that I am not able to look up; yea, they are more in number than the hairs of my head, and my heart hath failed me.

14 O Lord, let it be Thy pleasure to deliver me; O Lord, attend unto my help.

15 Let them be ashamed, and confounded together, that seek after my soul to destroy it; let

them be driven backward, and put to rebuke, that wish me evil.

¹⁶ Let them quickly receive shame for their reward, that say unto me, Well, well.

¹⁷ Let all them that seek Thee be joyful and glad in Thee, O Lord, and let such as love Thy salvation say always, The Lord be praised.

¹⁸ As for me, I am poor and needy, but the Lord will care for me; My helper and my defender art Thou, O my God, make no long tarrying.

Glory be to the Father, and to the Son, and to the Holy Spirit; both now, and ever, and unto the ages of ages. Amen.

Alleluia, alleluia, alleluia. Glory be to Thee, O God. *Thrice.*

Lord, have mercy. *Thrice.*

Glory be to the Father, and to the Son, and to the Holy Spirit; both now, and ever, and unto the ages of ages. Amen.

Second Stasis

Psalm 40. *Beatus qui intelligit.*
Unto the end, a Psalm of David.

BLESSED is he that considereth the poor and needy; the Lord shall deliver him on the evil day.

³ The Lord preserve him, and keep him alive,

and bless him upon the earth, and deliver him not into the hands of his enemies.

⁴ The Lord comfort him on his sick-bed; Thou hast turned all his bed in his sickness.

⁵ I said, Lord, have mercy on me; heal my soul, for I have sinned against Thee.

⁶ Mine enemies spake evil of me, When shall he die, and his name perish?

⁷ And if he came to see me, he spake vanity in his heart, he gathered iniquity to himself; he went forth and spake in like manner.

⁸ All mine enemies whispered against me; even against me did they imagine this evil.

⁹ They spread a slanderous word against me, Now that he sleepeth, he shall not rise up again.

¹⁰ Yea, even mine own familiar friend, in whom I trusted, who did eat of my bread, hath lifted up his heel against me.

¹¹ But Thou, O Lord, have mercy upon me, and raise me up, and I shall pay them back.

¹² By this I know Thou favorest me, that mine enemy doth not triumph against me.

¹³ But Thou hast taken my side by reason of my innocence, and hast established me before Thee for ever.

¹⁴ Blessed be the Lord God of Israel from everlasting to everlasting. So be it. So be it.

Psalm 41. *Quemadmodum.*
Unto the end, for instruction, of the sons of
Korah, a Psalm of David.

IKE as the hart panteth after the water-brooks, so longeth my soul after Thee, O God.

3 My soul hath thirsted for the mighty living God; when shall I come and appear before God's face?

4 My tears have been my bread day and night, while they daily said unto me, Where is now thy God?

5 I thought upon these things, and poured out my soul within me, for I shall go over into the place of the wonderful tabernacle, even unto the house of God, with a voice of rejoicing and thanksgiving, the noise of such as keep holy-day.

6 Why art thou so full of sadness, O my soul? And why dost thou trouble me? Put thy trust in God, for I will yet give Him thanks, the salvation of my countenance, and my God.

7 My soul is vexed within me; therefore will I remember Thee from the land of Jordan and Hermon, from the little hill.

8 Deep unto deep calleth at the voice of Thy water-floods; all Thy billows and Thy waves are gone over me.

9 The Lord hath commanded His mercy by day,

and His song from me by night, a prayer unto the God of my life.

¹⁰ I will say unto God, Thou art my helper, why hast Thou forgotten me? Why go I thus mournfully, while the enemy oppresseth me?

¹¹ While my bones were broken, mine enemies reproached me, whilst they said daily unto me, Where is now thy God?

¹² Why art thou so full of sadness, O my soul? And why dost thou trouble me? Put thy trust in God, for I will yet give Him thanks, the salvation of my countenance, and my God.

Psalm 42. *Judica me, Deus.*
A Psalm of David. Without superscription in the Hebrew.

JUDGE me, O God, and defend my cause; from an unholy nation, from the unjust and crafty man, deliver me.

² For Thou, O God, art my strength; why hast Thou rejected me? And why go I so heavily, while the enemy oppresseth me?

³ O send out Thy light and Thy truth; they have led me, and brought me unto Thy holy hill, and to Thy dwellings.

⁴ And I will go in unto the altar of God, even unto the God who giveth joy to my youth; upon the harp will I give thanks unto Thee, O God, my God.

⁵ Why art thou so full of sadness, O my soul? And why dost thou trouble me? Put thy trust in God,

for I will yet give Him thanks, the salvation of my countenance, and my God.

Glory be to the Father, and to the Son, and to the Holy Spirit; both now, and ever, and unto the ages of ages. Amen.

Alleluia, alleluia, alleluia. Glory be to Thee, O God. Thrice.

Lord, have mercy. Thrice.

Glory be to the Father, and to the Son, and to the Holy Spirit; both now, and ever, and unto the ages of ages. Amen.

Third Stasis

Psalm 43. *Deus, auribus.*
Unto the end, of the sons of Korah,
for instruction.

GOD, we have heard with our ears, and our fathers have told us, the work which Thou hast done in their days, in the days of old;

³ How Thou hast driven out the heathen with Thy hand, and planted them in; how Thou didst afflict the people, and cast them out.

⁴ For they gat not the land in possession through their own sword, neither was it their own arm that saved them; but Thy right hand, and Thine arm, and the light of Thy countenance, because Thou hadst a favor unto them.

⁵ Thou art Thyself my King and my God, Who dost command the salvation of Jacob.

⁶ Through Thee will we gore our enemies as with horns, and in Thy Name will we wipe out them that rise up against us.

⁷ For I will not trust in my bow, and my sword shall not save me;

⁸ For Thou hast saved us from them that afflict us, and hast put them to shame that hate us.

⁹ We make our boast of God all day long, and in Thy Name we will give thanks for ever.

¹⁰ But now Thou hast rejected us and put us to shame, and goest not forth, O God, with our armies.

¹¹ Thou hast turned us back before our enemies, and they which hate us have plundered our goods.

¹² Thou hast given us to be eaten like sheep, and hast scattered us among the heathen.

¹³ Thou didst sell Thy people for naught, and there were not many at our auction.

¹⁴ Thou hast made us the rebuke of our neighbors, a scoff and derision of them that are round about us.

¹⁵ Thou hast made us to be a by-word among the nations, and that the peoples shake their heads at us.

¹⁶ All day long my confusion is before me, and my face is covered with shame,

¹⁷ At the voice of the slanderer and blasphemer, at the face of the enemy and avenger.

¹⁸ All this hath come upon us, yet have we not forgotten Thee, neither behaved ourselves frowardly in Thy covenant,

¹⁹ And our heart hath not turned back, but Thou hast turned aside our paths from Thy ways.

²⁰ For Thou hast humbled us in a place of affliction, and covered us with the shadow of death.

²¹ If we have forgotten the Name of our God, and if we have holden up our hands to any strange god,

²² Shall not God search it out? For He knoweth the very secrets of the heart.

²³ For Thy sake we are killed all the day long; we are accounted as sheep for the slaughter.

²⁴ Up, Lord, why sleepest Thou? Arise, and reject us not before the end.

²⁵ Wherefore hidest Thou Thy face? Dost Thou forget our poverty and our affliction?

²⁶ For our soul is humbled down into the dust; our belly cleaveth unto the ground.

²⁷ Arise, O Lord; help us, and deliver us for Thy Name's sake.

Psalm 44. *Eructavit cor meum.*

Unto the end, concerning the verses that are to be
alternated, of the sons of Korah, for instruction, a
Song of the Beloved.

MY heart hath poured forth a good Word; I
speak of my works unto the King. My tongue
is the pen of a ready writer.

3 Thou art fairer than the sons of men; full of
grace are Thy lips, therefore hath God blessed
Thee for ever.

4 Gird Thy sword upon Thy thigh, O Thou
most Mighty, according to Thy splendor and Thy
beauty,

5 And bend Thy bow, and prosper, and reign,
for the sake of truth, and meekness, and righteousness; and Thy right hand shall guide Thee
wonderfully.

6 Thy arrows are very sharp, O Thou most
Mighty, in the hearts of the king's enemies; the
peoples shall fall under Thee.

7 Thy throne, O God, is for ever and ever; the
scepter of Thy kingdom is a rod of justice.

8 Thou hast loved righteousness, and hated iniquity, wherefore God, even Thy God, hath anointed
Thee with the oil of gladness above Thy fellows.

9 Thy garments smell of myrrh, frankincense,
and cassia from the ivory palaces, from where
they have made Thee glad.

10 Kings' daughters are among Thy honorable

women. Upon Thy right hand did stand the queen; in garments of gold is she vested, wrought about with divers colors.

¹¹ Hearken, O daughter, and see, and incline thine ear, and forget thy people, and thy father's house.

¹² And the King shall greatly desire thy beauty; for He is thy Lord, and thou shalt worship Him,

¹³ And the daughters of Tyre with gifts; the rich among the people shall entreat thy countenance.

¹⁴ All the glory of the King's daughter is within; with gold fringes is she adorned, and needle-work of many colors.

¹⁵ The virgins in her train shall be brought unto the King; her companions shall be brought unto Thee.

¹⁶ With joy and gladness shall they be brought in; they shall be brought into the King's house.

¹⁷ In the place of thy fathers will be thy sons; thou shalt make them princes over all the earth.

¹⁸ I will remember thy name in every generation and generation; therefore shall the peoples give thanks unto thee for ever, and for ever and ever.

Psalm 45. *Deus noster refugium.*
Unto the end, of the sons of Korah, concerning hidden things.

GOD is our refuge and strength, a very present helper in the troubles which greatly afflict us.

3 Therefore will we not fear, when the earth be shaken, and the hills be cast into the midst of the sea.

4 The waters thereof did rage and swell, and the mountains shook at His power.

5 The rushings of the river gladden the city of God; the Most High hath sanctified His tabernacle.

6 God is in the midst of her, and she shall not be moved; God shall help her in the morning, and that right early.

7 The nations were troubled; kingdoms toppled; the Most High lifted up His voice; the earth quaked.

8 The Lord of hosts is with us; the God of Jacob is our protector.

9 O come hither, and behold the works of the Lord, what wonders He hath wrought on earth.

10 Making wars to cease in all the world, He breaketh the bow, and knappeth the spear in sunder, and burneth the shields in the fire.

11 Be still, and know that I am God; I will be

exalted among the nations, and I will be lifted up on the earth.

[12] The Lord of hosts is with us; the God of Jacob is our protector.

Glory be to the Father, and to the Son, and to the Holy Spirit; both now, and ever, and unto the ages of ages. Amen.

Alleluia, alleluia, alleluia. Glory be to Thee, O God. Thrice.

¶ After the Sixth Kathisma, the Trisagion Prayers, and these troparia, in Tone III:

Praise do I offer unto Thee, O Lord, and I cry out to Thee, turning away from all my transgressions: O God, have mercy upon me!

Glory be to the Father, and to the Son, and to the Holy Spirit.

Save me, O my God, as once Thou didst save the publican! O my Saviour, Who didst not disdain the tears of the harlot, accept also my sighs, and save me!

Both now, and ever, and unto the ages of ages. Amen.

As a servant I now flee to thy protection, O most immaculate one. Deliver me from the molten image of the passions, O Theotokos, in that thou gavest birth unto the Author of dispassion.

Lord, have mercy [40]. And this Prayer:

WE thank Thee, O Lord our God, for all Thy loving deeds which have been unto us, unworthy as we are, from our infancy up to the present hour, those we know and those of which we are ignorant, both manifest and hidden, which have come to us by word or by deed. O Thou Who hast loved us enough to be pleased to have given Thine only-begotten Son for us, vouchsafe even us to be worthy of Thy love. By Thy word grant us wisdom, and by the fear of Thee breathe into us strength from Thy power; and if, voluntarily or involuntarily, we have sinned, forgive us and take no account of our misdeeds; and keep our souls holy, and set them before Thy throne pure in conscience, and having had an end worthy of Thy love for mankind. And be Thou mindful, O Lord, of all that call upon Thy Name in truth; remember all that wish us good or evil, for we are all men, and every man is vain. Wherefore, we beseech Thee, O Lord, Grant us the great mercy of Thy lovingkindness. Amen.

The Seventh Kathisma

Psalm 46. *Omnes gentes, plaudite.*
Unto the end, of the sons of Korah, a Psalm.

LL ye peoples, clap your hands; O shout unto God with a voice of rejoicing.

³ For the Lord Most High is terrible, a great King over all the earth.

⁴ He hath subdued the peoples unto us, and the nations under our feet.

⁵ He hath chosen out His inheritance for us, even the goodness of Jacob, whom He loved.

⁶ God is gone up with a merry noise, the Lord with the sound of the trump.

⁷ O sing unto our God, sing ye; O sing unto our King, sing ye.

⁸ For God is the King of all the earth, sing ye with understanding.

⁹ God reigneth over the nations; God sitteth upon His holy throne.

¹⁰ The princes of the peoples are gathered together, even with the God of Abraham; for God's mighty in the land are very high exalted.

Psalm 47. *Magnus Dominus.*
A Psalm and Song of the sons of Korah,
on the second day of the week.

 REAT is the Lord, and highly to be praised, in the city of our God, even upon His holy hill,

³ The well-situated joy of the whole world. The hills of Zion are the northern sides; the city of the great King.

⁴ God is known in her towers, when He cometh to her help.

⁵ For lo, the kings of the earth did gather, and come together.

⁶ They marveled to see her thus; they were troubled; they were shaken.

⁷ Fear came upon them; there was pain, as upon a woman in her travail.

⁸ With a stormy wind shalt Thou break the ships of Tarshish.

⁹ Like as we have heard, so have we seen in the city of the Lord of hosts, in the city of our God; God hath established her for ever.

¹⁰ We have received Thy mercy, O God, in the midst of Thy temple.

¹¹ According to Thy Name, O God, even so is Thy praise unto the ends of the earth; Thy right hand is full of righteousness.

¹² Let Mount Zion rejoice, and let the daughters

of Judah be glad, because of Thy judgments, O Lord.

¹³ Walk about Zion, and go round about her, and tell the towers thereof.

¹⁴ Set your hearts on her strength, and consider her houses, that ye may tell it to another generation.

¹⁵ For He is our God for ever, even for ever and ever; He shall be our shepherd for evermore.

Psalm 48. *Audite hæc, omnes.*
Unto the end, of the sons of Korah, a Psalm.

 HEAR this, all ye nations; take heed, all ye that dwell in the world;

³ High and low, rich and poor, one with another.

⁴ My mouth shall speak wisdom, and the meditation of my heart shall be of understanding.

⁵ I will incline mine ear to the parable, and show my dark speech upon the harp.

⁶ Wherefore should I fear in the evil day, when the wickedness at my heels shall compass me round about?

⁷ There be some that put their trust in their own strength, and boast themselves in the multitude of their riches.

⁸ A brother doth not redeem; shall a man redeem? He cannot give ransom to God even for himself,

⁹ Nor the price of redemption of his own soul, though he hath labored long,

¹⁰ And shall live until the end, and not see corruption,

¹¹ When he will see the wise also dying; together with the ignorant and foolish shall they perish, and leave their riches for other.

¹² And their graves shall be their houses for ever; their dwelling-places from one generation to another; they named the land after their names.

¹³ But man, being in honor, understood it not; he shall be compared unto the brute beasts, and is become like unto them.

¹⁴ This way of theirs is a stumbling-block unto them, yet afterwards they wish well with their mouths.

¹⁵ They are driven to hell like sheep; death shall be their shepherd, and the righteous shall have dominion over them in the morning, and their help shall rot in hell; they have been cast out from their glory.

¹⁶ But God will deliver my soul from the hand of hell, when He receiveth me.

¹⁷ Be not thou afraid, though a man be made rich, or though the glory of his house be increased;

¹⁸ For when he dieth, he shall carry nothing away, neither shall his pomp follow him.

¹⁹ For while he liveth, he counteth himself a happy man; he will speak well of Thee, so long as Thou doest good unto him.

²⁰ He shall go in even to the generation of his fathers; he shall never see the light.

²¹ But man, being in honor, understood it not; he shall be compared unto the brute beasts, and is become like unto them.

Glory be to the Father, and to the Son, and to the Holy Spirit; both now, and ever, and unto the ages of ages. Amen.

Alleluia, alleluia, alleluia. Glory be to Thee, O God. Thrice.

Lord, have mercy. Thrice.

Glory be to the Father, and to the Son, and to the Holy Spirit; both now, and ever, and unto the ages of ages. Amen.

Second Stasis

Psalm 49. *Deus deorum.*
A Psalm for Asaph.

THE God of gods, even the Lord, hath spoken, and summoned the earth, from the rising up of the sun, unto the going down thereof.

² Out of Zion is the splendor of His perfect beauty.

³ God shall plainly come, even our God, and He shall not keep silence; there shall burn before Him a consuming fire, and a mighty tempest is round about Him.

⁴ He shall summon the heavens from above, and the earth, that He may judge His people.

⁵ Gather His saints together unto Him, those that have made a covenant with Him for sacrifice,

⁶ And the heavens shall declare His righteousness, for God is Judge.

⁷ Hear, O my people, and I will speak unto you, and I will testify against thee, O Israel; I am God, even thy God.

⁸ I will not reprove thee because of thy sacrifices, for thy whole-burnt offerings are always before Me.

⁹ I will take no bullock out of thine house, nor he-goat out of thy folds.

¹⁰ For all the beasts of the forest are Mine, and so are the cattle upon a thousand hills, and the oxen.

¹¹ I know all the fowls of the heavens, and the beauty of the field is with Me.

¹² If I be hungry, I will not tell thee; for the whole world is Mine, and the fullness thereof.

¹³ Shall I eat bulls' flesh? Or drink the blood of goats?

¹⁴ Offer unto God a sacrifice of praise, and pay thy vows unto the Most High.

¹⁵ And call upon Me in the day of thy trouble, and I will deliver thee, and thou shalt glorify Me.

¹⁶ But unto the sinners God said, Why dost thou preach My statutes, and takest My covenant in thy mouth?

¹⁷ For thou hast hated correction, and hast cast My words behind thee.

¹⁸ If thou sawest a thief, thou didst run with him, and hast been partaker with the adulterer.

¹⁹ Thy mouth hath embroidered evil, and thy tongue hath woven lies.

²⁰ Sitting, thou didst slander thy brother, and hast laid temptation on thine own mother's son.

²¹ These things hast thou done, and I held My tongue; thou thoughtest wickedly, that I could be even such a one as thyself; I will reprove thee, and set thy sins before thy face.

²² Therefore consider this, ye that forget God, lest He pluck you away, and there be none to deliver.

²³ The sacrifice of praise shall glorify Me; and there is the way, by which I will show him My salvation.

Psalm 50. *Miserere mei, Deus.*
Unto the end, a Psalm of instruction by David,
when Nathan the prophet came unto him,
after he had gone in to Bathsheba, the wife
of Uriah.

HAVE mercy upon me, O God, after Thy great goodness, and according to the multitude of Thy mercies do away mine offences.

⁴ Wash me thoroughly from my wickedness, and cleanse me from my sin.

⁵ For I know my fault, and my sin is ever before me.

⁶ Against Thee only have I sinned, and done evil before Thee, that Thou mightest be justified in Thy words, and prevail when Thou art judged.

⁷ For behold, I was conceived in wickedness, and in sins did my mother bear me.

⁸ For behold, Thou hast loved truth; the hidden and secret things of Thy wisdom hast Thou revealed unto me.

⁹ Thou shalt sprinkle me with hyssop, and I shall be made clean; Thou shalt wash me, and I shall become whiter than snow.

¹⁰ Thou shalt give joy and gladness to my hearing; the bones that have been humbled will rejoice.

¹¹ Turn Thy face from my sins, and put out all my misdeeds.

¹² Make me a clean heart, O God, and renew a right spirit within me.

¹³ Cast me not away from Thy presence, and take not Thy Holy Spirit from me.

¹⁴ O give me the comfort of Thy salvation, and stablish me with Thy governing Spirit.

¹⁵ Then shall I teach Thy ways unto the wicked, and the ungodly shall be converted unto Thee.

¹⁶ Deliver me from blood-guiltiness, O God, the God of my salvation, and my tongue shall rejoice in Thy righteousness.

¹⁷ O Lord, open Thou my lips, and my mouth shall show forth Thy praise.

¹⁸ For if Thou hadst desired sacrifice, I would have given it; but Thou delightest not in burnt offerings.

¹⁹ The sacrifice unto God is a contrite spirit; a contrite and humble heart God shall not despise.

²⁰ O Lord, be favorable in Thy good will unto Zion, and let the walls of Jerusalem be builded up.

²¹ Then shalt Thou be pleased with the sacrifice of righteousness, with oblation and whole-burnt offerings; then shall they offer young bullocks upon Thine altar.

Glory be to the Father, and to the Son, and to the Holy Spirit; both now, and ever, and unto the ages of ages. Amen.

Alleluia, alleluia, alleluia. Glory be to Thee, O God. Thrice.

Lord, have mercy. Thrice.

Glory be to the Father, and to the Son, and to the Holy Spirit; both now, and ever, and unto the ages of ages. Amen.

Third Stasis

Psalm 51. *Quid gloriaris?*
Unto the end, a Psalm of David, for instruction,
when Doeg the Edomite came and told Saul,
and said unto him, David is come to the house
of Abimelech.

HY boastest thou thyself in evil, thou tyrant, and in mischief all day?

⁴ Thy tongue imagineth wickedness; thou hast stropped lies like a sharp razor.

⁵ Thou hast loved evil more than goodness; falsehood, more than to speak the truth.

⁶ Thou hast loved all words that may do hurt, O thou false tongue.

⁷ Therefore shall God destroy thee utterly; He shall pluck thee out, and tear thee from thy dwelling, and thy root from the land of the living.

⁸ The righteous shall see, and be afraid, and shall laugh at him, and say,

⁹ Behold the man that took not God for his helper, but trusted unto the multitude of his riches, and puffed up his vanity.

¹⁰ But I am like a fruitful olive-tree in the house of God; I have trusted in God's mercy for ever, and for ever and ever.

¹¹ I will always give thanks unto Thee for that Thou hast done, and I will wait upon Thy Name, for it is good before Thy saints.

Psalm 52. *Dixit insipiens.*
Unto the end, concerning Mahalath, an
instruction of David.

HE fool hath said in his heart, There is no
God. Corrupt are they, and become abominable in their wickedness, there is none that doeth
good.

3 God looked down from heaven upon the children of men, to see if there were any that did
understand, or seek after God.

4 They are all gone astray; they are altogether
become unprofitable; there is none that doeth
good, no not one.

5 Will they never understand, all that work
wickedness, who eat up my people as they would
eat bread? They have not called upon the Lord.

6 There were they afraid, where no fear was; for
God hath scattered the bones of the man-pleas-
ers; they were put to confusion, because God hath
despised them.

7 Oh, who will give the salvation of Israel out of
Zion? When God shall turn back the captivity of
His people, Jacob shall rejoice, and Israel shall be
right glad.

Psalm 53. *Deus, in nomine.*

Unto the end, among the songs of instruction by David, when the Ziphites came and said to Saul, Lo, is not David hid with us?

GOD, in Thy Name save me, and judge me by Thy power.

⁴ Hear my prayer, O God; hearken unto the words of my mouth.

⁵ For strangers are risen up against me, and mighty men have sought after my soul, which have not set God before them.

⁶ For behold, God helpeth me, and the Lord is the defender of my soul.

⁷ He shall repay mine enemies for their evil; destroy Thou them by Thy truth.

⁸ Willingly shall I sacrifice unto Thee; I will praise Thy Name, O Lord, for it is good.

⁹ For Thou hast delivered me out of every trouble, and mine eye hath looked upon mine enemies.

Psalm 54. *Exaudi, Deus.*

Unto the end, among the songs of instruction for Asaph, a Psalm.

EAR my prayer, O God, and despise not my petition.

³ Take heed unto me, and hear me; I mourned in my grief, and was vexed

⁴ By the voice of the enemy, and by the

oppression of the sinner, for they minded to do me mischief; and have wrathfully set themselves against me.

⁵ My heart is disquieted within me, and the fear of death is fallen upon me.

⁶ Fearfulness and trembling are come upon me, and darkness hath covered me.

⁷ And I said, Who will give me wings like a dove's? And I will fly away, and be at rest.

⁸ Lo, I ran away far off, and dwelt in the wilderness.

⁹ I waited for God, Who saveth me from faint-heartedness and from tempest.

¹⁰ Drown their voices, O Lord, and divide their tongues, for I have seen mischief and strife in the city.

¹¹ Day and night they go about the walls thereof; mischief also and hardship are in the midst of it, and injustice,

¹² And neither usury nor fraud go out of its streets.

¹³ For if an enemy had reviled me, I could have borne it; or if he that hateth me had blustered against me, then I would have hid myself from him.

¹⁴ But it was even thou, a man of like mind, my guide, and my own familiar friend,

¹⁵ Who took sweet counsel with me at table; we walked in the house of God in concord.

¹⁶ Let death come upon them, and let them go

down alive into hell; for wickedness is in their dwellings, and in their midst.

¹⁷ As for me, I called upon God, and the Lord heard me.

¹⁸ Evening, and morning, and noon-day will I call out, and cry aloud, and He shall hear my voice.

¹⁹ He will deliver my soul in peace from them that draw nigh against me, for they were with me in crowds.

²⁰ God will hear, and He that is before the ages shall humble them; there is no change with them, for they have not feared God.

²¹ He hath stretched forth His hand for retribution; they have defiled His covenant.

²² They were divided at the wrath of His countenance, and their hearts drew nigh; their words were smoother than oil, and yet are they arrows.

²³ O cast thy care upon the Lord, and He shall nourish thee; He shall never suffer the righteous to stumble.

²⁴ But Thou, O God, shalt bring them into the pit of destruction; the blood-thirsty and deceitful men shall not live out half their days, but I shall trust in Thee, O Lord.

Glory be to the Father, and to the Son, and to the Holy Spirit; both now, and ever, and unto the ages of ages. Amen.

Alleluia, alleluia, alleluia. Glory be to Thee, O God. Thrice.

¶ After the Seventh Kathisma, the Trisagion Prayers, and these troparia, in Tone V:

When the Judge taketh His seat, and the angels stand up, when the trumpet soundeth, and the flame is kindled, what shall I do, O my soul, when I am led to trial? For then thy wicked deeds will be presented for judgment and thy secret offenses will be revealed. Wherefore, before the end cry out to the Judge: O God, cleanse me and save me!

Glory be to the Father, and to the Son, and to the Holy Spirit.

Let us all keep watch and go forth to meet Christ with lighted lamps and a great quantity of oil, that we may be accounted worthy to enter the bridal chamber; for he that is overtaken outside the doors will cry out in vain unto God: Have mercy upon me!

Both now, and ever, and unto the ages of ages. Amen.

Lying upon the bed of mine offenses, I am bereft of hope for my salvation, for the sleep of my slothfulness bringeth torment to my soul. Yet, O God Who wast born of the Virgin, raise me up to praise Thee, that I may glorify Thee!

Lord, have mercy [40]. And this Prayer:

LORD my God, as Thou art good and the Lover of mankind, Thou hast accomplished many mercies for me, which I did not expect to see. And what shall I render unto Thy beneficence, O Lord, my Lord? I give thanks for Thine inexpressible long-suffering; and now do Thou help and aid me, and shelter me, O Master, from all the sins I have ever committed before Thee. For Thou knowest my folly, Thou knowest those things which I have done knowingly or unknowingly, voluntarily or involuntarily, at night or during the day, in mind and thought; therefore, as Thou art a good God Who lovest mankind, wash them away with the dew of Thy mercy, O all-good Lord, and save us for the sake of Thy holy Name, through the judgments which Thou knowest. For Thou art Light, and Truth, and Life, and unto Thee do we send up glory, to the Father, and to the Son, and to the Holy Spirit; both now, and ever, and unto the ages of ages. Amen.

The Eighth Kathisma

Psalm 55. *Miserere mei, Deus.*
Unto the end, concerning the people that were
removed from the sanctuary, a pillar inscription
of David, when the Philistines took him in Gath.

HAVE mercy upon me, O God, for man hath
trodden me down; fighting all day, he hath
pressed me sore.

3 Mine enemies have trodden on me all day
long, for there be many that fight against me from
on high.

4 I will not be afraid by day, for I will trust in
Thee.

5 My words shall speak praise concerning God;
I have put my trust in God, I will not fear what flesh
can do unto me.

6 They had a loathing unto my words all day; all
their thoughts were for evil against me.

7 They linger and lurk, they dog my heels,
because they are lying in wait for my soul.

8 By no means shalt Thou save them, Thou wilt
cast down peoples in displeasure.

⁹ O God, I have made known my life unto Thee; Thou hast put my tears before Thee, even as in Thy promise.

¹⁰ Let my enemies turn back on the very day that I call upon Thee; Lo, I have come to know that Thou art my God.

¹¹ My talk shall be of God's praise; my speech shall be in praise of the Lord.

¹² In God have I put my trust; I will not fear what man can do unto me.

¹³ In me, O God, are vows, which I will pay in Thy praise.

¹⁴ For Thou hast delivered my soul from death, mine eyes from tears, and my feet from slipping, that I may be acceptable before God in the light of the living.

Psalm 56. *Miserere mei, Deus.*
Unto the end, destroy not: by David, for a pillar inscription, when he fled from the presence of Saul into the cave.

HAVE mercy upon me, O God, have mercy upon me, for in Thee hath my soul trusted, and in the shadow of Thy wings shall I hope, until wickedness be over-past.

³ I will call unto the most high God, even unto the God that doeth good things for me.

⁴ He sent from heaven and saved me, He hath given over to reproof them that trod me down; God hath sent forth His mercy, and His truth.

⁵ And He hath delivered my soul from the midst of the lions' whelps; troubled, I slept my sleep. As for the children of men, their teeth are spears and arrows, and their tongue is a sharp sword.

⁶ Be Thou exalted above the heavens, O God, and Thy glory above all the earth.

⁷ They have laid a net for my feet, and pressed down my soul; they have digged a pit before me, and are fallen into it themselves.

⁸ My heart is ready, O God, my heart is ready; I will chant and sing in my glory.

⁹ Awake up, my glory; awake, psaltery and harp; I myself will awake right early.

¹⁰ I will give thanks unto Thee among the peoples, O Lord; I will sing unto Thee among the nations.

¹¹ For the greatness of Thy mercy reacheth unto the heavens, and Thy truth even unto the clouds.

¹² Be Thou exalted above the heavens, O God, and Thy glory above all the earth.

Psalm 57. *Si vere utique.*
Unto the end, destroy not: a pillar inscription of David.

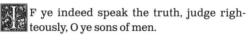

I F ye indeed speak the truth, judge righteously, O ye sons of men.

³ For ye imagine mischief in your heart upon the earth, and your hands weave wickedness.

⁴ Sinners are froward from the womb, even

from the belly have they gone astray, and spoken lies.

⁵ Their venom is like that of a serpent, even like the deaf adder, that stoppeth her ears;

⁶ Which refuseth to hear the voice of the charmer, charm he never so wisely.

⁷ God will break their teeth in their mouths; the Lord hath crushed the jaw-bones of the lions.

⁸ They shall go down like water that runneth out; He shall bend his bow until they falter.

⁹ Like melting wax shall they vanish away; fire hath fallen on them, and they shall not see the sun.

¹⁰ Before your briars can feel the thorn, He shall swallow them up alive in His wrath.

¹¹ The righteous man shall rejoice when he seeth the vengeance; he shall wash his hands in the blood of the sinner.

¹² And a man shall say, If indeed there is a reward for the righteous, then verily there is a God that judgeth them on earth.

Glory be to the Father, and to the Son, and to the Holy Spirit; both now, and ever, and unto the ages of ages. Amen.

Alleluia, alleluia, alleluia. Glory be to Thee, O God. Thrice.

Lord, have mercy. Thrice.

Glory be to the Father, and to the Son, and to the

Holy Spirit; both now, and ever, and unto the ages of ages. Amen.

Second Stasis

Psalm 58. *Eripe me de inimicis.*
Unto the end, destroy not: a pillar inscription of David, when Saul sent, and they watched the house to kill him.

ESCUE me from mine enemies, O God, and deliver me from them that rise up against me.

³ O deliver me from the wicked-doers, and save me from the blood-thirsty men.

⁴ For lo, they have seized my soul, the mighty men have fallen upon me; neither is it my wrong-doing, nor my fault, O Lord.

⁵ Without misdemeanor have I run and directed my steps; rise up to meet me and see.

⁶ And Thou, O Lord God of hosts, the God of Israel, be attentive to visit all the heathen, and be not merciful unto them that do wickedness.

⁷ They shall go to and fro in the evening, and scavenge like a dog, and run about through the city.

⁸ Behold, they speak with their mouth, and a sword is in their lips, for who hath heard?

⁹ But Thou, O Lord, shalt have them in derision; Thou shalt humble all the heathen.

¹⁰ I will save my strength for Thee, for Thou, O God, art my defender.

¹¹ My God, His mercy shall go before me; my God, He will flaunt me over mine enemies.

¹² Slay them not, that they may never forget Thy Law, but scatter them abroad by Thy power, and bring them down, O Lord, my defender,

¹³ For the sin of their mouth, and for the words of their lips; let them be taken in their pride, and they shall be notorious for their cursing and lies in the end.

¹⁴ Wrath is the end of them, and they shall be no more, and they shall know that God ruleth Jacob, and the ends of the world.

¹⁵ They shall go to and fro in the evening, and scavenge like a dog, and run about through the city.

¹⁶ They will run here and there for food, and grudge if they be not satisfied.

¹⁷ As for me, I will sing of Thy power, and will rejoice in Thy mercy betimes in the morning, for Thou hast been my defender and my refuge in the day of my trouble.

¹⁸ Thou art my helper; unto Thee will I sing, for Thou, O God, art my defender, and my merciful God.

Psalm 59. *Deus, repulisti nos.*
Unto the end, concerning the verses to be
alternated, a pillar inscription of David, for
instruction,when he had burned Mesopotamian
Syria and Syria Zobah, when Joab returned,
and smote of Edom in the Valley of Salt twelve
thousand.

GOD, Thou hast cast us out, and overthrown us; Thou hast been displeased with us and hast been merciful unto us.

⁴ Thou hast shaken the earth, and troubled it; heal the distress thereof, for it hath been stirred up.

⁵ Thou hast showed Thy people hard things; Thou hast made us drink the wine of contrition.

⁶ Thou hast given a sign unto such as fear Thee, that they may flee from before the bow.

⁷ That Thy beloved may be delivered, help me with Thy right hand, and hear me.

⁸ God hath spoken in His holiness, I will rejoice, and divide Shechem, and measure out the valley of Succoth.

⁹ Gilead is mine, and Manasseh is mine; Ephraim also is the strength of my head; Judah is my scepter.

¹⁰ Moab is the laver of my hope; over Edom will I stretch forth my shoe; the Philistines have submitted themselves unto me.

¹¹ Who will lead me into the strong city, or who will bring me into Edom?

¹² Wilt not Thou, O God, Who hast cast us out? And wilt not Thou, O God, go out with our hosts?

¹³ O give us help from affliction, for vain is the salvation of man.

¹⁴ Through God will we do mightily, and He shall wipe out them that afflict us.

Psalm 60. *Exaudi, Deus.*
Unto the end, among the Hymns of David.

HEAR my petition, O God; heed my prayer.
³ From the ends of the earth have I called upon Thee, when my heart was in heaviness, and Thou didst lift me up and set me upon a rock.

⁴ For Thou hast been my hope, and a tower of strength against the face of the enemy.

⁵ I will dwell in Thy tabernacle for ever; I will hide myself under the shelter of Thy wings.

⁶ For Thou, O God, hast heard my prayers, and hast given an inheritance unto those that fear Thy Name.

⁷ Thou shalt grant the King a long life, that his years may endure throughout all generations.

⁸ He shall abide before God for ever. Who can search out His mercy and truth?

⁹ So will I always sing praise unto Thy Name, that I may daily perform my vows.

Glory be to the Father, and to the Son, and to the

Holy Spirit; both now, and ever, and unto the ages of ages. Amen.

Alleluia, alleluia, alleluia. Glory be to Thee, O God. Thrice.

Lord, have mercy. Thrice.

Glory be to the Father, and to the Son, and to the Holy Spirit; both now, and ever, and unto the ages of ages. Amen.

Third Stasis

Psalm 61. *Nonne Deo?*

Unto the end, for Jeduthun, a Psalm of David.

OTH not my soul wait still upon God? For of Him cometh my salvation.

³ Yea, He is my God, and my Saviour, He is my defender; I shall no more be moved.

⁴ How long will ye threaten a man? Ye kill, all of you; yea, as ye might push over a leaning wall, or a broken rampart.

⁵ Moreover, they took counsel to impugn my honor; they ran in greed; they spake good words with their mouth, but cursed with their heart.

⁶ O my soul, wait thou still upon God, for from Him is my patient endurance.

⁷ Yea, He is my God, and my Saviour, He is my defender; I shall no more be moved.

⁸ In God is my salvation, and my glory; He is the God of my help, and in God is my trust.

⁹ O put your trust in Him, all ye congregation of

people; pour out your hearts before Him, for God is our helper.

¹⁰ But the children of men are vain; the children of men are deceitful upon the weights, that they may deal crookedly; they are altogether vanity.

¹¹ O trust not in wrong and do not imagine robbery; if riches increase, set not your heart upon them.

¹² God spake once, and twice I have heard the same, that power belongeth unto God,

¹³ And Thine, O Lord, is the mercy; for Thou rewardest every man according to his work.

Psalm 62. *Deus, Deus meus.*
A Psalm of David, when he was in the wilderness of Judah.

GOD, my God, early will I seek Thee. My soul hath thirsted for Thee, and how my flesh also hath longed after Thee in a barren and empty land where no water is.

³ Thus have I looked for Thee in the sanctuary, that I might behold Thy power and Thy glory.

⁴ For Thy mercy is better than life itself; my lips shall praise Thee.

⁵ I will bless Thee in my life on this manner: I will lift up my hands in Thy Name.

⁶ For my soul shall be satisfied, even as it were with marrow and fatness, and my mouth shall praise Thee with joyful lips.

⁷ If I remembered Thee upon my bed, in the morning I would take comfort in Thee,

⁸ Because Thou hast been my helper, and in the shelter of Thy wings will I rejoice.

⁹ My soul hath hanged upon Thee; Thy right hand hath upholden me.

¹⁰ These also that in vain seek my soul shall go under the earth.

¹¹ They shall be given over to the hand of the sword; they shall be a portion for foxes.

¹² But the King shall rejoice in God; every one that sweareth by Him shall be commended, for the mouth of them that speak lies hath been stopped.

Psalm 63. *Exaudi, Deus.*
Unto the end, a Psalm of David.

HEAR my voice, O God, when I pray unto Thee; deliver my soul from fear of the enemy.

³ Hide me from the gathering together of the froward; and from the mob of wicked doers,

⁴ Who have whet their tongues like a sword; they have bent their bow, a bitter thing,

⁵ That they may privily shoot at the innocent man. Suddenly will they shoot at him, and fear not.

⁶ They have set themselves up by a deceitful word, and have communed among themselves how they may lay snares; they said, Who shall see them?

⁷ They have searched out wickedness, they have

grown weary in their seeking of it; a man shall come, and a deep heart,

⁸ And God shall rise up; their wounds were as if made by the arrows of babes.

⁹ Yea, their tongues were weakened against them; all who saw them were troubled.

¹⁰ And every man was afraid; and they proclaimed the works of God, and understood His creation.

¹¹ The righteous man shall rejoice in the Lord, and shall put his trust in Him, and all they that are true of heart shall be praised.

Glory be to the Father, and to the Son, and to the Holy Spirit; both now, and ever, and unto the ages of ages. Amen.

Alleluia, alleluia, alleluia. Glory be to Thee, O God. Thrice.

¶ After the Eighth Kathisma, the Trisagion Prayers, and these troparia, in Tone V:

The threefold waves of despair toss me about, who have been dragged down into the abyss of sin; but as Thou art almighty, O Christ, Pilot of all, go Thou before me and guide me into the calm haven of dispassion, O Saviour, and save me in Thy loving-kindness.

Glory be to the Father, and to the Son, and to the Holy Spirit.

O my soul, who art here but a while, but shall

remain there everlastingly, I behold the tribunal, and the Judge seated upon His throne, and I tremble at the sentence. O my soul, change henceforth, for the trial is inevitable.

Both now, and ever, and unto the ages of ages. Amen.

O hope of the hopeless, help of the helpless, and aid of them that place their hope in thee, O holy Lady Theotokos, extend thy helping hand unto us!

Lord, have mercy [40]. And this Prayer:

COMPASSIONATE and merciful Lord, Who art long-suffering and of great mercy, hear my prayer and hearken unto the voice of my supplication; work with me a sign unto good; guide me to Thy path, that I may walk in the truth; gladden Thou my heart, that I may fear Thy holy Name. For great art Thou, Who workest wonders! Thou only art God, and there is none like unto Thee among the gods, O Lord, Who art mighty in mercy and good in strength, to help, to comfort, and to save all that trust in Thy Name, of the Father, and of the Son, and of the Holy Spirit; now, and ever, and unto the ages of ages. Amen.

The Ninth Kathisma

Psalm 64. *Te decet hymnus.*
Unto the end, a Psalm and Song of David,
sung by Jeremiah and Ezekiel and the people,
when they were about to be led captive away.

UNTO Thee, O God, belongeth praise in Zion, and unto Thee shall the vow be performed in Jerusalem.

3 Hear my prayer; unto Thee shall all flesh come.

4 The words of the ungodly have overpowered us, but Thou shalt wash away our impiety.

5 Blessed is the man whom Thou hast chosen and taken unto Thyself; he shall dwell in Thy courts. We shall be satisfied with the pleasures of Thy house; Thy temple is holy,

6 Wonderful in truth; hear us, O God of our salvation, the hope of all the ends of the earth, and of them that are afar off at sea.

7 Raising up the mountains by His strength, He is girded with power;

8 Stirring up the depths of the sea, who can

abide the noise of its waves? The heathen shall be brought to confusion.

⁹ They also that dwell in the uttermost parts of the earth shall be afraid at Thy signs; Thou dost embellish the outgoings of the morning and evening.

¹⁰ Thou didst visit the earth, and water it, Thou hast greatly enriched it; the river of God is full of water. Thou hast prepared food for them, for such is Thy providence.

¹¹ Water her furrows; increase her crops; the shoots shall rejoice in her showers.

¹² Thou shalt bless the crown of the year with Thy goodness, and Thy fields shall be full of plenty.

¹³ The beauty of the wilderness shall grow lush, and the little hills shall be girded with rejoicing on every side.

¹⁴ The sheep will be clothed with wool, and the valleys also shall stand so thick with wheat, that they shall laugh and sing.

Psalm 65. *Jubilate Deo.*
Unto the end, a Song or Psalm of Resurrection.

MAKE a joyful noise unto the Lord, all the earth, and sing unto His Name; make His praise to be glorious.

³ Say unto God, O how wonderful are Thy works! In the greatness of Thy power shall Thine enemies bow down unto Thee.

⁴ Let all the world worship Thee, and sing unto Thee; let it also praise Thy Name, O Most High.

⁵ O come hither, and behold the works of God, how wonderful He is in His counsels more than the children of men.

⁶ Who turneth the sea into dry land, so that they go through the river on foot; there shall we rejoice in Him,

⁷ Who by His power ruleth for ever; His eyes watch over the nations, let those who grieve Him be not exalted in themselves.

⁸ O bless our God, ye peoples, and make the voice of His praise to be heard;

⁹ Who hath set my soul unto life, and hath not suffered my feet to slip.

¹⁰ For Thou hast proved us, O God; Thou hast tried us, like as silver is tried.

¹¹ Thou broughtest us into the snare, and laidest trouble upon our back.

¹² Thou sufferedst men to ride over our heads; we went through fire and water, and Thou broughtest us out into refreshment.

¹³ I will go into Thine house with a whole-burnt offering, and will pay Thee my vows,

¹⁴ Which I promised with my lips, and spake with my mouth, when I was in trouble.

¹⁵ I will offer unto Thee fat whole-burnt sacrifices with incense, and rams; I will bring bullocks and goats unto Thee.

¹⁶ O come hither and hearken, all ye that fear

God, and I will tell you what He hath done for my soul.

¹⁷ I called unto Him with my mouth, and gave Him praises with my tongue.

¹⁸ If I regarded falsehood in mine heart, may the Lord not hear me.

¹⁹ Wherefore God hath heard me, and considered the voice of my prayer.

²⁰ Blessed be God, who hath not set aside my prayer, nor His mercy from me.

Psalm 66. *Deus misereatur.*
Unto the end, in verses, a Psalm or Song of David.

GOD, be merciful unto us, and bless us; shine the light of Thy countenance upon us, and have mercy upon us,

³ That Thy way may be known upon earth, Thy salvation among all nations.

⁴ Let the peoples give thanks unto Thee, O God; let all the peoples give thanks unto Thee.

⁵ O let the nations rejoice and be glad, for Thou shalt judge the folk with justice, and govern the nations upon earth.

⁶ Let the peoples give thanks unto Thee, O God; let all the peoples give thanks unto Thee.

⁷ The earth hath brought forth her increase; bless us, O God, our God.

⁸ Bless us, O God, and let all the ends of the world fear Him.

Glory be to the Father, and to the Son, and to the Holy Spirit; both now, and ever, and unto the ages of ages. Amen.

Alleluia, alleluia, alleluia. Glory be to Thee, O God. Thrice.

Lord, have mercy. Thrice.

Glory be to the Father, and to the Son, and to the Holy Spirit; both now, and ever, and unto the ages of ages. Amen.

Second Stasis

Psalm 67. *Exurgat Deus.*
Unto the end, a Psalm or Song of David.

ET God arise, and let His enemies be scattered, and let them that hate Him flee from before His face.

³ Like as smoke vanisheth, so let them vanish; like as wax melteth at the presence of fire, so let sinners perish at the presence of God,

⁴ But let the righteous be glad, and let them rejoice before God; let them take pleasure in gladness.

⁵ O sing unto God, sing unto His Name; prepare ye the way for Him that rideth upon the setting of the sun, LORD is His Name, and rejoice before Him.

⁶ Let them be troubled at the presence of Him, the Father of the fatherless, and the defender of the widow, even God in His holy habitation.

⁷ He is the God that maketh men to be of one mind in an house, leading forth the fettered with courage, and likewise the distressed living in the sepulchers.

⁸ O God, when Thou wentest forth before Thy people, when Thou wentest through the wilderness,

⁹ The earth quaked; indeed, the heavens dropped rain at the presence of the God of Sinai, at the presence of the God of Israel.

¹⁰ Thou dost withhold the bountiful rain, O God, from Thine inheritance, and it fainted, but Thou didst restore it.

¹¹ Thy creatures dwell therein; Thou hast prepared good things for the poor, O God.

¹² The Lord shall give speech with great power to them that preach the good tidings.

¹³ The king of the hosts of the Beloved shall divide the spoils for the beauty of the house.

¹⁴ If ye sleep within the boundary, ye shall be as a dove with silver wings, and her feathers like gleaming gold.

¹⁵ When the Heavenly One shall separate out kings over her, they shall be covered with snow in Zalmon.

¹⁶ God's hill is a rich mountain, a mountain of plenty, a rich mountain.

¹⁷ Why do ye ponder over mountains of plenty? This is the hill wherein it pleaseth God to dwell; yea, the Lord will abide in it for ever.

¹⁸ The chariots of God are ten thousand more than the thousand of those living in prosperity; the Lord is among them at Sinai, in the holy place.

¹⁹ Thou art gone up on high, Thou hast led captivity captive; Thou hast received gifts among men, even the disobedient, that Thou mightest settle Thyself in.

²⁰ The Lord God is blessed. Blessed be the Lord day by day; the God of our salvation shall speed us on our way.

²¹ Our God is the God that saveth, and of the Lord's Lord is the escape from death.

²² But God shall crush the heads of His enemies, and the hairy scalp of such a one as goeth on still in his wickedness.

²³ The Lord said, I will turn from Bashan; I will turn in the depths of the sea,

²⁴ That thy foot may be drenched in the blood of thine enemies, and that the tongue of thy dogs may be red from it.

²⁵ Thy goings were seen, O God, the processions of God my King in the sanctuary.

²⁶ The princes go before, the singers follow after, in the midst of damsels playing the timbrels.

²⁷ In churches bless ye God, the Lord from the fountains of Israel.

²⁸ There is Benjamin the younger in ecstasy, and the princes of Judah their rulers, the princes of Zebulun, and the princes of Naphtali.

[29] Declare Thyself, O God, by Thy might; stablish the thing, O God, which Thou hast wrought in us,

[30] For Thy temple's sake at Jerusalem shall kings bring presents unto Thee.

[31] Drive off the wild beasts with reeds, the herd of bulls among the kine of the people, to shut away those tempted by silver; scatter the nations that take pleasure in the field of battle.

[32] Ambassadors shall come out of Egypt; Ethiopia shall hasten to stretch out her hands unto God.

[33] Sing unto God, O ye kingdoms of the earth, sing praises unto the Lord,

[34] Unto Him Who hath gone into the heaven of heavens in the east; lo, He shall give to His voice the voice of power.

[35] Give ye glory to God; His majesty is upon Israel, and His power is upon the clouds.

[36] Wonderful is God in His saints, the God of Israel; He will give power and might unto His people. Blessed be God.

Glory be to the Father, and to the Son, and to the Holy Spirit; both now, and ever, and unto the ages of ages. Amen.

Alleluia, alleluia, alleluia. Glory be to Thee, O God. Thrice.

Lord, have mercy. Thrice.

Glory be to the Father, and to the Son, and to the

Holy Spirit; both now, and ever, and unto the ages of ages. Amen.

Third Stasis

Psalm 68. *Salvum me fac.*
Unto the end, concerning those that shall be changed, a Psalm of David.

 AVE me, O God, for the waters are come in, even unto my soul.

³ I was stuck fast in the deep mire, where no ground is; I am come into deep waters, and a tempest hath run over me.

⁴ I am weary of crying, my throat is become hoarse; my sight hath failed me, because I have been waiting so long upon my God.

⁵ They that hate me without a cause are become more than the hairs of my head; mine enemies, which persecute me unjustly, are become mighty. I paid them, then, for things I never took.

⁶ God, Thou knowest my foolishness, and my faults are not hid from Thee.

⁷ Let not them that wait upon Thee, O Lord, Lord of hosts, be ashamed because of me; let not those that seek Thee be confounded through me, O God of Israel.

⁸ For Thy sake have I suffered reproof; shame hath covered my face.

⁹ I am become a stranger unto my brethren, even an alien unto my mother's children.

¹⁰ For the zeal of Thine house hath eaten me up, and the rebukes of them that rebuked Thee are fallen upon me.

¹¹ I chastened my soul with fasting, and that was turned to my reproof.

¹² I put on sackcloth also, and they jested upon me.

¹³ They that sit in the gate amused themselves against me, and the drunkards made songs upon me.

¹⁴ But I make my prayer unto Thee, O God, at the acceptable time; O God, in the multitude of Thy mercy, hear me, even in the truth of Thy salvation.

¹⁵ Save me out of the mire, that I sink not; O let me be delivered from them that hate me, and out of the deep waters.

¹⁶ Let not the water-flood drown me, neither let the deep swallow me up, and let not the pit shut her mouth upon me.

¹⁷ Hear me, O Lord, for Thy mercy is gracious; turn Thee unto me according to the multitude of Thy loving-kindnesses.

¹⁸ Turn not Thy face from Thy servant, for I am in trouble; O quickly hearken unto me.

¹⁹ Draw nigh unto my soul, and deliver it; O deliver me, because of mine enemies.

²⁰ For Thou knowest my reproof, and my shame, and my dishonor; mine adversaries are all before Thee.

²¹ My soul was expecting rebuke, and misery; so I looked for some to have pity on me, but there was no one, neither found I any to comfort me.

²² They gave me also gall to eat, and when I was thirsty they gave me vinegar to drink.

²³ Let their table be made a snare to take themselves withal, and for a recompense, and an occasion of falling.

²⁴ Let their eyes be darkened, that they see not, and their backs be always bent.

²⁵ Pour out Thine indignation upon them, and let Thy wrathful displeasure take hold of them.

²⁶ Let their habitation be desolate, and no man to dwell in their tents.

²⁷ For they persecuted him whom Thou hast smitten, and have added to the pain of my wounds.

²⁸ Add iniquity unto their wickedness, and let them not come into Thy righteousness.

²⁹ Let them be blotted out of the book of the living, and not be written among the righteous.

³⁰ I am poor and in heaviness; let Thy salvation, O God, lift me up.

³¹ I will praise the Name of my God with a song; and I will magnify Him with praise.

³² And this shall please the Lord, better than a bullock that hath horns and hoofs.

³³ Let the humble consider this, and be glad; seek ye after God, and your soul shall live.

³⁴ For the Lord hath heard the poor and hath not despised His prisoners.

³⁵ Let heaven and earth praise Him, the sea, and all that liveth therein.

³⁶ For God will save Zion, and build the cities of Judah, and they shall dwell there, and have it in possession.

³⁷ The posterity also of Thy servants shall inherit it, and they that love Thy Name shall dwell therein.

Psalm 69. *Deus in adjutorium.*
Unto the end, by David for remembrance, that the Lord may save me.

 GOD, make speed to save me; O Lord, make haste to help me.

³ Let them be ashamed and confounded that seek after my soul. Let them be turned backward and be ashamed that wish me evil.

⁴ Let them for their reward be soon brought to shame that say over me, Well, well.

⁵ Let all those that seek Thee be joyful and glad in Thee, O God, and let all such as delight in Thy salvation say always, The Lord be praised.

⁶ But I am poor and needy, O God; help me! Thou art my helper and my redeemer, O Lord; make no long tarrying.

Glory be to the Father, and to the Son, and to the

Holy Spirit; both now, and ever, and unto the ages of ages. Amen.

Alleluia, alleluia, alleluia. Glory be to Thee, O God. Thrice.

¶ After the Ninth Kathisma, the Trisagion Prayers, and these troparia, in Tone VI:

I think upon the dreadful day, and weep for my evil deeds. How shall I answer the immortal King? Or with what boldness shall I look upon the Judge, prodigal that I am? O compassionate Father, only-begotten Son and Holy Spirit, have mercy upon me!

Glory be to the Father, and to the Son, and to the Holy Spirit.

In the vale of tears, at the place which Thou hast appointed for when Thou shalt take Thy seat to render Thy righteous judgment, O Merciful One, condemn not my secret sins, nor put me to shame before the angels; but take pity on me, O God, and have mercy on me!

Both now, and ever, and unto the ages of ages. Amen.

O Theotokos, thou hope and mighty protection of them that have recourse unto thee, good intercession for the world: with the incorporeal ones earnestly entreat God, Who loveth mankind, to Whom thou gavest birth, that our souls be delivered from every threat, O thou only blessed one.

Lord, have mercy [40]. And this Prayer:

MASTER Lord our God, Who alone knowest the sickness of my wretched soul and the healing thereof, Heal it, as Thou knowest, for the sake of the greatness of Thy mercy and Thy compassion, for there is no salve, or ointment, or binding, which may be applied thereto because of my deeds. But do Thou, Who camest not to call the righteous, but sinners, to repentance, have mercy and compassion, and forgive it; tear up the account of my many shameful deeds, and guide me to Thy straight path, that, walking in Thy truth, I may be able to escape the arrows of the evil one, and thus stand uncondemned before Thy dread throne, glorifying and praising Thy most holy name for ever. Amen.

The Tenth Kathisma

Psalm 70. *In te, Domine, speravi.*
David's, a Psalm of the sons of Jonadab and of the
first to be taken captive. Without superscription
in the Hebrew.

 N Thee, O Lord, have I put my trust, let me never be confounded.

² Rescue me in Thy righteousness, and deliver me; incline Thine ear unto me, and save me.

³ Be Thou unto me a defending God, and a strong-hold to save me, for Thou art my buttress and my safe haven.

⁴ O my God, deliver me out of the hands of the sinner, out of the hands of the law-breaker and the offender.

⁵ For Thou art the thing that I long for, O Lord; O Lord, Thou art my hope, even from my youth.

⁶ Through Thee have I been holden up from the womb, from my mother's belly art Thou my protector; my praise shall be always of Thee.

⁷ I am become as it were a spectacle unto many, but Thou art my strong helper.

⁸ O let my mouth be filled with Thy praise, that I may sing unto Thy glory, and all day unto Thy majesty.

⁹ Cast me not away in the time of old age; forsake me not when my strength faileth me.

¹⁰ For mine enemies spake against me, and they that lay wait for my soul took their counsel together.

¹¹ They said, God hath forsaken him; persecute him, and take him, for there is none to deliver him.

¹² O my God, go not far from me; my God, haste Thee to help me.

¹³ Let them be confounded and wiped out that are against my soul; let them be covered with shame and confusion that seek to do me evil.

¹⁴ But I shall always hope in Thee, and will set myself to praise Thee more and more.

¹⁵ My mouth shall speak of Thy righteousness, and all day of Thy salvation, because I have not learned the art of writing.

¹⁶ I will go forth in the strength of the Lord; O Lord, I will remember Thy righteousness only.

¹⁷ O my God, which hath taught me from my youth up even until now, I will declare Thy wondrous works,

¹⁸ Yea, forsake me not, O my God, even unto mine old age, when I am gray-headed, until I have made known Thy strength unto every generation that is yet to come.

¹⁹ Thy power and Thy righteousness, O God, are very high, for Thou hast done great things for me. O God, who is like unto Thee?

²⁰ O what great troubles and adversities hast Thou showed me! And yet didst Thou turn and revive me, and broughtest me up from the depths of the earth.

²¹ Thou hast heaped Thy majesty upon me, and Thou hast returned to comfort me, and broughtest me up again from the depths of the earth.

²² Therefore will I confess Thy truth to Thee among the people, O Lord, upon instruments of psalmody; I will sing unto Thee upon the harp, O God, Thou Holy One of Israel.

²³ My lips will be glad when I sing unto Thee, and so will my soul whom Thou hast delivered.

²⁴ My tongue also shall be occupied in Thy righteousness all the day long, when they are confounded and brought unto shame that seek to do me evil.

Psalm 71. *Deus, judicium.*
Concerning Solomon, a Psalm of David.

IVE the King Thy judgment, O God, and Thy righteousness unto the King's son,

² To judge Thy people according unto justice, and Thy poor with judgment.

³ Let the mountains stand witness for peace unto the people, and the little hills for justice.

⁴ He shall judge the simple folk, and shall

save the children of the poor, and humble the slanderer.

⁵ Even as long as the sun shall He endure, and before the moon, from one generation to another.

⁶ He shall come down like the rain upon a fleece of wool, even as the drops that water the earth.

⁷ In His days shall righteousness flourish, and abundance of peace, so long as the moon endureth.

⁸ He shall have dominion also from sea to sea, and from the rivers unto the world's end.

⁹ The Ethiopians shall kneel before Him, and His enemies shall lick the dust.

¹⁰ The kings of Tarshish and of the isles shall give presents, the kings of Arabia and Sheba shall bring gifts.

¹¹ Yea, all the kings of the earth shall fall down before Him, all nations shall do Him service.

¹² For He hath delivered the poor from the mighty, and the needy, that had no helper.

¹³ He shall spare the simple and needy, and shall save the souls of the poor.

¹⁴ He shall deliver their souls from usury and from injustice, and His Name shall be precious in their sight.

¹⁵ And He shall live, and unto Him shall be given of the gold of Arabia, and they shall ever pray concerning Him; they shall bless Him the day long.

¹⁶ There shall be a firmament on the earth upon the tops of the mountains; above Lebanon shall

the fruit thereof be exalted, and they of the city shall flourish like the grass of the earth.

¹⁷ His Name shall be blessed for ever; His Name shall abide before the sun; and all the tribes of the earth shall be blessed in Him; all the nations shall bless Him.

¹⁸ Blessed be the Lord God of Israel, Who alone worketh wonders,

¹⁹ And blessed be the Name of His glory for ever, and for ever and ever, and all the earth shall be filled with His glory. So be it. So be it.

The Songs of David the son of Jesse are ended.

Glory be to the Father, and to the Son, and to the Holy Spirit; both now, and ever, and unto the ages of ages. Amen.

Alleluia, alleluia, alleluia. Glory be to Thee, O God. Thrice.

Lord, have mercy. Thrice.

Glory be to the Father, and to the Son, and to the Holy Spirit; both now, and ever, and unto the ages of ages. Amen.

Second Stasis

Psalm 72. *Quam bonus Israel!*
A Psalm for Asaph.

OW good is God unto Israel, unto them of an upright heart!

² Nevertheless, my feet were almost moved; my steps had well-nigh slipped,

³ For I was envious of the wicked, seeing the peace of sinners,

⁴ For there is no fear in their death, and they are steadfast under the knout.

⁵ They are not in the labor of other folk, neither are they plagued like other men.

⁶ Therefore hath their pride mastered them utterly; they have clothed themselves in their unrighteousness and impiety.

⁷ Their injustice swelleth out like fat; they have surpassed even the lust of their heart.

⁸ They have thought and spoken in craftiness; they have spoken injustice in the high place.

⁹ They set their mouth against the heavens, and their tongue goeth throughout the world.

¹⁰ Therefore shall my people turn hither; and full days shall come to them.

¹¹ And they said, How should God see it? and, Is there knowledge in the Most High?

¹² Lo, these are the sinners and the prosperous of this age, and they have riches in possession.

¹³ And I said, Then in vain have I cleansed my heart and washed mine hands in innocency.

¹⁴ For I have been scourged all day, and chastened every morning.

¹⁵ If I said, I will speak thus, lo, I would have been faithless to the generation of Thy children.

¹⁶ And I sought to understand, but it was too hard for me,

¹⁷ Until I went into the sanctuary of God; then understood I their end,

¹⁸ Namely, that Thou hast laid evil upon them for their fraud; Thou didst cast them down, when they vaunted themselves.

¹⁹ Oh, such was their desolation! They were suddenly wiped out; they perished because of their lawlessness.

²⁰ Like as a dream when one awaketh, O Lord, so didst Thou make their image to vanish out of Thy city.

²¹ For my heart was kindled, and my insides were changed.

²² And I was humbled, and did not understand; I became as a beast before Thee.

²³ Nevertheless, I am always with Thee, for Thou hast holden me by my right hand,

²⁴ And hast guided me by Thy counsel, and with glory hast Thou received me.

²⁵ For what have I in heaven, and what have I desired upon earth from Thee?

²⁶ My flesh and my heart have failed, O God of my heart, but Thou art my portion, O God, for ever.

²⁷ For lo, they that go far from Thee shall perish; Thou hast destroyed all them that are unfaithful against Thee.

²⁸ But it is good for me to cleave unto God, to

put my trust in the Lord, that I may declare all Thy praises in the gates of the daughter of Zion.

Psalm 73. *Ut quid, Deus?*
Of instruction, for Asaph.

GOD, why hast Thou so utterly rejected us? Why hath Thy wrath been so hot against the sheep of Thy pasture?

² O remember Thy congregation, which Thou hast purchased of old; by Thy staff hast Thou delivered Thine inheritance, this holy hill of Zion, wherein Thou hast dwelt.

³ Lift up Thy hands against their overweening pride, all that the enemy hath done wickedly in Thy sanctuary.

⁴ Even they that hate Thee have boasted in the midst of Thy holy-day; they set up their banners; banners, though they knew it not,

⁵ As in the going-forth on high. Like as in the oak forest the tree hath been hewn down by the axe,

⁶ So with the doors thereof; with axes and hammers they demolished it.

⁷ They burned with fire Thy sanctuary on earth; they defiled the dwelling-place of Thy Name.

⁸ They said in their hearts, the brood of them together, Come, and let us abolish all the festivals of God from the earth.

⁹ We have not seen our signs, there is no more any prophet, nor will he any more acknowledge us.

¹⁰ How long, O God, shall the enemy carry on? Shall the adversary blaspheme Thy Name for ever?

¹¹ Why dost Thou utterly withdraw Thy hand and Thy right hand out of the midst of Thy bosom?

¹² But God is our King before the ages; He hath wrought salvation in the midst of the earth.

¹³ Thou didst establish the sea through Thy power; Thou brakest the heads of the dragons in the waters.

¹⁴ Thou smotest the heads of Leviathan in pieces; Thou gavest him as food for the people of Ethiopia.

¹⁵ Thou hast disrupted the springs and streams; Thou hast dried up the rivers of Etham.

¹⁶ Thine is the day, and Thine is the night; Thou hast perfected the light and the sun.

¹⁷ Thou hast fixed all the borders of the earth; the harvest and the spring, Thou hast established them.

¹⁸ Remember this, the enemy hath reviled the Lord, and a foolish people hath blasphemed Thy Name.

¹⁹ O deliver not the soul that confesseth Thee unto the wild beasts; forget not the souls of the poor for ever.

²⁰ Give refuge unto Thy covenant, for the dark places of the earth are filled with houses of iniquity.

²¹ O let not the meek be turned away ashamed; the poor and needy shall praise Thy Name.

²² Arise, O God, defend Thine own cause; remember the blasphemy against Thee, which is from the foolish man all day.

²³ Forget not the voice of Thy suppliants; the arrogance of them that hate Thee increaseth ever more and more.

Glory be to the Father, and to the Son, and to the Holy Spirit; both now, and ever, and unto the ages of ages. Amen.

Alleluia, alleluia, alleluia. Glory be to Thee, O God. Thrice.

Lord, have mercy. Thrice.

Glory be to the Father, and to the Son, and to the Holy Spirit; both now, and ever, and unto the ages of ages. Amen.

Third Stasis

Psalm 74. *Confitebimur tibi.*
Unto the end, destroy not, a Psalm or Song
for Asaph.

E will give thanks unto Thee, O God; we will give thanks unto Thee, and call upon Thy Name; we will declare all Thy wondrous works.

³ In a time of my reckoning, I shall judge according unto right.

⁴ The earth is growing weak, and all who live on it; I have shored up the pillars thereof.

⁵ I said unto the lawless, Deal not so lawlessly, and to the sinners, Lift not up the horn.

⁶ Set not up your horn on high, and speak not injustice against God;

⁷ For justice cometh neither from the coming forth of the sun, nor from the west, nor yet from the barren hills,

⁸ For God is judge; He putteth down one, and setteth up another.

⁹ For the cup in the hand of the Lord is wine unmingled, full to overflowing, and He hath swirled it to and fro, but the dregs thereof did not settle out; all the sinners of the earth shall drink them up.

¹⁰ But I shall rejoice for ever; I shall sing unto the God of Jacob.

¹¹ And I will break all the horns of sinners, but the horn of the righteous shall be exalted.

Psalm 75. *Notus in Judæa.*
Unto the end, among the songs, a Psalm for Asaph, a Song concerning the Assyrian.

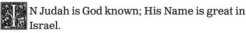I N Judah is God known; His Name is great in Israel.

³ And His place hath been at Salem, and His tabernacle in Zion.

⁴ There brake He the power of the bow, the shield and the sword, and the battle.

⁵ Thou dost shine wondrously from the ever-lasting hills.

⁶ All the simple-hearted were troubled, they slept their sleep, and all the men of wealth found nothing in their hands.

⁷ At Thy rebuke, O God of Jacob, all those mounted on horse-back slumbered.

⁸ Thou art terrible, and who may stand against Thee? From that time is Thy wrath.

⁹ Thou didst cause judgment to be heard from heaven; the earth trembled in fear, and was still,

¹⁰ When God arose to judgment, to save all the meek of the earth.

¹¹ For the thought of man shall turn unto Thee in thanksgiving, and the remainder of the thought shall keep festival unto Thee.

¹² Make a vow unto the Lord our God, and keep it; all that are round about Him shall bring presents,

¹³ Unto Him that is terrible and taketh away the spirits of princes, unto Him that is to be feared among the kings of the earth.

Psalm 76. *Voce mea ad Dominum.*
Unto the end, concerning Jeduthun, a Psalm for Asaph.

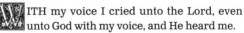ITH my voice I cried unto the Lord, even unto God with my voice, and He heard me.

³ In the day of my trouble I reached out to God

with my hands by night before Him, and I was not deceived; my soul refused to be comforted.

⁴ I remembered God, and I was glad; I mused, and my spirit faltered.

⁵ Mine eyes anticipated the morning watches; I was troubled and spake not.

⁶ I considered the days of old, and remembered the years of ages past, and I pondered.

⁷ By night I communed with mine own heart, and searched my soul.

⁸ Will the Lord be contemptuous for ever, and will He be no more favorably disposed?

⁹ Or will He cut off His mercy for ever, His word from generation to generation?

¹⁰ Will God forget to be gracious, or will He withhold His loving-kindness in His displeasure?

¹¹ And I said, Now have I begun; this change is of the right hand of the Most High.

¹² I remembered the works of the Lord, for I will be mindful of Thy wonders from the beginning.

¹³ And I will ponder all Thy works, and muse upon Thy undertakings.

¹⁴ Thy way, O God, is in the sanctuary; who is so great a god as our God?

¹⁵ Thou art the God that doest wonders; Thou hast declared Thy power among the peoples.

¹⁶ With Thine arm hast Thou delivered Thy people, even the sons of Jacob and Joseph.

¹⁷ The waters saw Thee, O God, the waters saw Thee, and were afraid; the depths were troubled.

¹⁸ Great was the noise of the waters; the clouds gave voice, for Thine arrows shall pass.

¹⁹ The voice of Thy thunder is in the wheel, Thy lightnings lit up the whole world; the earth trembled and shook.

²⁰ Thy ways are in the sea, and Thy paths in many waters, and Thy footsteps shall not be known.

²¹ Thou leddest Thy people like sheep, by the hand of Moses and Aaron.

Glory be to the Father, and to the Son, and to the Holy Spirit; both now, and ever, and unto the ages of ages. Amen.

Alleluia, alleluia, alleluia. Glory be to Thee, O God. Thrice.

¶ After the Tenth Kathisma, the Trisagion Prayers, and these troparia, in Tone VI:

I am in terror of the day of Thy dread coming, O Lord Christ, and fear Thine impartial tribunal; in fear and trembling am I, for I have a multitude of sins. But before the end convert me, as Thou art a merciful God, and save me, O my most merciful Saviour.

Glory be to the Father, and to the Son, and to the Holy Spirit.

When the thrones are set for judgment, O Lord, and men stand before Thy tribunal, a king will find no more favor than a soldier, the master will not be preferred to the slave. For each will be either glorified or put to shame by his own deeds.

Both now, and ever, and unto the ages of ages. Amen.

Great gifts hast thou been vouchsafed, O pure Virgin Mother of God, for thou gavest birth in the flesh unto One of the Trinity, Christ the Giver of life, unto the salvation of our souls.

Lord, have mercy [40]. And this Prayer:

LORD our God, Who art rich in mercy and Who hast no equal with respect to Thy compassion, Who alone art sinless by nature and becamest man, though without sin, for our sakes, Hearken at this hour unto this, my painful entreaty, for I am poor and bereft of good works, and my heart is troubled within me. For Thou knowest, O King most high, Lord of heaven and earth, that I have wasted all my youth in sins and, following after the lusts of my flesh, have become wholly an object of scorn to the demons. Continually have I followed wholly after the Devil, wallowing in the mire of the passions; for darkened in mind from my childhood, and even unto the present time, I have never desired to do Thy holy will; but, held wholly captive by the passions which assail me, I am become the butt of the mockery and scorn of the demons, being in no way mindful of the threat of Thine unendurable wrath against sinners and the fiery Gehenna which awaiteth. As one who hath thus fallen into despair and is in no way capable of conversion, I am become empty and naked of Thy friendship. For what manner of sin have I not committed? What demonic work have I not done? In what shameful and prodigal activity have I not indulged with relish and zeal? I have polluted my mind with lustful thoughts; I have sullied my body with intercourse; I have defiled my spirit by entertaining; every member of my wretched flesh have I loved to serve and enslave to sin. And who now will not lament me, wretch that I am? Who will not bewail me who am condemned? For I alone, I, O Master, have stirred up Thy wrath; I alone have kindled Thine anger against me; I alone have done that which is evil in Thy sight, having surpassed and outdone all the sinners of ages past, having sinned without rival and unforgivably. Yet, because Thou art most merciful and compassionate, O Lover of mankind, and awaitest the conversion of man, Lo! I throw myself before Thy dread and unendurable judgment seat, and, as it were, clutching Thy most pure feet, cry out from the depths of my soul: Cleanse me, O Lord! Forgive me, O Thou Who art readily reconciled! Have mercy upon my weakness; condescend unto my perplexity; hearken unto my supplication; and receive not my tears in silence. Accept me who repenteth, and turn me back who am gone astray; embrace me who am returning, and forgive me who prayeth. For Thou hast not appointed repentance for the righteous, nor hast Thou appointed forgiveness for them that have not sinned; but it is for me, a sinner, that Thou hast appointed repentance for those things wherein I have caused Thee displeasure, and I stand before Thee, naked and stripped bare, O Lord, Who knowest the hearts of men, confessing my sins; for I am unable to lift up mine eyes to gaze upon the height of heaven, being weighed down by the heavy burden of my sins. Enlighten, therefore, the eyes of my heart, and grant me remorse unto repentance, and contrition unto amendment of life, that, with good hope and true confidence, I may proceed to the world beyond, continually praising and blessing Thy most holy name: of the Father, and of the Son, and of the Holy Spirit; now, and ever, and unto the ages of ages. Amen.

The Eleventh Kathisma

Psalm 77. *Attendite, popule.*
A Psalm of instruction, for Asaph.

 EED my Law, O my people; incline your ears unto the words of my mouth.

2 I will open my mouth in parables; I will declare hard sayings of old;

3 Which we have heard, and known, and our fathers have told us;

4 They were not hidden from their children in another generation, declaring the praises of the Lord, and His mighty deeds, and the wonderful works that He hath done.

5 He made a covenant with Jacob, and gave Israel a Law, which He commanded our fathers to teach their children;

6 That another generation might know it, children as yet unborn, and they shall grow up and show their children the same;

7 That they might put their trust in God, and not forget the works of God, but search after His commandments.

8 Let them not be as their fathers, a perverse and

vexing generation, a generation that amended not their heart, and whose spirit was not faithful unto God;

9 Like as the sons of Ephraim, bending and shooting the bow, who turned back in the day of battle;

10 They kept not the covenant of God and would not walk in His Law.

11 And they forgat His good deeds, and the wonderful works that He had showed for them;

12 Marvelous things did He in the sight of their fathers, in the land of Egypt, even in the field of Tanis.

13 He divided the sea, and led them through; He held up the waters as in a wine-skin.

14 In the daytime also He led them with a cloud, and all the night through with a light of fire.

15 He clave a hard rock in the wilderness, and gave them drink, as it had been out of the great deep.

16 And He brought water out of the stony rock, and made the waters run down like rivers.

17 Yet they sinned still more against Him; they provoked the Most High in the desert.

18 And they tempted God in their hearts, asking for food for their souls.

19 They spake against God also, and said, Shall God be able to prepare a table in the wilderness?

20 He smote the stony rock indeed, and the waters gushed out, and the streams overflowed;

but can He give food also, or set a table for His people?

²¹ Wherefore the Lord heard and was wroth, and a fire was kindled in Jacob, and there came up heavy displeasure against Israel;

²² Because they believed not in God, nor trusted in His salvation.

²³ Yet He commanded the clouds above, and opened the doors of heaven;

²⁴ He rained down manna also upon them for to eat, and gave them bread of heaven.

²⁵ Angel's bread did man eat; He sent them their fill of food.

²⁶ He revoked the south wind from heaven, and by His power He brought in the south-west wind;

²⁷ And He rained flesh upon them as thick as dust, and feathered fowls like as the sand of the sea.

²⁸ And they fell in the midst of their camp, even round about their habitations.

²⁹ So did they eat, and were well filled, and their wish was brought unto them.

³⁰ They were not deprived of their desire. The food was still in their mouths,

³¹ And the heavy wrath of God came upon them, and slew the fattest of them, and the chosen of Israel He put in bonds.

³² In all this they sinned yet more, and believed not His wondrous works;

³³ And their days melted away in vanity, and their years in striving.

³⁴ When He slew them, they sought Him, and repented and performed their morning prayer unto God.

³⁵ And they remembered that God was their helper, and the most high God was their redeemer.

³⁶ Yet they did but flatter Him with their mouth, and dissembled unto Him with their tongue.

³⁷ For their heart was not whole with Him, neither continued they steadfast in His covenant.

³⁸ But He is merciful, and will cleanse their sins, and destroy them not; yea, many a time will He turn His wrath away, and will not kindle all His displeasure.

³⁹ For I will remember that they are but flesh, with a spirit that goeth forth, and returneth not again.

⁴⁰ How often did they provoke Him in the wilderness, and anger Him in the desert?

⁴¹ They both turned back, and tempted God, and provoked the Holy One of Israel.

⁴² And they remembered not His hand in the day when He delivered them from the hand of the tyrant;

⁴³ How He laid down His signs in Egypt, and His wonders in the field of Tanis,

⁴⁴ And turned into blood their rivers and their springs, that they might not drink.

⁴⁵ He sent swarms of flies against them, and they devoured them up, and frogs, and they corrupted them.

⁴⁶ And He gave their fruits to the caterpillar, and their labors to the locust.

⁴⁷ He killed their grapevines with hailstones, and their mulberry trees with frost.

⁴⁸ He gave over their cattle also to the hail, and their possessions to the fire.

⁴⁹ He sent down upon them the furiousness of His wrath: anger, and displeasure, and grief, the message of fierce angels.

⁵⁰ He laid the path for His indignation, and spared not their souls from death; their cattle also ended in death.

⁵¹ And He smote every first-born in the land of Egypt, the first-fruits of all their labor in the dwellings of Ham.

⁵² But His own people He drove like sheep, and led them forth into the wilderness like a flock.

⁵³ And He set them up unto faith, and they were not afraid, and the sea covered their enemies.

⁵⁴ And He brought them to the mountain of His holiness, even to the mountain which His right hand had purchased.

⁵⁵ He cast out the heathen also before them, and gave them the land by lot with a line of division, and settled the tribes of Israel in their tents.

⁵⁶ Yet they tempted and displeased the most high God, and kept not His testimonies;

⁵⁷ But turned backward, and fell away like their fathers, becoming like a sprung bow.

⁵⁸ And they angered Him in their hill places, and vexed Him with their idols.

⁵⁹ God heard and turned away, and greatly disparaged Israel.

⁶⁰ And He forsook the tabernacle in Shiloh, even the tent that He had pitched among men.

⁶¹ And delivered their power into captivity, and their beauty into the hands of the enemy.

⁶² He consigned His people also unto the sword, and disregarded His inheritance.

⁶³ Fire consumed their young men, and their maidens were not tearful.

⁶⁴ Their priests fell by the sword, and their widows will not be mournful.

⁶⁵ And the Lord rose up as one out of sleep, like one strong and rowdy from wine.

⁶⁶ And He smote His enemies backwards; He put them to perpetual shame.

⁶⁷ And He refused the tabernacle of Joseph, and chose not the tribe of Ephraim;

⁶⁸ But chose the tribe of Judah, even the hill of Zion, which He loved.

⁶⁹ And like a unicorn He set up His sanctuary on earth; He established it for ever.

⁷⁰ He chose David also His servant, and took him away from the sheepfolds.

⁷¹ From the freshening ewes He took him, that

he might tend Jacob His servant, and Israel His inheritance.

⁷² And he tended them in the innocence of his heart, and guided them by the skillfulness of his hands.

Glory be to the Father, and to the Son, and to the Holy Spirit; both now, and ever, and unto the ages of ages. Amen.

Alleluia, alleluia, alleluia. Glory be to Thee, O God. Thrice.

Lord, have mercy. Thrice.

Glory be to the Father, and to the Son, and to the Holy Spirit; both now, and ever, and unto the ages of ages. Amen.

Second Stasis

Psalm 78. *Deus, venerunt.*
A Psalm for Asaph.

 GOD, the heathen are come into Thine inheritance; they have defiled Thy holy temple.

² They have made Jerusalem as a root cellar; the dead bodies of Thy servants have they given to be meat unto the fowls of the air, and the flesh of Thy saints unto the beasts of the land.

³ Their blood have they poured out like water on every side of Jerusalem, and there was none to bury them.

⁴ We are become an open shame to our neigh-

bors, a very scorn and derision unto them that are round about us.

5 How long, O Lord, wilt Thou be angry? For ever? Will Thy jealousy kindle like a fire?

6 Pour out Thine indignation upon the nations that have not known Thee, and upon the kingdoms that have not called upon Thy Name.

7 For they have devoured Jacob, and laid waste his dwelling-place.

8 O remember not our old sins; but let Thy mercy overtake us, for we are come to great poverty.

9 Help us, O God our Saviour, for the glory of Thy Name; O Lord, deliver us, and wash away our sins, for Thy Name's sake,

10 Lest the nations say, Where is now their God? And let the vengeance of Thy servants' blood that hath been shed be openly showed upon the nations in our eyesight.

11 O let the sorrowful sighing of the prisoners come before Thee; according to the greatness of Thy power, preserve Thou the sons of the slain.

12 Reward Thou unto our neighbors seven-fold into their bosom for their blasphemy, wherewith they have blasphemed Thee, O Lord.

13 For we are Thy people, and the sheep of Thy pasture. We shall give Thee thanks, O God, for ever; from generation to generation will we show forth Thy praise.

Psalm 79. *Qui regis Israel.*

Unto the end, concerning the antiphons, a
testimony for Asaph, a Psalm concerning
the Assyrian.

HEAR, O Thou Shepherd of Israel, Thou that
leadest Joseph like a sheep; show Thyself,
Thou that sittest upon the Cherubim.

3 Before Ephraim, and Benjamin, and Manasseh
stir up Thy strength, and come to save us.

4 Convert us, O God; show the light of Thy countenance, and we shall be saved.

5 O Lord God of hosts, how long wilt Thou be
angry over the prayer of Thy servants?

6 Thou feedest us with the bread of sorrow, and
givest us tears to drink in full measure.

7 Thou hast made us a very strife unto our
neighbors, and our enemies laugh us to scorn.

8 O Lord God of hosts, convert us; show the light
of Thy countenance, and we shall be saved.

9 Thou hast brought a vine out of Egypt; Thou
hast cast out the heathen, and planted it.

10 Thou didst lay the way before it, and hast
planted the roots thereof, and it filled the land.

11 The shadow thereof covered the hills, and its
boughs God's cedar-trees.

12 She stretched out her runners unto the sea,
and her shoots even unto the river.

13 Why hast Thou then broken down her fence,
and all they that go by pluck off her grapes?

¹⁴ The wild boar out of the wood hath rooted it up, and the shy beast of the forest hath devoured it.

¹⁵ O God of hosts, turn Thee again, and look down from heaven, and see, and visit this vine,

¹⁶ And perfect that which Thy right hand hath planted, and upon the son of man, whom Thou hast strengthened for Thyself.

¹⁷ Burnt with fire, and digged up, at the rebuke of Thy countenance shall they perish.

¹⁸ Let Thy hand be upon the man of Thy right hand, and upon the son of man, whom Thou hast strengthened for Thyself.

¹⁹ And we shall not depart from Thee; Thou shalt quicken us, and we shall call upon Thy Name.

²⁰ O Lord God of hosts, convert us; show the light of Thy countenance, and we shall be saved.

Psalm 80. *Exultate Deo.*
Unto the end, a Psalm for Asaph, concerning the wine-presses.

REJOICE unto God our helper; make a joyful noise unto the God of Jacob.

³ Take the psalm, bring hither the timbrel, the merry harp with the psaltery.

⁴ Blow the trumpet in the new-moon, on the appointed day of our solemn feast.

⁵ For this is a statute for Israel, and a judgment to the God of Jacob.

⁶ This He ordained in Joseph for a testimony,

when he came out unto Him from the land of Egypt; he heard a language which he knew not.

⁷ He eased his back of the burden; his hands had labored at the straw.

⁸ Thou calledst upon Me in troubles, and I delivered thee, I heard thee in the thick darkness, I tested thee also at the waters of Meribah.

⁹ Hear, O My people, and I will testify unto thee, O Israel, if thou wilt hearken unto Me,

¹⁰ There shall not be another god in thee, neither shalt thou worship any strange god.

¹¹ For I am the Lord Thy God, who brought thee out of the land of Egypt; open thy mouth wide, and I shall fill it.

¹² But My people would not hear My voice, and Israel would not heed Me.

¹³ So I gave them up unto their hearts' lusts; they shall walk in their own imaginations.

¹⁴ O that My people would have hearkened unto Me, for if Israel had walked in My ways,

¹⁵ I should soon have put down their enemies, and laid My hand upon their adversaries.

¹⁶ The enemies of the Lord have lied to Him, and their time shall be for ever.

¹⁷ He fed them also with wheaten flour, and with honey out of the stony rock did He satisfy them.

Glory be to the Father, and to the Son, and to the Holy Spirit; both now, and ever, and unto the ages of ages. Amen.

Alleluia, alleluia, alleluia. Glory be to Thee, O God. Thrice.

Lord, have mercy. Thrice.

Glory be to the Father, and to the Son, and to the Holy Spirit; both now, and ever, and unto the ages of ages. Amen.

Third Stasis

Psalm 81. *Deus stetit.*
A Psalm for Asaph.

GOD standeth in the gathering of the gods, for in the midst of the gods He shall judge.

2 How long will ye judge unjustly, and accept the persons of sinners?

3 Judge for the fatherless and the poor, do right unto such as are humble and needy.

4 Rescue the needy and the poor, out of the hand of the sinner deliver him.

5 They have not known, nor understood. They walk in darkness; let all the foundations of the earth be shaken.

6 I said, Ye are gods, and ye are all children of the Most High.

7 But ye shall die like men, and like one of the princes shall ye fall.

8 Arise, O God; judge the earth, for Thou shalt be heir in all nations.

Psalm 82. *Deus, quis similis?*
A Song or Psalm for Asaph.

GOD, who is like unto Thee? Keep not still silence, neither refrain Thyself, O God.

³ For lo, Thine enemies have made a murmuring, and they that hate Thee have lift up their head.

⁴ They have imagined craftily against Thy people, and taken counsel against Thy saints.

⁵ They have said, Come, and let us root them out from among the nations, and that the name of Israel may be no more in remembrance.

⁶ For they have put their heads together with one consent, and made a covenant against Thee;

⁷ The tabernacles of the Edomites, and the Ishmaelites, the Moabites, and Hagarenes;

⁸ Gebal, and Ammon, and Amalek, and the Philistines, with them that dwell at Tyre.

⁹ For Assur also is come with them, they have been a defense for the children of Lot.

¹⁰ Do Thou to them as unto the Midianites and unto Sisera, as unto Jabin at the brook of Kishon.

¹¹ They perished at Endor, they became as dung for the earth.

¹² Make their princes like Oreb and Zeeb, and Zebah and Zalmunna, all their princes;

¹³ Who said, Let us take to ourselves God's sanctuary for an inheritance.

¹⁴ O my God, make them like unto a wheel, as stubble before the face of the wind,

¹⁵ Like as a fire burning the forest, as a flame burning up the mountains.

¹⁶ So shalt Thou persecute them with Thy tempest, and trouble them with Thy wrath.

¹⁷ Make their faces ashamed, O Lord, and they shall seek Thy Name.

¹⁸ Let them be confounded and vexed for ever and ever; let them be put to shame, and perish.

¹⁹ And let them know that Thy Name is LORD; Thou only art the Most High over all the earth.

Psalm 83. *Quam dilecta.*
Unto the end, concerning the wine-presses,
of the sons of Korah, a Psalm.

HOW amiable are Thy dwellings, O Lord of hosts!

³ My soul desireth and longeth for the courts of the Lord; my heart and my flesh have rejoiced in the living God.

⁴ Yea, the sparrow hath found her an house, and the dove a nest where she may lay her young, even Thy altars, O Lord of hosts, my King and my God.

⁵ Blessed are they that dwell in Thy house, for ever and ever will they praise Thee.

⁶ Blessed is the man whose help is from Thee, in his heart he hath proposed ascents

⁷ Into the valley of tears, unto the place which

he hath appointed, for the lawgiver shall give the blessing.

⁸ They will go from strength to strength; the God of gods shall appear in Zion.

⁹ O Lord God of hosts, hear my prayer; hearken, O God of Jacob.

¹⁰ Behold, O God, our defender, and look upon the face of Thy Christ.

¹¹ For one day in Thy courts is better than a thousand; I have preferred to be a doorkeeper in the house of my God, than to dwell in the tents of sinners.

¹² For the Lord loveth mercy and truth, God will give grace and glory; the Lord shall withhold no good thing from them that walk innocently.

¹³ O Lord God of hosts, blessed is the man that putteth his trust in Thee.

Psalm 84. *Benedixisti, Domine.*
Unto the end, of the sons of Korah, a Psalm.

 THOU hast been gracious, O Lord, unto Thy land, Thou hast turned back the captivity of Jacob.

³ Thou hast forgiven the offenses of Thy people; Thou hast covered all their sins.

⁴ Thou hast curtailed all Thy displeasure; Thou hast relented from the wrath of Thine indignation.

⁵ Convert us, then, O God of our salvation, and let Thine anger cease from us.

⁶ Wilt Thou be displeased at us for ever? Or wilt Thou stretch out Thy wrath from one generation to another?

⁷ O God, Thou shalt stay Thyself; Thou shalt revive us, and Thy people shall rejoice in Thee.

⁸ Show us, O Lord, Thy mercy, and grant us Thy salvation.

⁹ I will hear what the Lord God will say concerning me; for He shall speak peace unto His people, and to His saints, and to them that turn their hearts unto Him.

¹⁰ Surely His salvation is nigh them that fear Him, that glory may dwell in our land.

¹¹ Mercy and truth are met together, justice and peace have kissed each other.

¹² Truth hath flourished out of the earth, and justice hath looked down from heaven.

¹³ For the Lord shall show loving-kindness, and our land shall give her increase.

¹⁴ Justice shall go before Him, and shall set His steps in the way.

Glory be to the Father, and to the Son, and to the Holy Spirit; both now, and ever, and unto the ages of ages. Amen.

Alleluia, alleluia, alleluia. Glory be to Thee, O God. Thrice.

¶ After the Eleventh Kathisma, the Trisagion Prayers, and these troparia, in Tone VII:

Possessed of the healing remedy of repentance, O my soul, draw nigh with tears, crying out and sighing, O Physician of souls and bodies, O Lover of mankind, free me from my many sins; reckon me with the harlot, the thief, and the publican, O God; grant me forgiveness of my sins, and save me!

Glory be to the Father, and to the Son, and to the Holy Spirit.

I have not emulated the repentance of the publican, nor have I acquired the tears of the harlot; for because of my blindness I am at a loss for such amendment. Yet save me by Thy compassion, O Christ God, in that Thou art the Lover of mankind!

Both now, and ever, and unto the ages of ages. Amen.

O undefiled Virgin Theotokos, with the heavenly hosts entreat thy Son, that before the end He grant us forgiveness of transgressions and great mercy.

Lord, have mercy [40]. And this Prayer:

SHINE forth the incorruptible light of Thy divine knowledge in our hearts, O Lord, Lover of mankind, and open Thou the eyes of our minds to the understanding of Thy Gospel preaching; yea, instill in us the fear of Thy blessed commandments, that, having defeated all the lusts of the flesh, we may lead a spiritual life, being mindful of, and doing, all things such as are well-pleasing unto Thee. For Thou art the enlightenment of our souls and bodies, O Christ God, and unto Thee do we ascribe glory, together with Thine unoriginate Father, and Thy most holy, good and life-creating Spirit; now, and ever, and unto the ages of ages. Amen.

The Twelfth Kathisma

Psalm 85. *Inclina, Domine.*
A Prayer of David.

BOW down Thine ear, O Lord, and hear me, for I am poor and in misery.

² Preserve Thou my soul, for I am holy; save Thy servant, O my God, that putteth his trust in Thee.

³ Have mercy upon me, O Lord, for I will call upon Thee all day.

⁴ Give joy to the soul of Thy servant, for unto Thee have I lifted up my soul.

⁵ For Thou, Lord, art good and gentle, and of great mercy unto all them that call upon Thee.

⁶ Give ear, Lord, unto my prayer, and heed the voice of my supplication.

⁷ In the day of my trouble I called upon Thee, for Thou hast heard me.

⁸ Among the gods there is none like unto Thee, O Lord, nor are there any deeds according unto Thy deeds.

⁹ All nations whom Thou hast made shall come

and bow down before Thee, O Lord, and shall glorify Thy Name.

¹⁰ For Thou art great, and doest wondrous things; Thou art God alone.

¹¹ Guide me, O Lord, in Thy way, and I will walk in Thy truth; O let my heart rejoice to fear Thy Name.

¹² I will thank Thee, O Lord my God, with all my heart, and I will praise Thy Name for evermore.

¹³ For great is Thy mercy toward me, and Thou hast delivered my soul from the nethermost hell.

¹⁴ O God, the wicked are risen against me, and the congregations of the mighty have sought after my soul, and have not set Thee before them.

¹⁵ But Thou, O Lord my God, art compassionate and merciful, long-suffering, and greatly charitable and true.

¹⁶ O look upon me, and have mercy upon me, give Thy strength unto Thy servant, and help the son of Thine handmaid.

¹⁷ Work some sign upon me for good, that they who hate me may see, and be ashamed, because Thou, Lord, hast holpen me, and comforted me.

Psalm 86. *Fundamenta ejus.*
A Psalm and Song of the sons of Korah.

HER foundations are upon the holy hills; the Lord loveth the gates of Zion more than all the dwellings of Jacob.

³ Very glorious things are spoken of thee, O city of God.

⁴ I will speak of Rahab and Babylon with them that know me; behold, the Philistines also, and Tyre, with the Ethiopians, such were there.

⁵ Mother Zion, shall a man say, and the man was born in her, and the Most High Himself hath founded her.

⁶ The Lord shall tell in writing of the peoples and the princes that were in her,

⁷ How joyful are all they whose habitation is in thee!

Psalm 87. *Domine Deus.*
A Song and Psalm by the sons of Korah, unto the end, for the Mahalath to respond, of instruction to Heman the Ezrahite.

 LORD God of my salvation, by day have I cried, and by night before Thee.

³ O let my prayer come in before Thee; incline Thine ear unto my calling.

⁴ For my soul is full of trouble, and my life hath drawn nigh unto hell.

⁵ I have been counted as one of them that go down into the pit; I have become even as a man without help,

⁶ Free among the dead; like the wounded sleeping in the grave, whom Thou rememberest no more, and which have been cast away from Thy hand.

⁷ They laid me in the lowest pit, in the darkness and shadow of death.

⁸ Upon me hath Thine anger fixed itself, and all Thy waves hast Thou aimed at me.

⁹ Thou hast put away mine acquaintances far from me, they have made me to be an abomination unto them; I was betrayed, and did not go forth.

¹⁰ Mine eyes are grown weak from poverty. I called upon Thee, O Lord, all day; I stretched forth my hands unto Thee.

¹¹ Shalt Thou indeed work wonders with the dead? Or shall physicians revive them, and they shall praise Thee?

¹² Shall any in the grave declare Thy mercy and Thy truth in perdition?

¹³ Shall Thy wondrous works be known in the dark, and Thy righteousness in the Land of Oblivion?

¹⁴ But unto Thee have I cried, O Lord, and in the morning shall my prayer come before Thee.

¹⁵ Lord, why abhorrest Thou my soul? Why turnest Thou Thy face from me?

¹⁶ I am poor, and in hardship from my youth; having risen up, I have humbled myself and become utterly worn down.

¹⁷ Thy wrathful displeasure goeth over me; Thy terrors have undone me.

¹⁸ They came round about me like water; all day they compassed me about together.

¹⁹ Friend and neighbor hast Thou put away

from me, and mine acquaintances, because of sufferings.

Glory be to the Father, and to the Son, and to the Holy Spirit; both now, and ever, and unto the ages of ages. Amen.

Alleluia, alleluia, alleluia. Glory be to Thee, O God. Thrice.

Lord, have mercy. Thrice.

Glory be to the Father, and to the Son, and to the Holy Spirit; both now, and ever, and unto the ages of ages. Amen.

Second Stasis

Psalm 88. *Misericordias Domini.*
Of instruction, by Ethan the Ezrahite.

I SHALL sing of Thy mercy, O Lord, for ever; from one generation to another I will proclaim Thy truth with my mouth.

³ For Thou hast said, Mercy shall be set up for ever; Thy truth shall be stablished in the heavens.

⁴ I have made a covenant with My chosen; I have sworn unto David My servant,

⁵ Thy seed will I stablish for ever, and set up thy throne from one generation to another.

⁶ The heavens shall declare Thy wondrous works, O Lord, even Thy truth in the church of the saints.

⁷ For who among the clouds shall be compared

unto the Lord? Who among the sons of the gods shall be like unto the Lord?

⁸ We shall glorify God in the council of the saints; great and terrible is He over all them that are round about Him.

⁹ O Lord God of hosts, who is like unto Thee? Thou art strong, O Lord, and Thy truth is round about Thee.

¹⁰ Thou rulest the power of the sea; Thou stillest the raging of its waves.

¹¹ Thou hast humbled the arrogant, as one wounded; Thou hast scattered Thine enemies with the might of Thy strength.

¹² The heavens are Thine, the earth also is Thine; Thou hast laid the foundation of the whole world, and all that therein is.

¹³ Thou hast made the north and the sea; Tabor and Hermon shall rejoice in Thy Name.

¹⁴ Thy arm is mighty; let Thy hand be strengthened, and Thy right hand be lifted up.

¹⁵ Justice and judgment are the pedestal of Thy throne; mercy and truth shall go before Thy face.

¹⁶ Blessed is the people that know jubilation; O Lord, they shall walk in the light of Thy countenance,

¹⁷ And in Thy Name shall they rejoice all day, and by Thy righteousness shall they be exalted.

¹⁸ For Thou art the glory of their strength, and in Thy good pleasure shall our horn be lifted up.

¹⁹ For defense is of the Lord, and of the Holy One of Israel, our King.

²⁰ Then spakest Thou in a vision unto Thy sons, and saidst, I have laid help upon one that is mighty; I have raised up the chosen one of My people.

²¹ I have found David My servant; with My holy oil have I anointed him.

²² For My hand shall hold him up, and My arm shall strengthen him.

²³ The enemy shall be able to do nothing against him, and the son of iniquity shall not be able to hurt him.

²⁴ And I will smite down his foes before his face, and vanquish them that hate him.

²⁵ My truth also and My mercy are with him, and in My Name shall his horn be exalted.

²⁶ I will set his hand also upon the seas, and his right hand in the rivers.

²⁷ He shall call Me, Thou art my Father, my God, and the defender of my salvation.

²⁸ And I will make him My first-born, higher than the kings of the earth.

²⁹ My mercy will I keep for him for evermore, and My covenant shall be true to him.

³⁰ His seed also will I stablish for ever and ever, and his throne as the days of heaven.

³¹ But if his children forsake My Law, and walk not in My judgments;

³² If they profane My statutes, and keep not My commandments,

³³ I will visit their offenses with the rod, and their sin with scourges.

³⁴ Nevertheless, My mercy will I not unbind from them, nor act harmfully in My truth,

³⁵ Neither will I profane my covenant, nor alter the thing that is gone out of My lips.

³⁶ I have sworn once by My holiness, that I will not lie unto David.

³⁷ His seed shall endure for ever, and his throne shall be like as the sun before Me,

³⁸ And as the moon, perfect for ever, and a faithful witness in heaven.

³⁹ But Thou hast rejected and humiliated, Thou hast been indignant with Thine anointed.

⁴⁰ Thou hast annulled the covenant of Thy servant; Thou hast profaned his sanctuary on earth.

⁴¹ Thou hast overthrown all his bulwarks; Thou hast put fear in his strong-holds.

⁴² All they that pass by on the way have despoiled him; he is become a shame to his neighbors.

⁴³ Thou hast raised the right hand of them that oppress him; Thou hast gladdened all his enemies.

⁴⁴ Thou hast turned away the help of his sword, and took not up for him in battle.

⁴⁵ Thou hast made an end of his purification; Thou hast cast his throne down to the ground.

⁴⁶ Thou hast shortened the span of his days; Thou hast drenched him with shame.

⁴⁷ How long, O Lord, wilt Thou turn Thyself away? For ever? Shall Thy wrath kindle like fire?

⁴⁸ O remember what my substance is, for hast Thou made all the children of men for naught?

⁴⁹ What man is he that liveth, and shall not see death? Shall he deliver his soul from the hand of hell?

⁵⁰ Where are Thy mercies of old, O Lord, which Thou swarest unto David in Thy truth?

⁵¹ Remember, Lord, the rebuke that Thy servants have, which I have borne in my bosom from many nations,

⁵² Wherewith Thine enemies have blasphemed, O Lord, wherewith they have slandered the change of Thine anointed.

⁵³ Blessed be the Lord for evermore. So be it. So be it.

Glory be to the Father, and to the Son, and to the Holy Spirit; both now, and ever, and unto the ages of ages. Amen.

Alleluia, alleluia, alleluia. Glory be to Thee, O God. Thrice.

Lord, have mercy. Thrice.

Glory be to the Father, and to the Son, and to the Holy Spirit; both now, and ever, and unto the ages of ages. Amen.

Third Stasis

Psalm 89. *Domine, refugium.*
A Prayer of Moses the man of God.

ORD, Thou hast been our refuge from generation to generation.

³ Before ever the mountains were formed, or the earth and the world were created, even from age to age Thou art.

⁴ Turn not man away unto humiliation; yea, Thou hast said, Be converted, ye children of men.

⁵ For a thousand years before Thine eyes, O Lord, are but as yesterday when it is past, and as a watch in the night.

⁶ Fleeting shall their years be; he shall go by in the morning like the grass; in the morning it shall flourish, and grow up, but in the evening it shall fall away, and dry up, and wither.

⁷ For we consumed away in Thy displeasure, and were troubled at Thy wrathful indignation.

⁸ Thou hast set our misdeeds before Thee, our years are in the light of Thy countenance.

⁹ For all our days are spent, and we have disappeared in Thy wrath;

¹⁰ Our years are spun out like a spider's web. The days of our age are threescore years and ten, or if we be so strong, fourscore years, and more than these is but labor and sorrow; for frailty shall come upon us, and we shall be chastened.

¹¹ Who knoweth the power of Thy wrath, and from fear of Thee, who can recount Thine anger?

¹² So make Thy right hand known to me, and to them that are bound by the heart in wisdom.

¹³ Turn Thee again, O Lord; how long? And be gracious unto Thy servants.

¹⁴ We were satisfied with Thy mercy in the morning, O Lord, and we rejoiced and were glad;

¹⁵ We were glad all our days; for the days wherein Thou didst humble us, the years wherein we saw adversity.

¹⁶ And look upon Thy servants, and upon Thy works, and guide their children,

¹⁷ And let the brightness of the Lord our God be upon us, and prosper Thou the work of our hands upon us; yea, prosper Thou our handy-work.

Psalm 90. *Qui habitat.*
A Praise-song of David. Without superscription in the Hebrew.

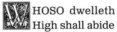 HOSO dwelleth in the help of the Most High shall abide in the shelter of the God of heaven.

² He will say unto the Lord, Thou art my defender, and my refuge, my God, and I will trust in Him.

³ For He shall deliver thee from the snare of the hunter, and from every mutinous word.

⁴ With His wings will He overshadow thee, and thou shalt be safe under His feathers; His truth shall compass thee round about like a shield.

⁵Thou shalt not be afraid for any terror by night, nor for the arrow that flieth by day;

⁶ For the thing that walketh in darkness, for sickness, or the demon of noon-day.

⁷A thousand shall fall beside thee, and ten thousand at thy right hand, but unto thee it shall not come nigh.

⁸ But thou shalt behold with thine eyes, and see the reward of sinners.

⁹ For Thou, Lord, art my hope; thou hast made the Most High thy refuge.

¹⁰ There shall no evil happen unto thee, neither shall any plague come nigh thy dwelling.

¹¹ For He shall give His angels charge over thee, to keep thee in all thy ways.

¹² They shall bear thee in their hands, that thou hurt not thy foot against a stone.

¹³ Thou shalt step upon the asp and basilisk; the lion and the serpent shalt thou tread under thy feet.

¹⁴ Because he hath set his hope upon Me, therefore will I deliver him; I will shelter him, because he hath known My Name.

¹⁵ He shall call upon Me, and I will hear him; yea, I am with him in trouble, I will deliver him, and bring him to glory.

¹⁶ With long life will I satisfy him, and show him My salvation.

Glory be to the Father, and to the Son, and to the

Holy Spirit; both now, and ever, and unto the ages of ages. Amen.

Alleluia, alleluia, alleluia. Glory be to Thee, O God. Thrice.

¶ After the Twelfth Kathisma, the Trisagion Prayers, and these troparia, in Tone VII:

O Lord, Who accepted the tears of the harlot and of Peter, and Who justified the publican who groaned from the depths of his heart, take pity on me who falleth down in contrition, O Saviour, and have mercy upon me!

Glory be to the Father, and to the Son, and to the Holy Spirit.

Receive me as the publican, O Lord, and cleanse me as the harlot, O Master; have mercy upon me as upon the Canaanite woman, according to Thy great mercy.

Both now, and ever, and unto the ages of ages. Amen.

O blessed Theotokos, Mother of the Light, entreat Christ God to shine forth the dawn, and great mercy upon our hearts.

Lord, have mercy [40]. And this Prayer:

LORD my God, Who alone art good and lovest mankind, Who alone art merciful and meek, Who alone art true and just, who alone art our compassionate and merciful God, May Thy power come upon me, who am a sinner and Thine unworthy servant, and may it strengthen my temple through the Gospel of Thy divine teaching, O Master and Lover of mankind, Who lovest the good, Who art full of loving-kindness. Enlighten my inmost parts and all my members by Thy will. Cleanse me of all enmity and sin; preserve me undefiled and unblemished by any intervention or activity of the Devil; and grant me, in Thy goodness, to understand those things which are of Thee, to think upon them, to live according to Thy will, to fear the fear of Thee, and to do what is pleasing unto Thee until my last breath, that according to Thine unutterable mercy, Thou mightest keep my soul and body, my mind and thoughts, a temple unexposed to all the wiles of the adversary. O Lord, my Lord, cover me with compassion and forsake not me a sinner, Thine impure and unworthy servant, for Thou art my Defender; O Lord, of Thee ever is my song, and unto Thee do we send up glory, to the Father, and to the Son, and to the Holy Spirit; now, and ever, and unto the ages of ages. Amen.

The Thirteenth Kathisma

Psalm 91. *Bonum est confiteri.*
A Psalm and Song for the Sabbath day.

IT is a good thing to give thanks unto the Lord, and to sing unto Thy Name, O Most High;

³ To tell of Thy mercy in the morning, and of Thy truth every night,

⁴ Upon the ten-stringed psaltery, and with a song upon the harp.

⁵ For Thou hast made me glad, O Lord, by Thy works, and in the operations of Thy hands will I rejoice.

⁶ How glorious are Thy works, O Lord; Thy thoughts are very deep.

⁷ These things an unwise man perceiveth not, and a fool doth not understand.

⁸ When sinners spring up as the grass, and when all the workers of wickedness do flourish, it is so they may be consumed for ever and ever.

⁹ But Thou art the Most High for evermore, O Lord.

¹⁰ For lo, Thine enemies, O Lord, for lo, Thine enemies shall perish, and all the workers of wickedness shall be driven off,

¹¹ But my horn shall be exalted like the horn of a unicorn, and my old age in plentiful oil.

¹² Mine eye also hath looked upon mine enemies, and mine ear shall hear the malignant that arise up against me.

¹³ The righteous shall flourish like a palm-tree, and shall spread abroad like a cedar in Lebanon.

¹⁴ Such as are planted in the house of the Lord, shall flourish in the courts of our God.

¹⁵ They shall bring forth fruit in ripe old age, and shall be well-acceptable,

¹⁶ That they may show how true the Lord our God is, and that there is no unrighteousness in Him.

Psalm 92. *Dominus regnavit.*
For the Sabbath day eve, when the earth was first inhabited, a Praise-song of David. Without superscription in the Hebrew.

THE Lord is King, He is clothed with majesty; the Lord is clothed in strength, and hath girt Himself, for He hath made the whole world so sure, that it shall not be moved.

² From the beginning is Thy throne prepared; Thou art from everlasting.

³ The rivers are risen, O Lord, the rivers have lift up their voices.

⁴ The rivers shall stir up their havoc; from the voices of many waters,

⁵ Wonderful are the heights of the sea; wonderful is the Lord on high.

⁶ Thy testimonies are very sure; holiness becometh Thine house, O Lord, unto length of days.

Psalm 93. *Deus ultionum.*
A Psalm of David, for the fourth day of the week.
Without superscription in the Hebrew.

OD is an avenging Lord; the God of vengeance hath acted freely.

² Arise, Thou Judge of the world, and reward the proud after their deserving.

³ Lord, how long shall sinners, how long shall sinners boast?

⁴ Shall they utter and speak untruth? Shall all speak that work iniquity?

⁵ They have humbled Thy peoples, O Lord, and embittered Thine inheritance.

⁶ They murder the widow, and the orphan, and put the pilgrim to death.

⁷ And they said, The Lord shall not see, neither shall the God of Jacob comprehend.

⁸ Take heed, ye thoughtless among the people, and ye fools, when will ye be wise?

⁹ He that planted the ear, shall He not hear? Or He that made the eye, shall He not see?

¹⁰ He that chasteneth the heathen, shall He not rebuke, He that teacheth man knowledge?

¹¹ The Lord knoweth the thoughts of man, that they are but vain.

¹² Blessed is the man whom Thou chastenest, O Lord, and teachest him out of Thy Law;

¹³ That Thou mayest give him relief from cruel days, until the pit be digged up for the sinner.

¹⁴ For the Lord will not reject His people, neither will He forsake His inheritance,

¹⁵ Until righteousness turn again unto judgment, and all such as are true in heart shall follow it.

¹⁶ Who will rise up for me against the evil-doers? Or who will stand up for me against the workers of iniquity?

¹⁷ If the Lord had not helped me, my soul had almost dwelt in hell.

¹⁸ If I said, My foot hath slipped, Thy mercy, O Lord, helped me.

¹⁹ According to the multitude of sorrows in my heart have Thy comforts refreshed my soul.

²⁰ Let not the throne of wickedness abide with Thee, which maketh trouble on command.

²¹ They shall seize upon the soul of the righteous, and condemn innocent blood.

²² But the Lord is become a refuge for me, and my God the help of my hope.

²³ And the Lord shall recompense them their wickedness, and according unto their own malice shall the Lord God destroy them.

Glory be to the Father, and to the Son, and to the Holy Spirit; both now, and ever, and unto the ages of ages. Amen.

Alleluia, alleluia, alleluia. Glory be to Thee, O God. Thrice.

Lord, have mercy. Thrice.

Glory be to the Father, and to the Son, and to the Holy Spirit; both now, and ever, and unto the ages of ages. Amen.

Second Stasis

Psalm 94. *Venite, exultemus Domino.*
A Praise-song of David. Without superscription in the Hebrew.

COME, let us rejoice unto the Lord; let us make a joyful noise unto God our Saviour.

² Let us come before His presence with thanksgiving, and rejoice unto Him in psalms.

³ For the Lord is a great God, and a great King over all the earth.

⁴ For in His hand are all the corners of the earth, and the heights of the hills are His also.

⁵ For the sea is His, and He made it, and His hands formed the dry land.

⁶ O come, let us worship and fall down before Him, and weep before the Lord that made us.

⁷ For He is our God, and we are the people of His pasture, and the sheep of His hand. Today if ye will hear His voice,

⁸ Harden not your hearts, as in the provocation, and as in the day of temptation in the wilderness;

⁹ When your fathers tempted Me, proved Me, and saw My works.

¹⁰ Forty years long was I grieved with that generation, and said, They do always err in their hearts, for they have not known My ways;

¹¹ So I swore in My wrath, that they should not enter into My rest.

Psalm 95. *Cantate Domino.*
A Praise-song of David, when the house was built after the Captivity. Without superscription in the Hebrew.

 SING unto the Lord a new song; sing unto the Lord, all the earth;

² Sing unto the Lord; bless His Name; be telling of His salvation from day to day.

³ Declare among the nations His glory, among all peoples His wonders.

⁴ For the Lord is great, and highly to be praised; He is more to be feared than all gods.

⁵ For all the gods of the heathen are demons, but the Lord made the heavens.

⁶ Thanksgiving and beauty are before Him; holiness and majesty are in His sanctuary.

⁷ Bring unto the Lord, O ye kindreds of the nations, bring unto the Lord glory and honor.

⁸ Bring unto the Lord the glory due unto His

Name; take up sacrifices, and enter into His courts.

⁹ O worship the Lord in His holy court; let the whole earth be shaken at His presence.

¹⁰ Tell it out among the heathen that the Lord is King, for He hath made the whole world, which shall not be moved; He shall judge the peoples with equity.

¹¹ Let the heavens be glad, and let the earth rejoice; let the sea be moved, and all that therein is.

¹² Let the fields be joyful, and all that is in them; then shall all the trees of the wood rejoice

¹³ At the presence of the Lord, for He cometh, for He cometh to judge the earth; to judge the whole world with righteousness, and the peoples with His truth.

Psalm 96. *Dominus regnavit.*

A Psalm of David, when the land was restored to him. Without superscription in the Hebrew.

THE Lord is King, let the earth rejoice; let the many isles be glad.

² Clouds and darkness are round about Him; righteousness and judgment are the restoration of His throne.

³ There shall go a fire before Him, and burn up His enemies on every side.

⁴ His lightnings shone forth upon the whole world; the earth saw, and trembled.

⁵ The hills melted like wax at the presence of the Lord, at the presence of the Lord of the whole earth.

⁶ The heavens have declared His righteousness, and all the people have seen His glory.

⁷ Confounded be all they that worship carved images, that boast of their idols; worship Him, all ye His angels.

⁸ Zion heard, and was glad, and the daughters of Judah rejoiced, because of Thy judgments, O Lord.

⁹ For Thou art the Lord Most High over all the earth; Thou art exalted far above all gods.

¹⁰ O ye that love the Lord, hate the thing which is evil. The Lord preserveth the souls of His saints; He shall deliver them from the hand of the sinner.

¹¹ There is sprung up a light for the righteous, and gladness for such as are true-hearted.

¹² Be glad in the Lord, ye righteous, and give thanks at the memory of His holiness.

Glory be to the Father, and to the Son, and to the Holy Spirit; both now, and ever, and unto the ages of ages. Amen.

Alleluia, alleluia, alleluia. Glory be to Thee, O God. Thrice.

Lord, have mercy. Thrice.

Glory be to the Father, and to the Son, and to the

Holy Spirit; both now, and ever, and unto the ages of ages. Amen.

Third Stasis

Psalm 97. *Cantate Domino.*
A Psalm of David.

 SING unto the Lord a new song, for the Lord hath done marvelous things; His own right hand hath saved Him, and His holy arm.

² The Lord hath declared His salvation; His righteousness hath He openly showed in the sight of the heathen.

³ He hath remembered His mercy to Jacob, and His truth to the house of Israel; all the ends of the earth have seen the salvation of our God.

⁴ Shout with jubilation unto God, all ye lands; chant ye, and be joyful; O sing ye.

⁵ Sing unto the Lord upon the harp, upon the harp with the voice of a psalm,

⁶ On forged trumpets and with the sound of a ram's horn; blow the horn before the Lord the King.

⁷ Let the sea be moved, and all that therein is, the whole world, and all they that dwell therein.

⁸ The rivers shall clap their hands together, and the hills shall be joyful

⁹ At the presence of the Lord, for He draweth nigh, yea, He cometh to judge the earth; to judge

the whole world in righteousness, and the peoples with equity.

Psalm 98. *Dominus regnavit.*
A Psalm of David. Without superscription in the Hebrew.

HE Lord is King, be the peoples never so impatient; He that sitteth upon the Cherubim, be the earth never so unquiet.

² The Lord is great in Zion, and high above all peoples.

³ Let them give thanks unto Thy great Name, for it is terrible and holy,

⁴ And the King's honor loveth judgment; Thou hast prepared justice, Thou hast executed judgment and righteousness in Jacob.

⁵ O magnify the Lord our God, and fall down at the footstool of His feet, for He is holy.

⁶ Moses and Aaron among His priests, and Samuel among such as call upon His Name; these called upon the Lord, and He heard them.

⁷ He spake unto them out of the cloudy pillar, for they kept His testimonies, and the ordinances that He gave them.

⁸ O Lord our God, Thou heardest them; O God, Thou wast merciful unto them, and vengeful unto all their provocations.

⁹ O magnify the Lord our God, and worship at His holy hill, for the Lord our God is holy.

Psalm 99. *Jubilate Deo.*
A Psalm of David, of thanksgiving.

BE joyful unto God, all the earth;

² Serve the Lord with gladness, and come in before Him with joy.

³ Know ye, that the Lord, He is our God; it is He that hath made us, and not we ourselves, for we are His people, and the sheep of His pasture.

⁴ Enter into His gates with thanksgiving, and into His courts with praise; be thankful unto Him, and praise His Name.

⁵ For the Lord is gracious; His mercy is everlasting, and His truth even from generation to generation.

Psalm 100. *Misericordiam et judicium.*
A Psalm of David.

MERCY and judgment shall be my song unto Thee, O Lord;

² I sing and understand in a blameless way; when wilt Thou come unto me? I have walked in the innocency of my heart in the midst of my house.

³ I have set no unlawful thing before mine eyes; I have hated the workers of iniquity.

⁴ A forward heart hath not cleaved unto me; I did not know the crafty man that turned away from me.

⁵ Whoso privily slandereth his neighbor, him

did I drive out; whoso hath a proud look and a greedy stomach, with such I did not eat.

⁶ Mine eyes look upon such as are faithful in the land, that they may dwell with me; whoso leadeth a godly life, he shall be my servant.

⁷ The proud doer hath not dwelt in the midst of my house; he that speaketh unjustly shall have no place in my sight.

⁸ In the morning I slew all the sinners of the land, to consume all the workers of lawlessness from the city of the Lord.

Glory be to the Father, and to the Son, and to the Holy Spirit; both now, and ever, and unto the ages of ages. Amen.

Alleluia, alleluia, alleluia. Glory be to Thee, O God. Thrice.

¶ After the Thirteenth Kathisma, the Trisagion Prayers, and these troparia, in Tone VIII:

With a compassionate eye look Thou upon my lowliness, O Lord, for in but a little while is my life wasted, and there is no salvation for me because of my deeds. Wherefore, I beseech Thee, With a compassionate eye look upon my lowliness, O Lord, and save Me.

Glory be to the Father, and to the Son, and to the Holy Spirit.

Take care, O my soul, and be thou mindful of the hour of the dreadful day, for the Judge standeth in readiness. For His judgment is without mercy for them that have not acted mercifully. Therefore, cry aloud unto Christ God: O Thou that knowest the hearts of men, before Thou condemnest me, have mercy upon me!

Both now, and ever, and unto the ages of ages. Amen.

Having in mind, day and night, Thy dreadful, terrible and impartial judgment, O Christ, I tremble as a shameless evil-doer, being guilty of deeds and cruel actions which I have committed with singular zeal. Therefore, in fear I fall down before Thee, crying aloud in sorrow: Through the prayers of her that bore Thee, O most Merciful One, save me!

Lord, have mercy [40]. And this Prayer:

HOLY Lord, Who livest in the highest and regardest all creation with Thine all-seeing eye: before Thee have we inclined the neck of body and soul, and Thee do we entreat, O Holy One of the holy, Stretch forth Thine invisible hand from Thy holy dwelling-place, and bless us all, and if we have committed any sin before Thee, knowingly or unknowingly, forgive us, in that Thou art good and lovest mankind, granting us the blessings of Thy peace. For Thine it is to have mercy and to save, O our God, and unto Thee do we ascribe glory, to the Father, and to the Son, and to the Holy Spirit; both now, and ever, and unto the ages of ages. Amen.

The Fourteenth Kathisma

Psalm 101. *Domine, exaudi.*

A Prayer of the poor man, when he is downcast, and poureth out his complaint before the Lord.

 LORD hear my prayer, and let my cry come unto Thee.

³ Turn not Thy face from me; in the day of my trouble, incline Thine ear unto me; in the day when I call upon Thee, quickly hearken unto me.

⁴ For my days have disappeared like smoke, and my bones are burnt up like kindling.

⁵ I have been smitten down like grass, and my heart is withered, for I forgot to eat my bread.

⁶ From the voice of my groaning hath my bone cleaved unto my flesh.

⁷ I am become like a pelican in the wilderness, I was like an owl in the ruins.

⁸ I have watched, and was even as it were a sparrow, that sitteth alone upon the house-top.

⁹ Mine enemies reviled me all the day long, and they that praised me swore at me.

¹⁰ For I have eaten ashes as it were bread, and mingled my drink with tears,

¹¹ Because of the face of Thine indignation and Thy wrath, for, having taken me up, Thou hast cast me down.

¹² My days are gone like a shadow, and I am withered like grass.

¹³ But, Thou, O Lord, shalt endure for ever, and Thy remembrance is unto generation and generation.

¹⁴ Thou shalt arise, and have mercy upon Zion, for it is time that Thou have mercy upon her, yea, the time is come.

¹⁵ For Thy servants have been well pleased by the stones thereof, and they shall be merciful unto her dust.

¹⁶ And the nations shall fear the Name of the Lord, and all the kings of the earth Thy glory.

¹⁷ For the Lord shall build up Zion, and reveal Himself in His glory.

¹⁸ He hath regarded the prayer of the humble, and hath not despised their petition.

¹⁹ Let this be written for another generation, and a people yet to be born shall praise the Lord;

²⁰ For He hath looked down from the height of His sanctuary; out of heaven did the Lord behold the earth,

²¹ To hear the moaning of such as are in shackles, to free the sons of the slain,

²² To declare the Name of the Lord in Zion, and His praise in Jerusalem,

²³ When the peoples are gathered together, and the kings also, to serve the Lord.

²⁴ He answered Him in the way of his strength; the fewness of my days shalt Thou make known unto me.

²⁵ O take me not away in the midst of my days; as for Thy years, they endure throughout all generations.

²⁶ In the beginning, O Lord, hast Thou laid the foundation of the earth, and the heavens are the work of Thy hands.

²⁷ They shall perish, but Thou shalt endure; yea, they all shall wax old as doth a garment, and as a vesture shalt Thou change them, and they shall be changed.

²⁸ But Thou art the same, and Thy years shall not fail.

²⁹ The sons of Thy servants shall abide, and their seed shall prosper for ever.

Psalm 102. *Benedic, anima mea.*
A Psalm of David.

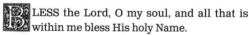

BLESS the Lord, O my soul, and all that is within me bless His holy Name.

² Bless the Lord, O my soul, and forget not all His benefits;

³ Who forgiveth all thine iniquities, and healeth all thy diseases;

⁴ Who redeemeth thy life from corruption, and crowneth thee with mercy and compassion;

⁵ Who satisfieth thy desire with good things; thy youth shall be renewed like the eagle's.

⁶ The Lord performeth deeds of mercy, and judgment for all them that are wronged.

⁷ He made known His ways unto Moses, His will unto the children of Israel.

⁸ The Lord is compassionate and merciful, long-suffering, and of great kindness.

⁹ He will not always be chiding, neither keepeth He His anger for ever.

¹⁰ He hath not dealt with us after our sins, nor rewarded us according to our wickednesses.

¹¹ For as high as the heaven is in comparison of the earth, so great is the Lord's mercy also toward them that fear Him.

¹² As wide as the east is from the west, so far hath He set our iniquity from us.

¹³ Like as a father pitieth his own children, even so hath the Lord been merciful unto them that fear Him.

¹⁴ For He knoweth whereof we are made; He remembereth that we are but dust.

¹⁵ As for man, his days are as the grass; for he flourisheth as a flower of the field.

¹⁶ For as soon as the wind goeth over it, it is gone; and it shall no more know the place thereof.

¹⁷ But the mercy of the Lord is from everlasting to everlasting upon them that fear Him,

¹⁸ And His righteousness upon sons of sons for

such as keep His covenant, and remember His commandments to do them.

¹⁹ The Lord hath prepared His throne in heaven, and His kingdom ruleth over all.

²⁰ O bless the Lord, all ye His angels, ye that excel in strength, ye that fulfill His commandment, to hearken unto the voice of His words.

²¹ O bless the Lord, all ye His hosts, ye servants of His that do His will.

²² O bless the Lord, all ye works of His, in every place of His dominion; bless the Lord, O my soul.

Glory be to the Father, and to the Son, and to the Holy Spirit; both now, and ever, and unto the ages of ages. Amen.

Alleluia, alleluia, alleluia. Glory be to Thee, O God. Thrice.

Lord, have mercy. Thrice.

Glory be to the Father, and to the Son, and to the Holy Spirit; both now, and ever, and unto the ages of ages. Amen.

Second Stasis

Psalm 103. *Benedic, anima mea.*
A Psalm of David, concerning the Genesis of
the World.

BLESS the Lord, O my soul. O Lord my God, Thou art become exceeding glorious; in honor and majesty hast Thou clothed Thyself,

² Wrapping Thyself with light as it were with a garment, and spreading out the heavens like a curtain,

³ Who covereth the beams of His chambers by the waters, Who appointeth the clouds for His going forth, Who walketh upon the wings of the wind,

⁴ Who maketh His angels spirits, and His ministers a flaming fire,

⁵ Whoso layeth the earth on its foundations, that it shall never be moved.

⁶ The deep like a garment is its clothing; the waters stand above the hills.

⁷ At Thy rebuke they shall flee; at the voice of Thy thunder they shall be afraid.

⁸ The hills shall go up and the plains shall go down, even unto the place which Thou hast appointed for them.

⁹ Thou hast set a boundary which they shall not pass, neither return again to cover the earth,

¹⁰ Who sendeth the springs into the valleys; the waters will run between the hills.

¹¹ All beasts of the field shall drink thereof, and the wild asses quench their thirst.

¹² Beside them shall the fowls of the air have their habitation; they shall sing among the rocks.

¹³ He watereth the hills from His heights; the earth shall be well-fed by the fruit of Thy works,

¹⁴ Who bringeth forth grass for the cattle, and

green herb for the service of men, to bring forth bread from the earth,

¹⁵ And wine maketh a man's heart glad; to anoint the face with oil, and bread strengtheneth man's heart.

¹⁶ The trees of the plain shall be full of sap, the cedars of Lebanon which He hath planted;

¹⁷ In them the birds shall make their nests; the home of the stork is chief among them.

¹⁸ The high hills are for the deer; the stony rock is a refuge for the conies.

¹⁹ He made the moon to mark the seasons; the sun knoweth his going down.

²⁰ Thou didst ordain darkness, and there was night, wherein all the beasts of the forest do move,

²¹ Young lions roaring after their prey and seeking their meat from God.

²² The sun arose, and they gathered together, and shall lie down in their dens.

²³ Man shall go forth to his work, and to his labor, until the evening.

²⁴ How great are Thy works, O Lord! In wisdom hast Thou made them all; the earth is filled with Thy handiwork.

²⁵ So is the great and wide sea also, wherein are things creeping innumerable, both small and great beasts.

²⁶ There go the ships, and that Leviathan, whom Thou hast made to take his pastime therein.

²⁷ These wait all upon Thee, that Thou mayest give them food in due season.

²⁸ When Thou givest it them, they shall gather it; when Thou openest Thy hand, all things shall be filled with good,

²⁹ But when Thou hidest Thy face, they shall be troubled; Thou shalt take away their spirit, and they shall pass away, and return again to their dust.

³⁰ Thou shalt send forth Thy Spirit, and they shall be made, and Thou shalt renew the face of the earth.

³¹ O let the glory of the Lord endure for ever; the Lord shall rejoice in His works,

³² Who looketh upon the earth, and it trembleth; Who toucheth the hills, and they smoke.

³³ I will sing unto the Lord as long as I live; I will praise my God while I have my being.

³⁴ Let my conversation be pleasing unto Him, for I shall be glad in the Lord.

³⁵ O that sinners should cease from the earth, and the ungodly, that they should be no more! Bless the Lord, O my soul.

Glory be to the Father, and to the Son, and to the Holy Spirit; both now, and ever, and unto the ages of ages. Amen.

Alleluia, alleluia, alleluia. Glory be to Thee, O God. Thrice.

Lord, have mercy. Thrice.

Glory be to the Father, and to the Son, and to the Holy Spirit; both now, and ever, and unto the ages of ages. Amen.

Third Stasis

Psalm 104. *Confitemini Domino.*
Alleluia.

 GIVE thanks unto the Lord, and call upon His Name; proclaim among the nations His deeds.

² O sing unto Him, and praise Him with psalms; tell of all His wondrous works.

³ Glory in His holy Name; let the heart of them be glad that seek the Lord.

⁴ Seek the Lord and be strengthened; seek His face always.

⁵ Remember the marvelous works that He hath done, His wonders, and the judgments of His mouth,

⁶ O ye seed of Abraham, His servants; ye children of Jacob, His chosen.

⁷ He is the Lord our God; His judgments are in all the world.

⁸ He hath been always mindful of His covenant, the promise that He made to a thousand generations;

⁹ That He made with Abraham, and His oath unto Isaac;

¹⁰ And appointed the same unto Jacob for an ordinance, and to Israel for an everlasting testament,

¹¹ Saying, Unto thee will I give the land of Canaan, the lot of your inheritance,

¹² When they were yet but few in number, of little consequence, and strangers therein.

¹³ And they went from one nation to another, from one kingdom to another people.

¹⁴ He suffered no man to do them wrong, and reproved even kings for their sakes, saying,

¹⁵ Touch not Mine anointed, and do My prophets no harm.

¹⁶ Moreover, He called for a famine upon the land, and destroyed all the provision of bread.

¹⁷ He sent a man before them, even Joseph, who was sold to be a slave.

¹⁸ They humbled his feet with fetters; he passed his life in irons,

¹⁹ Until his word came to pass; the word of the Lord tried him.

²⁰ The king sent, and released him, even the prince of the people, and let him go free.

²¹ He made him lord of his house, and ruler of all his substance;

²² To instruct his princes after his will, and teach his senators wisdom.

²³ Israel also came into Egypt, and Jacob was a stranger in the land of Ham.

²⁴ And He increased His people exceedingly, and made them stronger than their enemies;

²⁵ He turned their heart to hate His people; to deal craftily with His servants.

²⁶ He sent Moses His servant, and Aaron whom He had chosen.

²⁷ To them He committed the words of His signs and of His wonders in the land of Ham.

²⁸ He sent darkness, and it was dark, for they were galled by His words.

²⁹ He turned their waters into blood, and slew their fish.

³⁰ Their land was overrun with frogs, even in the storerooms of their kings.

³¹ He spake, and there came swarms of flies, and lice in all their quarters.

³² He gave them hail-stones for rain, and grievous fire in their land.

³³ He smote their vines also and their fig-trees, and brake every tree that was in their coasts.

³⁴ He spake, and the locusts came, and caterpillars innumerable,

³⁵ And did eat up all the grass in their land, and devoured all the fruit of their ground.

³⁶ He smote also all the first-born in their land, the first-fruit of all their labor.

³⁷ He brought them forth also with silver and gold, and there was not one feeble person among their tribes.

³⁸ Egypt was glad at their departing, for a fear of them had fallen upon her.

³⁹ He spread out a cloud to be a covering for them, and fire to give light unto them by night.

⁴⁰ They asked, and quails came, and He filled them with the bread of heaven.

⁴¹ He clave the rock of stone, and the waters flowed out, so that rivers ran in the dry places.

⁴² For He remembered His holy word, which He had given unto Abraham His servant.

⁴³ And He brought forth His people with joy, and His chosen with gladness.

⁴⁴ And gave them the lands of the heathen, and they took the labors of the peoples in possession;

⁴⁵ That they might keep His statutes, and seek out His Law.

Glory be to the Father, and to the Son, and to the Holy Spirit; both now, and ever, and unto the ages of ages. Amen.

Alleluia, alleluia, alleluia. Glory be to Thee, O God. Thrice.

¶ After the Fourteenth Kathisma, the Trisagion Prayers, and these troparia, in Tone VIII:

Like the harlot do I fall down before Thee, that I may receive forgiveness; and instead of myrrh I offer Thee tears from my heart, O Christ God, that Thou mayest have compassion upon me as Thou didst upon her, O Saviour, and grant me the cleansing of my sins. For like her I cry out to Thee: Deliver me from the mire of my deeds!

Glory be to the Father, and to the Son, and to the Holy Spirit.

Why art thou not mindful of death, O my soul? Why turnest thou not henceforth to amendment of life before the trumpets sound for the judgment? Then there shall be no time for repentance! Bring, then, to mind the publican and the harlot who cried: I have sinned against Thee, O Lord, have mercy upon me!

Both now, and ever, and unto the ages of ages. Amen.

O ever-virgin Theotokos, in that thou dost truly surpass the heavenly hosts by thy birth-giving, we that for thy sake have been enriched with divinity unceasingly magnify thee.

Lord, have mercy [40]. And this Prayer:

WE thank Thee, O Lord God of our salvation, for Thou doest all things for the benefit of our life; for Thou hast granted us rest in the nighttime which hath passed, and hast raised us up from our beds, and set us to worship Thine honored and glorious Name. Wherefore, we pray Thee, O Lord: grant us grace and power, that we may be accounted worthy to hymn Thee, the Saviour and Benefactor of our souls, working out our salvation with fear and trembling. Hearken, therefore, and have mercy upon us, O Compassionate One; crush beneath our feet the invisible foe and enemy; accept the thanks which we offer in accordance with our strength; grant us grace and power, that we may open our mouths, and teach us by Thy judgments. For we know not what we pray for, except Thou, O Lord, instruct us by Thy Holy Spirit. And if we have committed some sin before this present hour, by word, or deed, or in thought, knowingly or unknowingly, loose, remit and forgive. For if Thou takest note of iniquity, Lord, O Lord, who shall stand? For with Thee is purification, with Thee is deliverance; Thou only art holy, the mighty Helper and Defender of our life, and Thee do we bless for ever. Amen.

The Fifteenth Kathisma

Psalm 105. *Confitemini Domino.*
Alleluia.

 GIVE thanks unto the Lord, for He is good; for His mercy endureth for ever.

2 Who shall speak of the mighty acts of the Lord? Who shall make all His praise to be heard?

3 Blessed are they that keep judgment, and do righteousness always.

4 Remember us, O Lord, according to the favor that Thou bearest unto Thy people; O visit us with Thy salvation,

5 That we may see the goodness of Thy chosen, and be glad in the gladness of Thy nation, and glory with Thine inheritance.

6 We have sinned with our fathers; we have done amiss, and dealt wickedly.

7 Our fathers considered not Thy wonders in Egypt, neither kept they Thy great mercy in remembrance, but were disobedient when they went up to the Red Sea.

⁸ Nevertheless, He helped them for His Name's sake, that He might make His power to be known.

⁹ He rebuked the Red Sea also, and it was dried up, and He led them through the deep, as through a wilderness.

¹⁰ And He saved them from the hand of the adversaries, and delivered them from the hand of the enemy.

¹¹ The waters overwhelmed them that troubled them; there was not one of them left.

¹² Then believed they His words, and sang praise unto Him.

¹³ But within a while they forgat His works; they waited not for His counsel,

¹⁴ But they lusted with desire in the wilderness, and they tempted God in the desert.

¹⁵ And He gave them their desire, and sent satiety into their soul.

¹⁶ They angered Moses also in the camp, and Aaron the holy one of the Lord.

¹⁷ So the earth opened, and swallowed up Dathan, and covered the congregation of Abiram.

¹⁸ And a fire was kindled in their company; the flame burnt up the sinners.

¹⁹ They made a calf also in Horeb, and worshipped a graven image.

²⁰ Thus they turned His glory into the similitude of a calf that eateth hay.

²¹ And they forgat the God Who had saved them, Who had done so great things in Egypt;

²² Wondrous works in the land of Ham, and fearful things by the Red Sea.

²³ And He said He would have destroyed them, had not Moses His chosen stood before Him in the breach, to turn away His wrathful indignation, lest He should destroy them.

²⁴ Yea, they thought scorn of that longed-for land; they gave no credence unto His word,

²⁵ But murmured in their tents; they hearkened not unto the voice of the Lord.

²⁶ Therefore lifted He up His hand against them, to cast them down in the wilderness;

²⁷ To cast out their seed among the nations, and to scatter them in the lands.

²⁸ Then were they joined unto Baal-peor, and ate the sacrifices of the dead.

²⁹ And they provoked Him to anger with their undertakings, and the plague was great among them.

³⁰ Then stood up Phineas and made propitiation, and so the plague ceased.

³¹ And that was counted unto him for righteousness, from generation to generation for evermore.

³² They angered Him also at the waters of Meribah, and it went ill with Moses for their sakes;

³³ Because they provoked his spirit, and he spake unadvisedly with his lips.

³⁴ Neither destroyed they the heathen, as the Lord commanded them,

³⁵ But were mingled among the heathen, and learned their works,

³⁶ And they worshipped their graven images, and it became a stumbling-block unto them.

³⁷ Yea, they sacrificed their sons and their daughters unto demons,

³⁸ And shed innocent blood, even the blood of their sons and of their daughters, whom they sacrificed unto the graven images of Canaan, and the land was putrid with their blood.

³⁹ Thus was it defiled by their works; moreover, they played the whore in their doings.

⁴⁰ Therefore was the wrath of the Lord kindled against His people, and He abhorred His own inheritance.

⁴¹ And He gave them over into the hand the enemy, and they that hated them were lords over them.

⁴² Their enemies oppressed them also, and had them in subjection under their hands.

⁴³ Many a time did He deliver them, but they vexed Him by their obstinacy, and wallowed in their wickedness.

⁴⁴ But the Lord took notice, when they were being afflicted, when He heard their entreaty.

⁴⁵ And He remembered His covenant, and repented, according unto the abundance of His mercy;

⁴⁶ Yea, He caused them to be pitied in the sight of all those that led them away captive.

⁴⁷ Save us, O Lord our God, and gather us from among the nations, that we may give thanks unto Thy holy Name, and make our boast of Thy praise.

⁴⁸ Blessed be the Lord God of Israel from everlasting to everlasting, and all the people shall say, Amen. So be it.

Glory be to the Father, and to the Son, and to the Holy Spirit; both now, and ever, and unto the ages of ages. Amen.

Alleluia, alleluia, alleluia. Glory be to Thee, O God. Thrice.

Lord, have mercy. Thrice.

Glory be to the Father, and to the Son, and to the Holy Spirit; both now, and ever, and unto the ages of ages. Amen.

Second Stasis

Psalm 106. *Confitemini Domino.*
Alleluia.

 GIVE thanks unto the Lord, for He is good; for His mercy endureth for ever.

² So let them say, whom the Lord hath redeemed, whom He hath delivered from the hand of the enemy,

³ And gathered them out of the lands, from the east, and the west, and the north, and the sea.

⁴ They wandered in the waterless wilderness; they found no city to dwell in.

⁵ Hungry and thirsty, their soul fainted within them.

⁶ So they cried unto the Lord in their trouble, and He delivered them from their distress.

⁷ And He led them forth by the right way, that they might go to a habitable city.

⁸ O let them give thanks unto the Lord for His mercy, and for His wonderful works to the children of men!

⁹ For He hath filled the empty soul, and satisfied the hungry soul with goodness,

¹⁰ Such as sit in darkness, and in the shadow of death, fast bound in penury and iron,

¹¹ Because they rebelled against the words of God, and spurned the counsel of the Most High.

¹² He also brought down their heart through hard labor; they were used up, and there was none to help them.

¹³ So they cried unto the Lord in their trouble, and He saved them out of their distress,

¹⁴ And He brought them out of darkness, and the shadow of death, and brake their bonds in sunder.

¹⁵ O let them give thanks unto the Lord for His mercy, and for His wonderful works to the children of men!

¹⁶ For He hath shattered the gates of brass, and broken the bars of iron.

¹⁷ He took them from their path of wickedness, for because of their wickedness were they brought low.

¹⁸ Their soul abhorred all manner of food, and they were hard at death's door.

¹⁹ So they cried unto the Lord in their affliction, and He saved them out of their distress.

²⁰ He sent His Word, and healed them, and delivered them from their destruction.

²¹ O let them give thanks unto the Lord for His mercy, and for His wonderful works to the children of men!

²² And let them offer unto Him a sacrifice of praise, and proclaim His works with rejoicing!

²³ They that go down to the sea in ships, that do business in great waters;

²⁴ These men have seen the works of the Lord, and His wonders in the deep.

²⁵ He spake, and there stood up a stormy wind, and lifted up the waves thereof.

²⁶ They go up as high as the heavens, and they go down as far as the deep; their soul melted away because of the peril.

²⁷ They were tossed to and fro; they staggered like a drunken man, and were at their wit's end.

²⁸ So they cried unto the Lord in their trouble, and He delivered them out of their distress.

²⁹ And He commanded the storm, and it stood down into a calm, and the waves thereof grew still.

³⁰ Then were they glad, because they were at rest, and He guided them unto the haven of His will.

³¹ O let them give thanks unto the Lord for His mercy, and for His wonderful works to the children of men!

³² Let them exalt Him in the congregation of the people, and praise Him in the seat of the elders!

³³ He hath turned rivers into a desert, and springs of water into dry ground,

³⁴ A fruitful land into a salt marsh, because of the wickedness of them that dwell therein.

³⁵ He turned a desert into pools of water, and a parched land into springs of water.

³⁶ And there He settled in the hungry, and they built cities to dwell in;

³⁷ And they sowed the fields, and planted vineyards, and made a plentiful harvest.

³⁸ And He blessed them, and they multiplied exceedingly, and He suffered not their cattle to decrease.

³⁹ And again, they were minished, and brought low, through affliction, calamity, and suffering.

⁴⁰ Contempt was poured out upon their princes, and He caused them to wander out of the way in the wilderness.

⁴¹ Yet helped He the poor out of misery, and made His households like a flock of sheep.

⁴² The righteous will consider this, and be glad, and the mouth of all wickedness shall be stopped.

⁴³ Who is wise, and will keep these things? And will they understand the mercies of the Lord?

Glory be to the Father, and to the Son, and to the Holy Spirit; both now, and ever, and unto the ages of ages. Amen.

Alleluia, alleluia, alleluia. Glory be to Thee, O God. Thrice.

Lord, have mercy. Thrice.

Glory be to the Father, and to the Son, and to the Holy Spirit; both now, and ever, and unto the ages of ages. Amen.

Third Stasis

Psalm 107. *Paratum cor meum.*
A Song or Psalm of David.

Y heart is ready, O God, my heart is ready; I will chant and sing in my glory.

³ Awake, my glory; awake, psaltery and harp; I myself will awake right early.

⁴ I will give thanks unto Thee among the peoples, O Lord; I will sing praises unto Thee among the nations.

⁵ For Thy mercy is greater than the heavens, and Thy truth reacheth unto the clouds.

⁶ Be Thou exalted above the heavens, O God, and Thy glory over all the earth.

⁷ So that Thy beloved may be delivered, do Thou save with Thy right hand, and hear me.

⁸ God hath spoken in His holiness; I will be exalted therefore, and divide Shechem, and measure out the valley of Succoth.

⁹ Gilead is mine, and Manasseh is mine; Ephraim also is my helmet; Judah is my king.

¹⁰ Moab is the laver of my hope; over Edom will I stretch forth my shoe; the Philistines have submitted themselves unto me.

¹¹ Who will lead me into the strong city, and who will bring me into Edom?

¹² Wilt not Thou, O God, who hast forsaken us? And wilt not Thou, O God, go forth with our hosts?

¹³ O give us help from affliction, for vain is the help of man.

¹⁴ Through God we shall do great deeds, and it is He that shall wipe out our enemies.

Psalm 108. *Deus laudem.*
Unto the end, a Psalm of David.

GOD, be not silent of my praise,

² For the mouth of the ungodly, yea, the mouth of the deceitful is opened upon me, and they have spoken against me with a false tongue;

³ They compassed me about also with words of hatred, and fought against me without a cause.

⁴ Instead of the love that I had unto them, they would defame me, but I gave myself unto prayer.

⁵ And they rewarded me evil for good, and hatred for my love.

⁶ Set Thou a sinner to be ruler over him, and let the Devil stand at his right hand.

⁷ When sentence is given upon him, let him be condemned, and let his prayer be turned into sin.

⁸ Let his days be few, and let another take his office.

⁹ Let his children be fatherless, and his wife a widow.

¹⁰ Let his children be homeless wanderers, and beg their bread; let them be driven out of their homes.

¹¹ Let the usurer consume all that he hath, and let the stranger plunder his labor.

¹² Let there be no man to defend him, nor to have compassion upon his fatherless children.

¹³ Let his offspring be destroyed; in a single generation let his name be clean wiped out.

¹⁴ Let the wickedness of his fathers be had in remembrance in the sight of the Lord, and let not the sin of his mother be done away;

¹⁵ Let them always be before the Lord, and let the memory of them be rooted out from off the earth;

¹⁶ Because he remembered not to do mercy, but persecuted to death the poor helpless man, and him that was vexed at heart.

¹⁷ He loved cursing also, and it shall happen unto him, and he loved not blessing, therefore shall it be far from him.

¹⁸ And he clothed himself with cursing, like as

with a raiment, and it came into his bowels like water, and like oil into his bones.

¹⁹ Let it be unto him as the cloak that he hath upon him, and as the girdle that he is always girded withal.

²⁰ This is the dealing from the Lord unto them that slander me, and to those that speak evil against my soul.

²¹ But do Thou, Lord, O Lord, deal with me according unto Thy Name, for sweet is Thy mercy.

²² O deliver me, for I am poor and in misery, and my heart is wounded within me.

²³ I go hence like a shadow that departeth; I am driven away as the locust.

²⁴ My knees are weak from fasting; my flesh is dried up for want of oil.

²⁵ I became also a reproach unto them; they that looked upon me shaked their heads.

²⁶ Help me, O Lord my God, and save me according to Thy mercy;

²⁷ And let them know, how that this is Thy hand, and that Thou, Lord, hast done it.

²⁸ They shall curse, yet Thou shalt bless; let them be confounded that rise up against me, but Thy servant shall be glad.

²⁹ Let those who slander me be clothed with shame, and let them cover themselves with their own confusion, as with a cloak.

³⁰ I will give great thanks unto the Lord with my mouth, and praise Him among the multitude;

³¹ For He stood at the right hand of the poor, to save my soul from the persecutors.

Glory be to the Father, and to the Son, and to the Holy Spirit; both now, and ever, and unto the ages of ages. Amen.

Alleluia, alleluia, alleluia. Glory be to Thee, O God. Thrice.

¶ After the Fifteenth Kathisma, the Trisagion Prayers, and these troparia, in Tone I:

My many transgressions are like the great deep, O Saviour, and I have been cruelly drowned by mine offenses. Give me Thy hand, as Thou didst to Peter; save me, O God, and have mercy upon me!

Glory be to the Father, and to the Son, and to the Holy Spirit.

In that I have been condemned by my wicked thoughts and deeds, O my Saviour and God, grant me thought of converting, that I may cry: Save me, O good Benefactor, and have mercy upon me!

Both now, and ever, and unto the ages of ages. Amen.

O divinely blessed and most immaculate Maiden, cleanse me, wretch that I am, who have besmirched myself with wicked deeds and vile thoughts, O undefiled, pure and most holy Virgin Mother.

Lord, have mercy [40]. And this Prayer:

LORD and Master Jesus Christ, Thou art my helper; I am in Thy hands; help me. Leave me not to sin against Thee, for I am lost; and leave me not to follow the will of my flesh. Disdain me not, O Lord, for I am weak. Thou knowest what is profitable for me; leave me not to perish through my sins; leave me not, O Lord, depart not from me, for unto Thee have I fled. Teach me to do Thy will, for Thou art my God; heal Thou my soul, for I have sinned against Thee; save me for the sake of Thy mercy, for they that afflict me are before Thee, and I have no other refuge than Thee, O Lord. Therefore, let all that rise up against me and seek after my soul to destroy it be put to shame, for Thou alone art mighty, O Lord, in all things, and Thine is the glory for ever. Amen.

The Sixteenth Kathisma

Psalm 109. *Dixit Dominus.*
A Psalm of David.

THE Lord said unto my Lord, Sit Thou at my right hand, until I make Thine enemies the footstool of Thy feet.

² The Lord shall send the scepter of power unto Thee out of Zion; be Thou ruler, even in the midst of Thine enemies.

³ With Thee is dominion in the day of Thy power, in the splendor of Thy saints; from the womb before the morning star have I begotten Thee.

⁴ The Lord hath sworn, and will not repent, Thou art a Priest for ever, after the order of Melchizedek.

⁵ The Lord at Thy right hand hath broken kings in the day of His wrath.

⁶ He shall judge among the nations, He shall wreak havoc, He shall smite in sunder the heads of many on earth.

⁷ He shall drink of the brook in the way; therefore shall He lift up His head.

Psalm 110. *Confitebor Domino.*
Alleluia.

I will give thanks unto Thee, O Lord, with my whole heart, in the council of the righteous, and in the congregation.

² Great are the works of the Lord, sought out according unto all His will.

³ His work is praise and splendor, and His righteousness endureth for ever and ever.

⁴ He hath made His marvelous works to be remembered; the Lord is merciful and compassionate.

⁵ He hath given food unto them that fear Him; He shall ever be mindful of His covenant.

⁶ He hath showed His people the power of His works, that He may give them the inheritance of the nations.

⁷ The works of His hands are truth and judgment; all His commandments are faithful,

⁸ Confirmed for ever and ever, done in truth and equity.

⁹ He hath sent redemption unto His people, He hath established His covenant for ever; holy and terrible is His Name.

¹⁰ The fear of the Lord is the beginning of wisdom, a good understanding have all they that do thereafter; His praise endureth for ever and ever.

Psalm 111. *Beatus vir.*
Alleluia.

Blessed is the man that feareth the Lord, in His commandments shall he greatly delight.

² His seed shall be mighty upon earth, the generation of the righteous shall be blessed.

³ Glory and riches are in his house, and his righteousness endureth for ever and ever.

⁴ Unto the godly hath dawned a Light in the darkness; He is merciful, and compassionate, and righteous.

⁵ A good man showeth compassion, and giveth, he will guide his words with discretion, for he shall never be moved.

⁶ The righteous shall be had in everlasting remembrance;

⁷ He will not be afraid of evil tidings, his heart is ready to trust in the Lord.

⁸ His heart is firm, and will not shrink, until he looketh down upon his enemies.

⁹ He hath disbursed abroad, he hath given to the poor, and his righteousness endureth for ever and ever; his horn shall be exalted in glory.

¹⁰ The sinner shall see it, and be angry, he shall gnash with his teeth, and melt away; the desire of the sinner shall perish.

Glory be to the Father, and to the Son, and to the Holy Spirit; both now, and ever, and unto the ages of ages. Amen.

Alleluia, alleluia, alleluia. Glory be to Thee, O God. Thrice.

Lord, have mercy. Thrice.

Glory be to the Father, and to the Son, and to the Holy Spirit; both now, and ever, and unto the ages of ages. Amen.

Second Stasis

Psalm 112. *Laudate, pueri.*
Alleluia.

PRAISE the Lord, ye servants; O praise the Name of the Lord.

² Blessed be the Name of the Lord, from this time forth and for evermore.

³ From the rising up of the sun, unto the going down of the same, the Lord's Name is praised.

⁴ The Lord is high above all nations; His glory is above the heavens.

⁵ Who is like unto the Lord our God, that dwelleth on high,

⁶ And beholdeth the humble things that are in heaven and earth?

⁷ He raiseth up the beggar out of the dust, and lifteth the cripple out of the dump;

⁸ That He may set him with the princes, even with the princes of His people.

⁹ He maketh the barren woman to keep house, a joyful mother of children.

Psalm 113. *In exitu Israel.*
Alleluia.

WHEN Israel came out of Egypt, the house of Jacob from among a strange people,

² Judah was His sanctuary, and Israel His dominion.

³ The sea saw it, and fled; Jordan was driven back.

⁴ The mountains skipped like rams, and the little hills like lambs.

⁵ What aileth thee, O thou sea, that thou fleddest? Thou Jordan, that thou wast driven back?

⁶ Ye mountains, that ye skipped like rams, and ye little hills, like lambs?

⁷ The earth quaked at the presence of the Lord, at the presence of the God of Jacob,

⁸ Who turned the hard rock into pools of water, and the flinty stone into a gushing spring.

⁹ Not unto us, O Lord, not unto us, but unto Thy Name give the glory, for the sake of Thy mercy and Thy truth,

¹⁰ Lest the heathen should say, Where is now their God?

¹¹ But our God is in heaven and on earth; He hath done all whatsoever He pleased.

¹² The idols of the heathen are silver and gold, even the work of men's hands.

¹³ They have mouths, and speak not; eyes have they, and see not.

¹⁴ They have ears, and hear not; noses have they, and smell not.

¹⁵ They have hands, and handle not; feet have they, and walk not, neither speak they through their throat.

¹⁶ May they that make them become like unto them, and all such as do put their trust in them.

¹⁷ The house of Israel hath trusted in the Lord; He is their helper and defender.

¹⁸ The house of Aaron hath trusted in the Lord; He is their helper and defender.

¹⁹ They that fear the Lord have put their trust in the Lord; He is their helper and defender.

²⁰ The Lord hath been mindful of us, and hath blessed us; He hath blessed the house of Israel; He hath blessed the house of Aaron.

²¹ He hath blessed them that fear the Lord, both small and great.

²² May the Lord increase you more and more, you and your children.

²³ Ye are the blessed of the Lord, Who made heaven and earth.

²⁴ All the whole heavens are the Lord's; but the earth hath He given to the children of men.

²⁵ The dead praise not Thee, O Lord, neither all they that go down into hell.

²⁶ But we who live will bless the Lord, from this time forth and for evermore.

Psalm 114. *Dilexi, quoniam.*
Alleluia.

I WAS filled with love, because the Lord will hear the voice of my supplication.

² Because He hath inclined His ear unto me, therefore will I call upon Him as long as I live.

³ The pains of death compassed me round about, and the perils of hell gat hold upon me; I found grief and sorrow, and I called upon the Name of the Lord.

⁴ O Lord, deliver my soul; gracious is the Lord, and righteous, yea, our God is merciful.

⁵ The Lord preserveth the simple; I humbled myself, and He saved me.

⁶ Turn again then into thy rest, O my soul, for the Lord hath prospered thee.

⁷ For He hath delivered my soul from death, mine eyes from tears, and my feet from stumbling.

⁸ I will be well-pleasing before the Lord in the land of the living.

Glory be to the Father, and to the Son, and to the Holy Spirit; both now, and ever, and unto the ages of ages. Amen.

Alleluia, alleluia, alleluia. Glory be to Thee, O God. *Thrice.*

Lord, have mercy. *Thrice.*

Glory be to the Father, and to the Son, and to the Holy Spirit; both now, and ever, and unto the ages of ages. Amen.

Third Stasis

Psalm 115. *Credidi.*
Alleluia.

 BELIEVED, so I spake; but I was greatly humbled.

² I said in my confusion, All men are liars.

³ What shall I render unto the Lord, for all that He hath rendered unto me?

⁴ I will take the cup of salvation, and call upon the Name of the Lord.

⁵ I will pay my vows unto the Lord in the presence of all His people.

⁶ Precious in the sight of the Lord is the death of His saints.

⁷ O Lord, I am Thy servant; I am Thy servant, and the son of Thine handmaid; Thou hast broken my bonds in sunder.

⁸ I will offer unto Thee a sacrifice of thanksgiving, and will call upon the Name of the Lord.

⁹ I will pay my vows unto the Lord in the presence of all His people,

¹⁰ In the courts of the Lord's house, even in the midst of thee, O Jerusalem.

Psalm 116. *Laudate, Dominum.*
Alleluia.

 PRAISE the Lord, all ye nations; praise Him, all ye peoples,

² For His merciful kindness is ever more and more towards us, and the truth of the Lord endureth for ever.

Psalm 117. *Confitemini Domino.*
Alleluia.

 GIVE thanks unto the Lord, for He is good, for His mercy endureth for ever.

² Let the house of Israel now say that He is good, for His mercy endureth for ever.

³ Let the house of Aaron now say that He is good, for His mercy endureth for ever.

⁴ Let all them that fear the Lord now say that He is good, for His mercy endureth for ever.

⁵ I called upon the Lord out of grief, and He heard me at large.

⁶ The Lord is my helper, and I will not fear what man shall do unto me.

⁷ The Lord is my helper, and I shall look down upon mine enemies.

⁸ It is better to trust in the Lord, than to put any confidence in man.

⁹ It is better to trust in the Lord, than to put any confidence in princes.

¹⁰ All nations compassed me round about, but in the Name of the Lord have I driven them back.

¹¹ They kept me in on every side, but in the Name of the Lord have I driven them back.

¹² They came about me like bees on a honeycomb, and burned even as a fire among the thorns, and in the Name of the Lord have I driven them back.

¹³ Hard pressed, I turned to fall, and the Lord catcheth me.

¹⁴ The Lord is my strength, and my song, and is become my salvation.

¹⁵ The voice of joy and salvation is in the dwellings of the righteous; the right hand of the Lord hath brought mighty things to pass.

¹⁶ The right hand of the Lord lifted me up; the right hand of the Lord hath brought mighty things to pass.

¹⁷ I shall not die, but live, and declare the works of the Lord.

¹⁸ With chastening hath the Lord chastened me, but He hath not given me over unto death.

¹⁹ Open unto me the gates of righteousness,

that, having gone into them, I may give thanks unto the Lord.

²⁰ This is the gate of the Lord, the righteous shall enter into it.

²¹ I will thank Thee, for Thou hast heard me, and art become my salvation.

²² The stone which the builders refused, is become the head stone of the corner.

²³ This is the Lord's doing, and it is marvelous in our eyes.

²⁴ This is the day which the Lord hath made, let us rejoice and be glad therein.

²⁵ Save me now, O Lord! O Lord, make haste.

²⁶ Blessed is he that cometh in the Name of the Lord; we have blessed you out of the house of the Lord.

²⁷ God is the Lord, and hath appeared unto us; appoint a festival with branches, even unto the horns of the altar.

²⁸ Thou art my God, and I will give thanks unto Thee; Thou art my God, and I will exalt Thee; I will thank Thee, for Thou hast heard me, and wast for me unto salvation.

²⁹ O give thanks unto the Lord, for He is good; for His mercy endureth for ever.

Glory be to the Father, and to the Son, and to the Holy Spirit; both now, and ever, and unto the ages of ages. Amen.

Alleluia, alleluia, alleluia. Glory be to Thee, O God. Thrice.

¶ After the Sixteenth Kathisma, the Trisagion Prayers, and these troparia, in Tone I:

The other world awaiteth thee, O my soul, and the Judge wisheth to condemn thy secret and wicked deeds. Remain no longer in thy present ways, but go beforehand to the Judge, crying out: O God, cleanse me and save me!

Glory be to the Father, and to the Son, and to the Holy Spirit.

In that I am covered with sin and countless wounds, O Christ Saviour, while yet sinning I beseech Thy compassion: O Physician of the afflicted, visit, heal and save me!

Both now, and ever, and unto the ages of ages. Amen.

O my soul, why livest thou in negligence and slothfulness? Why hast thou no concern for the evil things thou hast done in this life? Take care to set all aright before the Lord closeth the door to thee. Make haste to the Theotokos, fall down and cry out: O most pure Lady, hope of the hopeless, save me who have sinned greatly against thee.

Lord, have mercy [40]. And this Prayer:

HOLY Lord, Who hast Thy dwelling so high, and yet humblest Thyself to regard all things that are in heaven and earth with Thine all-seeing eye, to Thee do we bow the neck of our soul and body, and to Thee do we pray, O Holy of Holies, Stretch forth Thine invisible hand from Thy holy dwelling-place on high, and bless us all, and forgive us all our trespasses, voluntary or involuntary, in word or in deed. Grant us contrition, O Lord; grant us spiritual tears unto the cleansing of our many sins; grant Thy great mercy unto Thy world, and unto us, Thine unworthy servants. For blessed and most glorious is Thy Name, of the Father, and of the Son, and of the Holy Spirit; now, and ever, and unto the ages of ages. Amen.

The Seventeenth Kathisma

Psalm 118. *Beati immaculati.*
Alleluia.

Octave 1: א ALEPH

BLESSED are the blameless in the way, who walk in the Law of the Lord.

² Blessed are they that search into His testimonies; with their whole heart shall they seek after Him.

³ For they who do no wickedness have walked in His ways.

⁴ Thou hast charged that we shall diligently keep Thy commandments.

⁵ O that my ways were so directed, as to keep Thy statutes!

⁶ Then should I not be confounded, when I consider all Thy commandments.

⁷ I will thank Thee with an unfeigned heart, when I shall have learned the judgments of Thy righteousness.

⁸ I will keep Thy statutes; O forsake me not utterly.

Octave 2: ⊐ Beth. *In quo corriget?*

OW shall a young man correct his way? By keeping Thy words.

¹⁰ With my whole heart have I sought Thee; O estrange me not from Thy commandments.

¹¹ Thy words have I hid within my heart, that I should not sin against Thee.

¹² Blessed art Thou, O Lord; teach me Thy statutes.

¹³ With my lips have I declared all the judgments of Thy mouth.

¹⁴ I have had as great delight in the way of Thy testimonies, as in all riches.

¹⁵ I will ponder Thy commandments, and understand Thy ways.

¹⁶ I will study Thy statutes; I will not forget Thy words.

Octave 3: ⅃ Gimel. *Retribue servo tuo.*

EWARD Thy servant; give me life, and I shall keep Thy words.

¹⁸ Open Thou mine eyes, that I may recognize the wondrous things of Thy Law.

¹⁹ I am a pilgrim upon earth, O hide not Thy commandments from me.

²⁰ My soul hath been consumed with longing for Thy judgments at all times.

²¹ Thou hast rebuked the proud; cursed are they that do err from Thy commandments.

²² O take from me rebuke and contempt, for I have sought Thy testimonies.

²³ For princes did sit and speak against me, but Thy servant occupied himself in Thy statutes.

²⁴ For Thy testimonies are my consolation, and Thy statutes are my counsel.

Octave 4: ד DALETH. *Adhæsit pavimento.*

Y soul cleaveth to the dust; O give me life, according to Thy word.

²⁶ I acknowledged my ways, and Thou heardest me; O teach me Thy statutes.

²⁷ Make me to understand the way of Thy statutes, and I shall ponder Thy wondrous works.

²⁸ My soul nodded off in weariness; sustain Thou me in Thy words.

²⁹ Take from me the way of injustice, and by Thy Law have mercy upon me.

³⁰ I have chosen the way of truth, and Thy judgments have I not forgotten.

³¹ I have stuck unto Thy testimonies, O Lord; confound me not.

³² I ran the way of Thy commandments, when Thou didst enlarge my heart.

Octave 5: ה HE. *Legem pone.*

AKE the way of Thy statutes a Law unto me, and I shall always seek it.

³⁴ Give me understanding, and I shall delve into Thy Law; yea, I shall keep it with my whole heart.

³⁵ Set me on the path of Thy commandments, for therein hath been my desire.

³⁶ Incline my heart unto Thy testimonies, and not to covetousness.

³⁷ O turn away mine eyes, lest they behold vanity; give me life in Thy way.

³⁸ O stablish Thy word in Thy servant unto fear of Thee.

³⁹ Take away my rebuke, which I have considered, for Thy judgments are good.

⁴⁰ Behold, I have desired Thy commandments; O give me life in Thy righteousness.

Octave 6: ו VAU. *Et veniat super me.*

ET Thy loving mercy come also unto me, O Lord, even Thy salvation, according unto Thy word.

⁴² So shall I have an answer for them that rebuke me, for I have trusted in Thy word.

⁴³ And take not the word of Thy truth out of my mouth utterly, for in Thy judgments have I hoped.

⁴⁴ So shall I always keep Thy Law; for ever, and for ever and ever.

⁴⁵ And I walked abroad, for I sought Thy commandments.

⁴⁶ I spake of Thy testimonies also before kings, and I was not ashamed.

⁴⁷ And my study was in Thy commandments, which I greatly loved.

⁴⁸ My hands also did I lift up unto Thy

commandments, which I have loved, and I occupied myself in Thy statutes.

Octave 7: ׳ ZAYIN. *Memor esto servi tui.*

REMEMBER Thy word unto Thy servant, by which Thou hast given me hope.

⁴⁹ The same hath comforted me in my humbleness, for Thy word hath given me life.

⁵¹ The proud have brazenly transgressed, yet have I not shrinked from Thy Law.

⁵² I remembered Thine everlasting judgments, O Lord, and was comforted.

⁵³ Grief hath taken me, because of the sinners that forsake Thy Law.

⁵⁴ Thy statutes have been my songs in the place of my pilgrimage.

⁵⁵ I have remembered Thy Name, O Lord, in the night-season, and have kept Thy Law.

⁵⁶ This befell me, because I sought Thy statutes.

Octave 8: ח HETH. *Portio mea, Domine.*

HOU art my portion, O Lord; I said, I would keep Thy Law.

⁵⁸ I entreated Thy countenance with my whole heart; have mercy upon me, according to Thy word.

⁵⁹ I considered Thy ways, and turned my feet unto Thy testimonies.

⁶⁰ I made ready, and was not ashamed to keep Thy commandments.

⁶¹ The cords of sinners have bound me, but I have not forgotten Thy Law.

⁶² At midnight I rose up to give thanks unto Thee, because of Thy righteous judgments.

⁶³ I am a part of all them that fear Thee, and of them that keep Thy commandments.

⁶⁴ The earth, O Lord, is full of Thy mercy; O teach me Thy statutes.

Octave 9: ט TETH. *Bonitatem fecisti.*

THOU hast dealt graciously with Thy servant, O Lord, according unto Thy word.

⁶⁶ O teach me goodness and correction and understanding, for I have believed Thy commandments.

⁶⁷ Before I submitted, I sinned; therefore have I kept Thy word.

⁶⁸ Thou art good, O Lord, and of Thy goodness teach me Thy statutes.

⁶⁹ The injustice of the proud increased against me, but I will look into Thy commandments with my whole heart.

⁷⁰ Their hearts have curdled like milk, but I have studied Thy Law.

⁷¹ It is good for me that Thou didst humble me, that I may learn Thy statutes.

⁷² The Law of Thy lips is better unto me, than thousands of gold and silver.

Glory be to the Father, and to the Son, and to the Holy Spirit; both now, and ever, and unto the ages of ages. Amen.

Alleluia, alleluia, alleluia. Glory be to Thee, O God. Thrice.

Lord, have mercy. Thrice.

Glory be to the Father, and to the Son, and to the Holy Spirit; both now, and ever, and unto the ages of ages. Amen.

Second Stasis

Octave 10: י JOD. *Manus tuæ fecerunt me.*

THY hands have made me and fashioned me; O give me understanding, and I shall learn Thy commandments.

74 They that fear Thee shall see me and be glad, because I have put my trust in Thy word.

75 I have understood, O Lord, that Thy judgments are righteousness, and justly didst Thou humble me.

76 But let Thy mercy comfort me, according to Thy word unto Thy servant.

77 O let Thy loving mercies come unto me, and I shall live, for Thy Law is my consolation.

78 Let the proud be confounded, for they have unfairly behaved lawlessly against me, but I will be occupied in Thy commandments.

79 Let such as fear Thee turn unto me, and them that know Thy testimonies.

⁸⁰ O let my heart be blameless in Thy statutes, that I be not ashamed.

Octave 11: ב CAPH. *Defecit anima mea.*

Y soul hath longed for Thy salvation; I have trusted in Thy word.

⁸² Mine eyes longed for Thy word, saying, O when wilt Thou comfort me?

⁸³ For I am become like a wine-skin in the frost, yet did I not forget Thy statutes.

⁸⁴ How many are the days of Thy servant? When wilt Thou avenge me of them that persecute me?

⁸⁵ The law-breakers told me tales, but not so Thy Law, O Lord.

⁸⁶ All Thy commandments are true; they persecuted me unjustly; O be Thou my help.

⁸⁷ They had almost made an end of me upon earth, but I have not forsaken Thy commandments.

⁸⁸ O give me life according to Thy mercy, and so shall I keep the testimonies of Thy mouth.

Octave 12: ל LAMED. *In æternum, Domine.*

LORD, Thy word abideth for ever in heaven.

⁹⁰ Thy truth is from generation to generation; Thou hast laid the foundation of the earth, and it abideth.

⁹¹ By Thine ordinance doth the day continue, for all things serve Thee.

⁹² For if my delight had not been in Thy Law, I should have perished in my humbleness.

⁹³ I will never forget Thy statutes, for in them Thou hast given me life.

Middle

⁹⁴ I am Thine, O save me; for I have sought Thy statutes.

⁹⁵ The sinners laid wait for me to destroy me, but I have understood Thy testimonies.

⁹⁶ I have seen the limit of all perfection, but Thy commandment is exceeding broad.

Octave 13: ‏מ‎ MEM. *Quomodo dilexi!*

 HOW I have loved Thy Law, O Lord; it is my study all day.

⁹⁸ Thou through Thy commandment hast made me wiser than mine enemies, for it is mine for ever.

⁹⁹ I have understood more than all my teachers, for Thy testimonies are my study.

¹⁰⁰ I have become wiser than an elder, because I sought Thy commandments.

¹⁰¹ I have refrained my feet from every evil way, that I may keep Thy word.

¹⁰² I have not turned aside from Thy judgments, for Thou didst appoint a Law for me.

¹⁰³ O how sweet are Thy words unto my throat; yea, sweeter than honey unto my mouth.

¹⁰⁴ Through Thy commandments I understood, therefore have I hated every way of untruth.

Octave 14: ♪ NUN. *Lucerna pedibus meis.*

THY Law is a lamp unto my feet, and a light unto my paths.

¹⁰⁶ I have sworn, and steadfastly resolved, to keep Thy righteous judgments.

¹⁰⁷ I was greatly humbled; give me life, O Lord, according to Thy word.

¹⁰⁸ Make acceptable the free-will offerings of my mouth, O Lord, and teach me Thy judgments.

¹⁰⁹ My soul is always in Thy hand, and I have not forgotten Thy Law.

¹¹⁰ The sinners laid a snare for me, yet I swerved not from Thy commandments.

¹¹¹ Thy testimonies have I claimed as my inheritance for ever, for they are the joy of my heart.

¹¹² In return, I have inclined mine heart to perform Thy statutes always.

Octave 15: ס SAMECH. *Iniquos odio habui.*

I HATED the law-breakers, but Thy Law have I loved.

¹¹⁴ Thou art my helper and my defender; I have trusted in Thy words.

¹¹⁵ Depart from me, ye wicked, and I will put the commandments of my God to the test.

¹¹⁶ O stand up for me according to Thy word,

that I may live, and let me not be disappointed of my hope.

¹¹⁷ Help me, and I shall be saved, and I shall ever delight in Thy statutes.

¹¹⁸ Thou hast despised all them that depart from Thy statutes, for their intent is iniquitous.

¹¹⁹ All the sinners of the earth I accounted as transgressors, therefore have I loved Thy testimonies.

¹²⁰ Nail my flesh to the fear of Thee, for I was afraid of Thy judgments:

Octave 16: ע AYIN. *Feci judicium.*

 HAVE done judgment and justice; O give me not over unto them that do me wrong.

¹²² Vouch for Thy servant unto good; let not the proud slander me.

¹²³ Mine eyes are wasted away with looking for Thy salvation, and for the word of Thy truth.

¹²⁴ O deal with Thy servant according unto Thy mercy, and teach me Thy statutes.

¹²⁵ I am Thy servant; O give me understanding, that I may know Thy testimonies.

¹²⁶ It is time for the Lord to act; for they have made void Thy Law.

¹²⁷ Therefore have I loved Thy commandments more than gold and topaz.

¹²⁸ Therefore have I held straight to all Thy commandments; I have hated every wrong way.

Octave 17: ‎ᴅ ᴘᴇ. *Mirabilia.*

HY testimonies are wonderful, therefore hath my soul searched them out.

¹³⁰ The manifestation of Thy words shall give light and understanding unto the simple.

¹³¹ I opened my mouth and sighed, because I was longing for Thy commandments.

Glory be to the Father, and to the Son, and to the Holy Spirit; both now, and ever, and unto the ages of ages. Amen.

Alleluia, alleluia, alleluia. Glory be to Thee, O God. Thrice.

Lord, have mercy. Thrice.

Glory be to the Father, and to the Son, and to the Holy Spirit; both now, and ever, and unto the ages of ages. Amen.

Third Stasis

¹³² O look Thou upon me, and have mercy upon me, according to the judgment of them that love Thy Name.

¹³³ Direct my steps according to Thy word, and let not any wickedness have dominion over me.

¹³⁴ O deliver me from the calumny of men, and I shall keep Thy commandments.

¹³⁵ Make Thy face to shine upon Thy servant, and teach me Thy statutes.

¹³⁶ Mine eyes gushed out streams of water, because I kept not Thy Law.

Octave 18: צ Tzaddi. *Justus es, Domine.*

RIGHTEOUS art Thou, O Lord, and true are Thy judgments.

¹³⁸ Thou hast enjoined as Thy testimonies exceeding righteousness and truth.

¹³⁹ Thy zeal hath used me up, because mine enemies have forgotten Thy word.

¹⁴⁰ Thy word is well tempered, and Thy servant hath loved it.

¹⁴¹ I am young, and of no account, yet have I not forgotten Thy statutes.

¹⁴² Thy righteousness is righteousness for ever, and Thy Law is truth.

¹⁴³ Grief and want have found me, yet are Thy commandments my comfort.

¹⁴⁴ The righteousness of Thy testimonies is everlasting; O give me understanding, and I shall live.

Octave 19: ק Coph. *Clamavi in toto corde meo.*

I CRIED with my whole heart, Hear me, O Lord, and I will seek Thy statutes.

¹⁴⁶ I cried unto Thee, Save me, and I shall keep Thy testimonies.

¹⁴⁷ I got up in the dead of night and cried, I trusted in Thy word.

¹⁴⁸ Mine eyes were open before dawn, that I might be occupied in Thy words.

¹⁴⁹ Hear my voice, O Lord, according unto Thy mercy; give me life, according unto Thy judgment.

¹⁵⁰ They drew nigh that persecute me with wickedness; they are far gone from Thy Law.

¹⁵¹ Thou art nigh at hand, O Lord, and all Thy ways are truth.

¹⁵² I have known long since from Thy testimonies, that Thou hast established them for ever.

Octave 20: ר RESH. *Vide humilitatem.*

SEE my humbleness, and spare me, for I have not forgotten Thy Law.

¹⁵⁴ Judge Thou my cause, and deliver me; give me life, because of Thy word.

¹⁵⁵ Salvation is far from sinners, for they sought not Thy statutes.

¹⁵⁶ Thy mercies are many, O Lord; give me life, according unto Thy judgment.

¹⁵⁷ Many there are that trouble me, and persecute me, yet have I not swerved from Thy testimonies.

¹⁵⁸ I looked upon them that did not understand, and grieved, because they kept not Thy words.

¹⁵⁹ See how I have loved Thy commandments, O Lord; give me life, according to Thy mercy.

¹⁶⁰ The beginning of Thy words is truth, and all

the judgments of Thy righteousness endure for evermore.

Octave 21: ש SHIN. *Principes persecuti sunt.*

PRINCES have persecuted me without a cause, but my heart standeth in awe of Thy words.

¹⁶² I am as glad of Thy words, as one that findeth great spoils.

¹⁶³ I have hated and loathed untruth, but Thy Law have I loved.

¹⁶⁴ Seven times a day have I praised Thee, because of Thy righteous judgments.

¹⁶⁵ Great peace have they who love Thy Law, and nothing can trip them up.

¹⁶⁶ I have looked for Thy salvation, O Lord, and I have loved Thy commandments.

¹⁶⁷ My soul hath kept Thy testimonies, and loved them exceedingly.

¹⁶⁸ I have kept Thy commandments and Thy testimonies, for all my ways are before Thee, O Lord.

Octave 22: ת TAU. *Appropinquet deprecatio.*

LET my petition come before Thee, O Lord; give me understanding, according to Thy word.

¹⁷⁰ Let my supplication come before Thee, O Lord; deliver me, according to Thy word.

¹⁷¹ My lips shall break out in song, when Thou hast taught me Thy statutes.

¹⁷² My tongue shall proclaim Thy words, for all Thy commandments are righteous.

¹⁷³ Let Thine hand be ready to save me, for I have chosen Thy commandments.

¹⁷⁴ I have longed for Thy salvation, O Lord, and Thy Law is my delight.

¹⁷⁵ My soul shall live, and shall praise Thee, and Thy judgments shall help me.

¹⁷⁶ I have gone astray like a sheep that is lost; O seek Thy servant, for I have not forgotten Thy commandments.

Glory be to the Father, and to the Son, and to the Holy Spirit; both now, and ever, and unto the ages of ages. Amen.

Alleluia, alleluia, alleluia. Glory be to Thee, O God. Thrice.

¶ After the Seventeenth Kathisma, the Trisagion Prayers, and these troparia, in Tone II:

Like the prodigal son have I sinned against Thee, O Saviour; accept me who repent, O Father, and have mercy upon me, O God!

Glory be to the Father, and to the Son, and to the Holy Spirit.

With the publican's voice do I cry unto Thee, O Saviour Christ; cleanse me as Thou didst him, and have mercy upon me!

Both now, and ever, and unto the ages of ages. Amen.

O Theotokos, disdain not me who am in need of thine aid, for in thee hath my soul trusted. Have mercy upon me!

Lord, have mercy [40]. And this Prayer:

ALMIGHTY Master and Lord, Creator of all, Father of compassion and God of mercy, Who fashioned man from the earth and showed him to be created according to Thine image and likeness, that thereby Thy majestic Name might be glorified on earth; and Who, when he had been uprooted by the violation of Thy commandment, didst fashion him anew and yet better in Thy Christ, and didst lead him up to heaven, I thank Thee that Thou hast not given me over utterly to mine enemies, which seek to cast me down to be lost in hell, nor hast left me to perish with mine iniquities. Now, therefore, O greatly merciful Lord, Who lovest that which is good, Who desirest not the death of the sinner, but awaitest his conversion and dost accept it, Who settest aright them that have been cast down, and healest the broken, turn even me unto repentance, set me aright who have been cast down, and heal me who am broken; be Thou mindful of Thy compassions and Thine incomparable goodness which hath been unto us from of old, and forget my countless iniquities which I have committed by thought, word and deed; remove the blinders of my heart, and grant me tears of remorse for the cleansing of my vile thoughts. Hearken, O Lord, and attend, O Lover of mankind; cleanse me, O Compassionate One, and free Thou my wretched soul from the tyranny of the passions which reign within me. And let sin have no more hold over me, nor let the warring demon prevail against me, neither let him lead me to do his will; but with Thy mighty hand, O Thou Who hast rescued me from his dominion, do Thou reign within me, O good Lord Who lovest mankind; and be Thou well pleased that I be wholly Thine, and that I live henceforth in accordance with Thy will. And by Thine ineffable goodness grant me cleansing of heart, a guard over my mouth, uprightness of activity, a humble mind, peace of thought, serenity of the powers of my soul, spiritual joy, true piety, long-suffering, goodness, meekness, unfeigned love, steadfast temperance; and fill me with every good fruit, through the gift of Thy Holy Spirit, and bring me not to the mid-point of my days unprepared, neither snatch away my unrepentant soul, but perfect me with Thy perfection, and thus lead me up from this present life, that, having passed through the principalities and powers of darkness without hindrance, even I may, through Thy grace, behold the ineffable beauty of Thine unapproachable glory, with all Thy saints, in whom Thy most honorable and majestic Name hath been glorified and sanctified, together with Thy Son, and Thy most holy, good and life-creating Spirit; now, and ever, and unto the ages of ages. Amen.

The Eighteenth Kathisma

Psalm 119. *Ad Dominum.*
A Song of Ascents.

HEN I was in trouble I called upon the Lord, and He heard me.

² O Lord, deliver my soul from lying lips, and from a deceitful tongue.

³ What shall be given unto thee, or what shall be aimed at thee, against a false tongue?

⁴ Even the sharp arrows of the mighty, with hot burning coals.

⁵ Woe is me, for my wandering hath been prolonged; I have dwelt among the tents of Kedar.

⁶ Long did my soul wander; with them that hate peace I was peaceable,

⁷ But when I spake unto them, they fought against me without a cause.

Psalm 120. *Levabo oculos.*
A Song of Ascents.

LIFTED up mine eyes unto the hills; from whence will my help come?

² My help cometh even from the Lord, Who hath made heaven and earth.

³ Suffer not thy feet to slip, nor Him that keepeth thee to slumber.

⁴ Behold, He that keepeth Israel shall neither slumber nor sleep.

⁵ The Lord Himself shall keep thee; the Lord is thy shelter upon thy right hand;

⁶ The sun shall not burn thee by day, neither the moon by night.

⁷ The Lord shall keep thee from all evil; yea, the Lord shall preserve thy soul.

⁸ The Lord shall preserve thy going out, and thy coming in, from this time forth, and for evermore.

Psalm 121. *Lœtatus sum.*
A Song of Ascents.

 WAS glad when they said unto me, Let us go into the house of the Lord.

² Our feet stood in thy gates, O Jerusalem.

³ Jerusalem is built as a city, whose sharing is in common.

⁴ For thither did the tribes go up, even the tribes of the Lord, the testimony of Israel, to give thanks unto the Name of the Lord.

⁵ For there sat the thrones of judgment, even the thrones of the house of David.

⁶ O pray for the peace of Jerusalem, and for prosperity to them that love thee.

⁷ Let there be peace in thy power, and prosperity within thy palaces.

⁸ For my brethren and neighbors' sake I spake peace concerning thee.

⁹ Because of the house of the Lord our God, I sought thy good.

Psalm 122. *Ad te levavi oculos meos.*
A Song of Ascents.

NTO Thee have I lifted up mine eyes, O Thou that dwellest in heaven.

² Behold, even as the eyes of servants are upon the hand of their masters, and as the eyes of a maid are upon the hand of her mistress, even so are our eyes upon the Lord our God, until He have pity upon us.

³ Have mercy upon us, O Lord, have mercy upon us, for we have had our fill of humiliation.

⁴ Our soul is fed up with the scornful reproof of the wealthy, and the disparaging of the proud.

Psalm 123. *Nisi quia Dominus.*
A Song of Ascents.

F the Lord Himself had not been on our side, may Israel now say,

² If the Lord Himself had not been on our side, when men rose up against us, then would they have swallowed us up alive;

³ When their wrath was kindled upon us, then would the waters have drowned us.

⁴ The stream would have gone over our soul;

⁵ The roiling waters would have gone even over our soul.

⁶ Blessed be the Lord, Who hath not given us over for a prey unto their teeth.

⁷ Our soul escaped even as a bird out of the snare of the fowler; the snare was broken, and we were delivered.

⁸ Our help is in the Name of the Lord, Who hath made heaven and earth.

Glory be to the Father, and to the Son, and to the Holy Spirit; both now, and ever, and unto the ages of ages. Amen.

Alleluia, alleluia, alleluia. Glory be to Thee, O God. *Thrice.*

Lord, have mercy. *Thrice.*

Glory be to the Father, and to the Son, and to the Holy Spirit; both now, and ever, and unto the ages of ages. Amen.

Second Stasis

Psalm 124. *Qui confidunt.*
A Song of Ascents.

THEY that trust in the Lord are as mount Zion; he that liveth in Jerusalem shall never be shaken.

² The hills are round about her; even so is the

Lord round about His people, from this time forth for evermore.

³ For the Lord shall not suffer the rod of sinners to rest upon the lot of the righteous, lest the righteous stretch forth their hand unto wickedness.

⁴ Do well, O Lord, unto those that are good and true of heart.

⁵ As for such as turn aside unto craftiness, the Lord shall lead them forth with the workers of wickedness; peace be upon Israel.

Psalm 125. *In convertendo.*
A Song of Ascents.

WHEN the Lord turned again the captivity of Zion, then were we like unto them that are comforted.

² Then was our mouth filled with joy, and our tongue with merry-making; then shall they say among the nations, The Lord hath done great things for them.

³ Yea, the Lord hath done great things for us already, whereof we rejoice.

⁴ Turn our captivity, O Lord, as the streams in the south.

⁵ They that sow in tears, shall reap in joy.

⁶ They went on their way and wept, sowing their seed, but they shall return in joy, bearing their sheaves.

Psalm 126. *Nisi Dominus.*
A Song of Ascents.

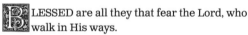XCEPT the Lord build the house, they labor in vain that build it; except the Lord keep the city, the watchman waketh but in vain.

² It is but lost labor that ye haste to rise up early, and so late take rest, and eat the bread of carefulness, when He shall give His beloved sleep.

³ Lo, children are the legacy of the Lord, the reward of the fruit of the womb.

⁴ Like as arrows in the hand of a giant, even so are the children of them that were cast out.

⁵ Blessed is he that hath his quiver full of them; they shall not be ashamed when they speak with their enemies in the gate.

Psalm 127. *Beati omnes.*
A Song of Ascents.

LESSED are all they that fear the Lord, who walk in His ways.

² For thou shalt eat the fruit of thy labors; blessed art thou, and it shall be well with thee.

³ Thy wife shall be as a fruitful vine upon the walls of thine house;

⁴ Thy children like newly-planted olive trees round about thy table.

⁵ Lo, thus shall the man be blessed that feareth the Lord.

⁶ The Lord from out of Zion shall bless thee, and

thou shalt see the good of Jerusalem all the days of thy life.

⁷ Yea, thou shalt see thy children's children. Peace be upon Israel.

Psalm 128. *Sæpe expugnaverunt.*
A Song of Ascents.

MANY a time have they fought against me from my youth up, may Israel now say;

² Yea, many a time have they fought against me from my youth up, but they have not prevailed against me.

³ The plowers plowed upon my back; they made long furrows.

⁴ But the righteous Lord hath hewn the necks of the sinners clean through.

⁵ Let them be confounded and turned backward, as many as have evil will at Zion.

⁶ Let them be even as the grass growing upon the house-tops, which withereth afore it be plucked up;

⁷ Whereof the mower filleth not his hand, neither he that bindeth up the sheaves his bosom.

⁸ Neither do they who go by say so much as, The blessing of the Lord be upon you, we have blessed you in the Name of the Lord.

Glory be to the Father, and to the Son, and to the Holy Spirit; both now, and ever, and unto the ages of ages. Amen.

Alleluia, alleluia, alleluia. Glory be to Thee, O God. Thrice.

Lord, have mercy. Thrice.

Glory be to the Father, and to the Son, and to the Holy Spirit; both now, and ever, and unto the ages of ages. Amen.

Third Stasis

Psalm 129. *De profundis.*
A Song of Ascents.

 UT of the depths have I cried unto Thee, O Lord; Lord, hear my voice.

² Let thine ears be attentive unto the voice of my supplication.

³ If Thou shouldest mark iniquities, O Lord; Lord, who shall stand? For with Thee there is forgiveness.

⁴ For Thy Name's sake have I waited for Thee, O Lord, my soul hath waited for Thy word; my soul hath hoped in the Lord.

⁵ From the morning watch until the night, from the morning watch, let Israel hope in the Lord.

⁶ For with the Lord there is mercy, and with Him is plenteous redemption, and He shall redeem Israel from all his iniquities.

Psalm 130. *Domine, non est.*
A Song of Ascents.

ORD, my heart is not haughty, nor mine eyes lofty,

² Neither have I exercised myself in great matters, nor in wonders too high for me.

³ If I had not been humble-minded, but had lifted up my soul, like as a child that is weaned against his mother, so wouldst Thou have done unto my soul.

⁴ Let Israel trust in the Lord, from this time forth and for evermore.

Psalm 131. *Memento, Domine.*
A Song of Ascents.

EMEMBER, O Lord, David, and all his meekness;

² How he sware unto the Lord, and vowed a vow unto the God of Jacob,

³ I will not go into the tabernacle of mine house, or climb up into the couch of my bed;

⁴ I will not suffer mine eyes to sleep, or mine eye-lids to slumber, or the temples of my head to take any rest,

⁵ Until I find out a place for the Lord, an habitation for the God of Jacob.

⁶ Lo, we heard of it at Ephratha, and we found it in the fields of the wood.

⁷ We will go into His tabernacle; we will bow down toward the place where His feet have stood.

⁸ Arise, O Lord, into Thy rest; Thou, and the Ark of Thy holiness.

⁹ Thy priests shall be clothed with righteousness, and Thy saints shall rejoice.

¹⁰ For Thy servant David's sake, turn not away the face of Thine anointed.

¹¹ The Lord hath made a faithful oath unto David, and He shall not shrink from it, Of the fruit of thy loins shall I set upon thy throne.

¹² If thy sons will keep My covenant, and these testimonies that I shall teach them, their sons also shall sit upon thy throne for evermore.

¹³ For the Lord hath chosen Zion; He hath desired it for an habitation for Himself.

¹⁴ This is My rest for ever and ever; here will I dwell, for I have desired it.

¹⁵ Blessing, I will bless her catch; I will satisfy her poor with bread.

¹⁶ I will clothe her priests with salvation, and her saints shall be glad with joy.

¹⁷ There shall I make the horn of David to grow; I have prepared a lamp for Mine anointed.

¹⁸ His enemies shall I clothe with shame, but upon him shall My holiness flourish.

Psalm 132. *Ecce, quam bonum!*
A Song of Ascents.

BEHOLD, what is so good, or what is so fine, but for brethren to dwell in unity?

² It is like the myrrh upon the head, that runneth down upon the beard, even Aaron's beard, and goeth down to the fringes of his clothing,

³ Like as the dew of Hermon, which falleth upon the hills of Zion; for there hath the Lord ordained blessing, and life for evermore.

Psalm 133. *Ecce nunc.*
A Song of Ascents.

BEHOLD now, bless ye the Lord, all ye servants of the Lord, that stand in the house of the Lord, even in the courts of the house of our God.

² Lift up your hands by night in the sanctuary, and bless the Lord.

³ The Lord bless thee out of Zion, Who hath made heaven and earth.

Glory be to the Father, and to the Son, and to the Holy Spirit; both now, and ever, and unto the ages of ages. Amen.

Alleluia, alleluia, alleluia. Glory be to Thee, O God. Thrice.

¶ After the Eighteenth Kathisma, the Trisagion Prayers, and these troparia, in Tone II:

Before Thou condemnest me, O Lord my Governor, grant me conversion and amendment of my many sins; grant me compunction of spirit, that I may cry out to Thee: O my compassionate God, Lover of mankind, save me!

Glory be to the Father, and to the Son, and to the Holy Spirit.

Having made myself like unto the irrational beasts, prodigal that I am, I have joined myself to them. Grant me conversion, O Christ, that I may receive from Thee great mercy!

Both now, and ever, and unto the ages of ages. Amen.

Turn not thy face away from me who entreat thee, O Lady; but as the compassionate Mother of the compassionate God, make haste to grant me conversion before the end, that, saved by thee, I may praise thee as my salvation and hope unashamed, O my Lady.

Lord, have mercy [40]. And this Prayer:

LORD, rebuke me not in Thine anger, neither chasten me in Thy wrath. O Master Lord Jesus Christ, Son of the Living God, have mercy upon me who am sinful, poor, naked, slothful, negligent, contrary, wretched, a fornicator, an adulterer, effeminate, a lyer with men, vile, lustful, ungrateful, unmerciful, cruel, a drunkard, consumed with a burning conscience, indifferent, cowardly, inexcusable, unworthy of Thy love for mankind, and worthy of every torment, and Gehenna, and torture. Subject me not to a multitude of torments because of the multitude of my great offenses, O Deliverer, but have mercy upon me, for I am weak, in soul, in body, in understanding, and in thought; O Thou with Whom are the scales of justice, save me, Thine unworthy servant, by the prayers of our most pure Lady, the Theotokos, and of all the saints who have pleased Thee well throughout the ages, for blessed art Thou for ever and ever. Amen.

The Nineteenth Kathisma

Psalm 134. *Laudate Nomen.*
Alleluia.

 PRAISE ye the Name of the Lord; O ye servants, praise the Lord,

² Ye that stand in the house of the Lord, in the courts of the house of our God.

³ O praise the Lord, for the Lord is good; O sing unto His Name, for it is good.

⁴ For the Lord hath chosen Jacob unto Himself, and Israel for His own possession.

⁵ For I have seen how great the Lord is, and that our Lord is above all gods.

⁶ All, whatsoever the Lord pleased, that hath He done, in heaven, and in earth, and in the seas, and in all deep places,

⁷ Bringing forth the clouds from the ends of the world, He made lightnings into rain, Who bringeth the winds out of His treasuries,

⁸ Who smote the first-born of Egypt, both man and beast.

⁹ He sent signs and wonders into the midst of

thee, O Egypt, upon Pharaoh, and upon all his servants.

[10] He smote many nations, and slew mighty kings;

[11] Sihon, king of the Amorites, and Og, the king of Bashan, and all the kingdoms of Canaan;

[12] And gave their land to be an inheritance, an inheritance unto Israel His people.

[13] O Lord, Thy Name endureth for ever, and Thy memory from generation to generation,

[14] For the Lord will judge His people, and be entreated concerning His servants.

[15] The idols of the heathen are but silver and gold, the work of men's hands.

[16] They have mouths, and speak not; eyes have they, and they see not.

[17] They have ears, and yet they hear not, neither is there any breath in their mouths.

[18] Let them that make them become like unto them, and all them that put their trust in them.

[19] O house of Israel, bless ye the Lord; bless the Lord, ye house of Aaron; bless the Lord, ye house of Levi.

[20] Ye that fear the Lord, bless the Lord.

[21] Blessed be the Lord out of Zion, who dwelleth at Jerusalem.

Psalm 135. *Confitemini.*
Alleluia.

GIVE thanks unto the Lord, for He is good, for His mercy endureth for ever.

² O give thanks unto the God of gods, for His mercy endureth for ever.

³ O give thanks unto the Lord of lords, for His mercy endureth for ever;

⁴ Who alone doeth great wonders, for His mercy endureth for ever;

⁵ Who by wisdom made the heavens, for His mercy endureth for ever;

⁶ Who fixed the earth upon the waters, for His mercy endureth for ever;

⁷ Who made the great lights, for His mercy endureth for ever;

⁸ The sun to rule the day, for His mercy endureth for ever;

⁹ The moon and the stars to govern the night, for His mercy endureth for ever;

¹⁰ Who smote Egypt with her first-born, for His mercy endureth for ever;

¹¹ And led forth Israel from among them, for His mercy endureth for ever;

¹² With a mighty hand and upstretched arm, for His mercy endureth for ever;

¹³ Who divided the Red Sea in two parts, for His mercy endureth for ever;

¹⁴ And led Israel through the midst of it, for His mercy endureth for ever;

¹⁵ But overthrew Pharaoh and his host in the Red Sea, for His mercy endureth for ever;

¹⁶ Who led His people through the wilderness, for His mercy endureth for ever;

¹⁷ Who smote great kings, for His mercy endureth for ever;

¹⁸ Yea, and slew mighty kings, for His mercy endureth for ever;

¹⁹ Sihon, king of the Amorites, for His mercy endureth for ever;

²⁰ And Og, the king of Bashan, for His mercy endureth for ever;

²¹ And gave their land for an inheritance, for His mercy endureth for ever;

²² An inheritance unto Israel His servant, for His mercy endureth for ever;

²³ For in our humbleness the Lord remembered us, for His mercy endureth for ever;

²⁴ And hath delivered us from our enemies, for His mercy endureth for ever;

²⁵ Who giveth food to all flesh, for His mercy endureth for ever.

²⁶ O give thanks unto the God of heaven, for His mercy endureth for ever.

Psalm 136. *Super flumina.*
David's, by Jeremiah.

BY the waters of Babylon, there we sat down and we wept, when we remembered Zion.

² Upon the willows in the midst thereof did we hang our harps.

³ For there they that had taken us captive asked us for the words of a song, and they that led us away for a melody, saying, Sing us one of the songs of Zion.

⁴ How shall we sing the Lord's song in a strange land?

⁵ If I forget thee, O Jerusalem, let my right hand be forgotten.

⁶ Let my tongue cleave to the back of my throat, if I remember thee not, if I prefer not Jerusalem above my chief joy.

⁷ Remember the children of Edom, O Lord, in the day of Jerusalem, how they said, Down with it, down with it, even to the foundation thereof.

⁸ O daughter of Babylon, thou cursed one, blessed shall he be that shall do unto thee, as thou hast done unto us.

⁹ Blessed is he that shall seize and dash thine infants against a rock.

Glory be to the Father, and to the Son, and to the Holy Spirit; both now, and ever, and unto the ages of ages. Amen.

Alleluia, alleluia, alleluia. Glory be to Thee, O God. Thrice.

Lord, have mercy. Thrice.

Glory be to the Father, and to the Son, and to the Holy Spirit; both now, and ever, and unto the ages of ages. Amen.

Second Stasis

Psalm 137. *Confitebor tibi.*
A Psalm of David, by Haggai and Zechariah.

I WILL give thanks unto Thee, O Lord, with my whole heart, and before the angels will I sing praise unto Thee, for Thou hast heard all the words of my mouth.

² I will worship toward Thy holy temple, and give thanks unto Thy Name, because of Thy mercy and Thy truth, for Thou hast magnified Thy holy Name above all.

³ In whatsoever day I may call upon Thee, quickly hear me; Thou shalt fortify me in my soul by Thy strength.

⁴ Let all earthly kings give thanks unto Thee, O Lord, for they have heard the words of Thy mouth.

⁵ Yea, let them sing in the byways of the Lord, for great is the glory of the Lord.

⁶ For the Lord is high, yet hath He respect unto the lowly, and the high He knoweth from afar off.

⁷ Though I walk in the midst of trouble, Thou

shalt refresh me; Thou hast stretched forth Thy hand upon the furiousness of mine enemies, and Thy right hand hath saved me.

⁸ The Lord shall make payment for me; O Lord, Thy mercy is for ever; despise not the works of Thy hands.

Psalm 138. *Domine, probasti.*
Unto the end, David's, a Psalm of Zechariah in the Dispersion.

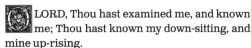 LORD, Thou hast examined me, and known me; Thou hast known my down-sitting, and mine up-rising.

² Thou hast understood my thoughts from afar off.

³ Thou hast searched into my path and my lot, and all my ways hast Thou foreseen.

⁴ For there is no guile in my tongue; Lo, O Lord, Thou hast known

⁵ All things, the last and the first; Thou hast made me and hast laid Thy hand upon me.

⁶ Thy knowledge is too wonderful for me; it is too hard, I cannot attain unto it.

⁷ Whither shall I go then from Thy Spirit? Or whither shall I flee from Thy presence?

⁸ If I climb up into heaven, Thou art there; if I go down to hell, Thou art there also.

⁹ If I take up my wings early, and dwell in the uttermost parts of the sea,

¹⁰ Even there also shall Thy hand lead me, and Thy right hand shall hold me.

¹¹ And I said, Peradventure the darkness shall hide me, and the night is light in my pleasures.

¹² For the darkness shall be no darkness with Thee, and the night shall be as bright as the day, for as is the darkness thereof, even so is the light of it.

¹³ For Thou hast made my reins; Thou didst take me from my mother's womb.

¹⁴ I will give thanks unto Thee, for Thou hast fearfully worked wonders; marvelous are Thy works, and that my soul knoweth right well.

¹⁵ My bones are not hid from Thee, which Thou didst make in secret, and my substance in the nether regions of the earth.

¹⁶ Thine eyes did see my unformed being, and in Thy book shall all be enrolled; in a day shall they be fashioned, when as yet there are none of them.

¹⁷ But Thy friends have been very dear to me, O God; their powers have been greatly strengthened.

¹⁸ I will count them, and they will be more in number than the sand; I woke up, and I am still with Thee.

¹⁹ Wilt Thou slay the sinners, O God? Depart from me, ye blood-thirsty men!

²⁰ For Thou shalt speak against contriving; they shall take Thy cities in vain.

²¹ Have I not hated them, O Lord, that hate Thee, and pined away because of Thine enemies?

²² With a perfect hatred have I hated them; they have been to me as enemies.

²³ Examine me, O God, and know my heart; test me, and understand my ways.

²⁴ And look well if there be any way of wickedness in me; and lead me unto the way everlasting.

Psalm 139. *Eripe me, Domine.*
Unto the end, a Psalm of David.

 AVE me, O Lord, from the evil man; from the wicked man deliver me,

² Who have imagined a lie in their heart, and stirred up strife all day.

³ They have sharpened their tongues like a serpent, adder's poison is under their lips.

⁴ Keep me, O Lord, from the hands of the sinner; save me from the wicked men, who have purposed to trip up my steps.

⁵ The proud have laid a snare for me, and spread a net abroad with cords for my feet.

⁶ They set traps in my way.

⁷ I said unto the Lord, Thou art my God; hear, O Lord, the voice of my supplication.

⁸ Lord, O Lord, Thou strength of my salvation, Thou hast overshadowed my head in the day of battle.

⁹ Give me not over to the sinner, O Lord, because

of my desire; they have plotted against me; forsake me not, lest they be too proud.

¹⁰ Let the mischief of their own lips fall upon the head of them that compass me about.

¹¹ Let hot burning coals fall upon them; Thou shalt cast them down into the torments, and they shall not stand.

¹² A garrulous man shall not prosper upon the land; evil shall hunt the wicked person unto extinction.

¹³ I know that the Lord will uphold the cause of the helpless, and avenge the poor.

¹⁴ Verily, the righteous shall give thanks unto Thy Name, and the just shall dwell in Thy presence.

Glory be to the Father, and to the Son, and to the Holy Spirit; both now, and ever, and unto the ages of ages. Amen.

Alleluia, alleluia, alleluia. Glory be to Thee, O God. Thrice.

Lord, have mercy. Thrice.

Glory be to the Father, and to the Son, and to the Holy Spirit; both now, and ever, and unto the ages of ages. Amen.

Third Stasis

Psalm 140. *Domine, clamavi.*
A Psalm of David.

LORD, I have cried unto Thee, hear me; receive the voice of my supplication when I cry unto Thee.

2 Let my prayer be set forth in Thy sight as incense, and let the lifting up of my hands be an evening sacrifice.

3 Set a watch, O Lord, over my mouth, and a door of restraint before my lips.

4 Incline not my heart unto evil words, to imagine excuses for sins with men who work wickedness; yea, I will have no doings with their elect.

5 The righteous shall chasten me with mercy, and reprove me, but let not the oil of the sinner anoint my head, for my prayer is yet more against their good favor.

6 Their judges were swallowed up close by the rock; they will hear my words, for they have prevailed.

7 As a clod of earth is broken upon the ground, so were their bones strewn beside hell.

8 For unto Thee, Lord, O Lord, are mine eyes; in Thee have I put my trust; O take not my soul away.

9 Keep me from the snare that they have laid for me, and from the traps of them that do wickedness.

¹⁰ The sinners shall fall into their own net; I am alone, until I have gone by.

Psalm 141. *Voce mea ad Dominum.*
An Instruction of David, when he was in the cave praying.

CRIED unto the Lord with my voice; with my voice unto the Lord did I make supplication.

³ I will pour out my petition before Him; I will declare before Him my trouble.

⁴ When my spirit would falter within me, then Thou knewest my paths; in this way wherein I walked have they privily laid a snare for me.

⁵ I looked upon my right hand and saw, and there was no man that would know me; I had no place to flee unto, and there was no one looking out for my soul.

⁶ I cried unto Thee, O Lord; I said, Thou art my hope; Thou art my portion in the land of the living.

⁷ Consider my petition, for I am brought very low; O deliver me from my persecutors, for they have become too strong for me.

⁸ Bring my soul out of prison, that I may give thanks unto Thy Name; the righteous await me, until Thou shalt requite me.

Psalm 142. *Domine, exaudi.*

A Psalm of David, when Absalom his son pursued him.

LORD, hear my prayer, consider my supplication in Thy truth; hearken unto me in Thy righteousness,

² And enter not into judgment with Thy servant, for before Thee shall no man living be justified.

³ For the enemy hath persecuted my soul; he hath smitten my life down to the ground; he hath laid me in the darkness, as those that have been long dead,

⁴ And my spirit is despondent within me, and my heart within me is vexed.

⁵ I remembered the days of old; I mused upon all Thy works; I exercised myself in the works of Thy hands.

⁶ I stretched forth my hands unto Thee; my soul gasped unto Thee as a thirsty land.

⁷ Hear me soon, O Lord, for my spirit faltereth; turn not Thy face from me, or I shall be like unto them that go down into the pit.

⁸ O let me hear Thy mercy in the morning, for in Thee have I trusted; tell me, O Lord, the way that I should walk in, for I lift up my soul unto Thee.

⁹ Deliver me from mine enemies, O Lord, for I have fled unto Thee.

¹⁰ Teach me to do Thy will, for Thou art my

God. Thy good Spirit shall lead me into the land of righteousness.

[11] For Thy Name's sake, O Lord, quicken me by Thy truth; Thou shalt bring my soul out of trouble.

[12] And of Thy mercy Thou shalt slay mine enemies, and destroy all them that vex my soul, for I am Thy servant.

Glory be to the Father, and to the Son, and to the Holy Spirit; both now, and ever, and unto the ages of ages. Amen.

Alleluia, alleluia, alleluia. Glory be to Thee, O God. Thrice.

¶ After the Nineteenth Kathisma, the Trisagion Prayers, and these troparia, in Tone VII:

In thanksgiving I glorify Thee, O my Saviour and God, for Thou hast bestowed repentance upon all sinners. When Thou comest to judge all the world, put me not to shame who have committed shameful deeds.

Glory be to the Father, and to the Son, and to the Holy Spirit.

Having sinned against Thee without measure, I await infinite torments. O my God, pity me and save me!

Both now, and ever, and unto the ages of ages. Amen.

Unto the multitude of thy mercies do I now flee,

O Theotokos; break asunder the chains of mine offenses.

Lord, have mercy [40]. And this Prayer:

MASTER Christ God, Who hast healed my passions by Thy Passion and hast cured my wounds by Thy Wounds, grant tears of remorse unto me who have sinned greatly against Thee. Prepare for my body some of the fragrance of Thy life-creating Body, and sweeten the bitterness of my soul by Thy precious Blood, wherewith vouchsafe me, who doth resist Thee, to drink. Raise aloft to Thee my mind which is drawn downwards, and lead it up from the depths of destruction, for I have no repentance, I have no remorse, I have no tears of comfort which lead children to their inheritance. I have been darkened in mind amid the passions of life, and am unable to lift up mine eyes to Thee in my pain; I cannot warm myself with tears of love for Thee. Yet, O Lord and Master, Jesus Christ, Treasury of blessings, grant me complete repentance and a heart diligent in searching for Thee. Grant me Thy grace, and renew in me the lineaments of Thine image. I have forsaken Thee; do not forsake me! Come Thou in search of me, and make me to lie down in Thy green pasture, and number me among the sheep of Thy chosen flock. Feed me with them on the living grass of Thy divine mysteries, through the prayers Thy most pure Mother and of all Thy saints. Amen.

The Twentieth Kathisma

Psalm 143. *Benedictus Dominus.*
A Psalm of David, concerning Goliath.

LESSED be the Lord my God, Who teacheth my hands to war, and my fingers to fight;

² My mercy and my refuge, my protector and my deliverer, my defender, and I have trusted in Him; Who subdueth my people under me.

³ Lord, what is man, that Thou hast had such respect unto him? Or the son of man, that Thou so regardest him?

⁴ Man is like to vanity; his days as a shadow pass away.

⁵ Bow the heavens, O Lord, and come down; touch the mountains, and they shall smoke.

⁶ Flash forth the lightning, and scatter them; shoot out Thine arrows, and vex them.

⁷ Send down Thine hand from above; rescue me, and deliver me out of the great waters, from the hand of the strange children,

⁸ Whose mouths speak vanity, and their right hand is the right hand of untruth.

⁹ I will sing a new song unto Thee, O God; upon a psaltery of ten strings will I sing unto Thee,

¹⁰ Who givest salvation unto kings, who deliverest David Thy servant from the evil sword.

¹¹ Deliver me, and rescue me from the hand of the strange children, whose mouths speak vanity, and their right hand is the right hand of untruth,

¹² Whose sons are like newly planted saplings in their youth; their daughters are refined, adorned like unto a temple.

¹³ Their garners are full, overflowing with all manner of store; their sheep are fruitful, abundant in their issue, and their cattle are fat.

¹⁴ There is no falling down of fences, no trespassing, neither is there clamor in their streets.

¹⁵ The people that are in such a case have been called blessed, but blessed are the people whose God is the Lord.

Psalm 144. *Exaltabo te, Deus.*
David's Psalm of praise.

I will exalt Thee, O my God, my King, and I will bless Thy Name for ever, yea, for ever and ever.

² Every day will I bless Thee, and I will praise Thy Name for ever, yea, for ever and ever.

³ Great is the Lord, and highly to be praised, and of His greatness there is no end.

⁴ Generation and generation shall praise Thy works, and declare Thy power.

⁵ They shall speak of the glorious majesty of Thy holiness, and tell of Thy wondrous works;

⁶ And of the might of Thy terrifying acts shall they speak, and tell of Thy greatness.

⁷ The memory of the abundance of Thy kindness shall they gush forth, and exult in Thy righteousness.

⁸ The Lord is merciful and gracious, long-suffering, and of great kindness.

⁹ The Lord is good unto all, and His mercies are upon all His works.

¹⁰ Let all Thy works praise Thee, O Lord, and let Thy saints bless Thee.

¹¹ They shall speak of the glory of Thy kingdom, and talk of Thy power,

¹² To make known unto the sons of men Thy power, and the glorious majesty of Thy kingdom.

¹³ Thy kingdom is an everlasting kingdom, and Thy dominion endureth throughout all ages; the Lord is faithful in all His words, and holy in all His works.

¹⁴ The Lord upholdeth all such as fall, and lifteth up all those that be bowed down.

¹⁵ The eyes of all look unto Thee, O Lord, and Thou givest them their food in due season.

¹⁶ Thou openest Thine hand, and fillest every living thing with benevolence.

¹⁷ The Lord is righteous in all His ways, and holy in all His works.

¹⁸ The Lord is nigh unto all them that call upon Him, to all such as call upon Him in truth.

¹⁹ He will fulfill the desire of them that fear Him, and He will hear their prayer, and save them.

²⁰ The Lord preserveth all them that love Him, but all the sinners will He consume.

²¹ My mouth shall speak the praise of the Lord, and let all flesh bless His holy Name for ever, yea, for ever and ever.

Glory be to the Father, and to the Son, and to the Holy Spirit; both now, and ever, and unto the ages of ages. Amen.

Alleluia, alleluia, alleluia. Glory be to Thee, O God. Thrice.

Lord, have mercy. Thrice.

Glory be to the Father, and to the Son, and to the Holy Spirit; both now, and ever, and unto the ages of ages. Amen.

Second Stasis

Psalm 145. *Lauda, anima mea.*
Alleluia. Of Haggai and Zechariah.

RAISE the Lord, O my soul;
   ² While I live will I praise the Lord; I will sing unto my God as long as I have being.

³ O put not your trust in princes, in the sons of men, in whom there is no salvation.

⁴ His spirit shall go forth, and he shall return again to his earth; in that day all his thoughts shall perish.

⁵ Blessed is he that hath the God of Jacob for his helper, whose hope is in the Lord his God;

⁶ Who made heaven and earth, the sea, and all that therein is, Who preserveth truth for ever;

⁷ Who rendereth judgment for the wronged, Who giveth food unto the hungry; the Lord looseth the fettered;

⁸ The Lord giveth wisdom to the blind; the Lord raiseth up the fallen; the Lord loveth the righteous;

⁹ The Lord preserveth the proselytes; He defendeth the fatherless and the widow, but the way of sinners shall He destroy.

¹⁰ The Lord shall reign for ever, Thy God, O Zion, unto generation and generation.

Psalm 146. *Laudate Dominum.*
Alleluia. Of Haggai and Zechariah.

PRAISE the Lord, for a psalm is a good thing; let our praise be sweet unto our God.

² The Lord Who doth build up Jerusalem, He shall gather together the dispersed of Israel,

³ Who healeth those that are broken in heart and bindeth up their wounds.

⁴ Who telleth the number of the stars, and calleth them all by their names.

⁵ Great is our Lord, and great is His power, and of His wisdom there is no end.

⁶ The Lord Who receiveth the meek, but Who humbleth the sinners down to the ground.

⁷ O begin unto the Lord in thanksgiving; sing unto our God upon the harp,

⁸ Who doth clothe the heaven with clouds, Who prepareth rain for the earth; Who maketh the grass to grow upon the mountains, and herb for the use of men;

⁹ Who giveth the cattle their fodder, and the young ravens that call upon Him.

¹⁰ He hath no pleasure in the strength of an horse, neither doth He favor any man's legs.

¹¹ The Lord favoreth them that fear Him, and that put their trust in His mercy.

Psalm 147. *Lauda, Ierusalem.*
Alleluia. Of Haggai and Zechariah.

RAISE the Lord, O Jerusalem! Praise thy God, O Zion!

² For He hath strengthened the bars of thy gates; He hath blessed thy children within thee;

³ Who maketh peace in thy borders, and filleth thee with flour of wheat;

⁴ Who sendeth forth His Word unto the earth; His Word runneth very swiftly;

⁵ Who giveth His snow like wool, and scattereth the hoar-frost like ashes;

⁶ Who scattereth His hail like bread; who is able to abide His frost?

⁷ He shall send out His Word, and melt them; His Wind shall blow, and the waters will run;

⁸ Who declareth His word unto Jacob, His statutes and ordinances unto Israel.

⁹ He hath not dealt so with every nation, neither hath He revealed His judgments unto them.

Glory be to the Father, and to the Son, and to the Holy Spirit; both now, and ever, and unto the ages of ages. Amen.

Alleluia, alleluia, alleluia. Glory be to Thee, O God. *Thrice.*

Lord, have mercy. *Thrice.*

Glory be to the Father, and to the Son, and to the Holy Spirit; both now, and ever, and unto the ages of ages. Amen.

Third Stasis

Psalm 148. *Laudate Dominum.*
Alleluia. Of Haggai and Zechariah.

 PRAISE the Lord from the heavens; praise Him in the heights.

² Praise Him, all ye His angels; praise Him, all ye His hosts.

³ Praise Him, sun and moon; praise Him, all ye stars and light.

⁴ Praise Him, ye heaven of heavens, and thou water that art above the heavens.

⁵ Let them praise the Name of the Lord; for He spake, and they came to be; He commanded, and they were created.

⁶ He hath established them for ever, and for ever and ever; He hath set an ordinance, and it shall not pass away.

⁷ Praise the Lord from the earth, ye dragons, and all deeps;

⁸ Fire and hail, snow and ice, the stormy wind, fulfilling His word;

⁹ Mountains and all hills, fruitful trees and all cedars;

¹⁰ Beasts and all cattle, creeping things and feathered fowls;

¹¹ Kings of the earth and all peoples, princes and all judges of the world;

¹² Young men and maidens, old men and children;

¹³ Let them praise the Name of the Lord, for His Name only is exalted; His praise is above heaven and earth.

¹⁴ And He shall exalt the horn of His people; this is a song for all His saints, for the children of Israel, for the people that draw nigh unto Him.

Psalm 149. *Cantate Domino.*

Alleluia.

SING unto the Lord a new song; His praise is in the church of the saints.

² Let Israel be glad in her Maker, and let the children of Zion exult in their King.

³ Let them praise His Name in the dance; let them sing praises unto Him with timbrel and psaltery.

⁴ For the Lord hath pleasure in His people; and shall lift up the meek unto salvation.

⁵ The saints shall boast in glory, and they will rejoice upon their beds.

⁶ Let the exultations of God be in their throats, and sharp two-edged swords in their hands,

⁷ To do vengeance among the heathen, and rebuke among the peoples;

⁸ To bind their kings in chains, and their nobles with manacles of iron.

⁹ To do among them the judgment written. This glory shall be to all His saints.

Psalm 150. *Laudate Dominum.*
Alleluia.

PRAISE God in His sanctuary, praise Him in the firmament of His power.

² Praise Him for His mighty acts, praise Him according to the magnitude of His greatness.

³ Praise Him with the sound of the trumpet, praise Him upon the psaltery and harp.

⁴ Praise Him with the timbrel and dance, praise Him upon the strings and pipe.

⁵ Praise Him upon the well-tuned cymbals, praise Him upon the cymbals of jubilation.

⁶ Let every thing that hath breath praise the Lord.

Glory be to the Father, and to the Son, and to the Holy Spirit; both now, and ever, and unto the ages of ages. Amen.

Alleluia, alleluia, alleluia. Glory be to Thee, O God. Thrice.

Psalm 151. *Pusillus eram inter fratres meos.*
This psalm was specially written by David, when he fought in single combat against Goliath, and is outside the number of the 150 psalms.
Not read in church.

WAS small among my brethren, and the youngest in my father's house; I tended my father's sheep.

³ My hands made an organ, and my fingers fashioned a psaltery.

⁴ And who will tell my Lord? The Lord Himself, He shall hear it.

⁵ He Himself sent His Angel, and took me from my father's flock, and anointed me with the oil of His anointing.

⁶ My brethren were tall and fair, but the Lord took no pleasure in them.

⁷ I went forth to meet the Philistine, and he cursed me by his idols.

⁸ But I took the sword from him and cut off his head; and I took away reproach from the sons of Israel.

¶ After the Twentieth Kathisma, the Trisagion Prayers, and these troparia, in Tone VIII:

O my Christ, fullness of all good things, fill Thou my soul with joy and gladness, and save me, for Thou alone art great in mercy.

Glory be to the Father, and to the Son, and to the Holy Spirit.

Though I have sinned before Thee, O Christ my Saviour, yet I have not known any God save Thee, and I make bold to appeal to Thy mercy: O compassionate Father, only-begotten Son and Holy Spirit, accept me who turn to Thee, and save me!

Both now, and ever, and unto the ages of ages. Amen.

Apart from thee I have known no other refuge or fervent intercessor. As thou hast boldness before Him that was born of thee, O Lady, help and save me, thy servant!

Lord, have mercy [40]. And this Prayer:

LORD Jesus Christ my God, have mercy upon me, a sinner, and forgive me, Thine unworthy servant, for as many sins as I have committed throughout all the time of my life, unto this very hour, however I have sinned as a man: my transgressions voluntary and involuntary, in word and deed, in mind and thought, with delight and carelessly, and my great slothfulness and indifference. And if I have sworn by Thy name, if I have sworn falsely or blasphemed in thought; or if I have offended, or slandered, or grieved, or angered anyone in any way, or have stolen, or indulged my lust, or lied, or eaten secretly; or if a friend came to me and I rejected him; or if I have troubled or embittered my brother; or if, when standing in prayer and psalmody, my wicked mind hath wandered in the thicket of evil thoughts, or if I have indulged in pleasures more than is seemly, or laughed thoughtlessly, or spoken blasphemously; or have been vainglorious, or haughty, or have set my gaze upon vain beauty and been seduced by it; or if I have given my mind over to things which are harmful to it; if I have in any way been negligent concerning prayer, or have not kept the commandments of my spiritual father, or have spoken idly, or done ought else which is evil; for all these things and more have I done, and things which I cannot even recall: Have mercy, O Lord, and forgive me all, that I may sleep and rest in peace, praising, and blessing, and glorifying Thee, together with Thine unoriginate Father, and Thy most holy, good and life-creating Spirit; now, and ever, and unto the ages of ages. Amen.

Prayers After Reading the Psalter

¶ After the completion of several kathismata, or the whole Psalter, we say,

IT is truly meet to bless thee, O Theotokos, ever-blessed and most pure, and the Mother of our God. More honorable than the Cherubim, and incomparably more glorious than the Seraphim; who without corruption gavest birth to God the Word, the very Theotokos, thee do we magnify. And a prostration.

¶ But during the Great Fast, or on a day when the Liturgy of St. Basil is appointed, we say, instead,

IN thee rejoiceth, O thou who art full of grace, all creation, the angelic assembly, and the race of man; O sanctified temple and noetical paradise, praise of virgins, of whom God was incarnate, and became a child, He that was before the ages, even our God; for of thy body a throne He made, and thy womb more spacious than the heavens did He form. In thee rejoiceth, O thou who art full of grace, all creation: glory to thee. Then,

The Trisagion

Holy God, Holy Mighty, Holy Immortal, have mercy upon us. Thrice, with bows.

Glory be to the Father, and to the Son, and to the Holy Spirit; both now, and ever, and unto the ages of ages. Amen. Bow.

O Most Holy Trinity, have mercy upon us. O Lord, wash away our sins. O Master, pardon our transgressions. O Holy One, visit and heal our infirmities for Thy Name's sake.

Lord, have mercy. Thrice.

Glory be to the Father, and to the Son, and to the Holy Spirit; both now, and ever, and unto the ages of ages. Amen. Bow.

The Lord's Prayer

OUR Father, Who art in heaven, hallowed be Thy Name. Thy kingdom come. Thy will be done, on earth as it is in heaven. Give us this day our daily bread. And forgive us our debts, as we forgive our debtors. And lead us not into temptation; but deliver us from the evil one.

If there is a priest, he says,

For Thine is the kingdom, the power, and the glory: of the Father, and of the Son, and of the Holy Spirit; Now, and ever, and unto the ages of ages. Amen.

But, if not, say,

O Lord Jesus Christ, Son of God, have mercy upon us. Amen.

And these troparia, in Tone VI:

Have mercy upon us, O Lord, have mercy upon us; for, at a loss for any defense, we sinners offer unto Thee, as Master, this prayer, Have mercy upon us!

Glory be to the Father, and to the Son, and to the Holy Spirit,

The Church hath shown forth the honored feast of Thy prophet, O Lord, to be as heaven, for thereon the angels join chorus with men. Through his prayers, O Christ God, guide our life in peace, that we may chant unto Thee: Alleluia!

Both now, and ever, and unto the ages of ages. Amen.

Many are the multitudes of my sins, O Theotokos; unto thee have I fled, imploring salvation, O most pure one. Do thou visit my feeble soul, and entreat thy Son and our God to grant me pardon for the evil I have done, O thou only blessed one.

¶ Then Lord, have mercy [40]. And, having made as many prostrations as we are able, we say,

¶ Here, during the Great Fast, except on Saturdays and Sundays, as well as during the other fasts, and also during Cheesefare Week on Wednesday and Friday, we say:

The Prayer of Our Holy Venerable Father, Ephraim the Syrian

O Lord and Master of my life, take from me the spirit of sloth, despondency, avarice and idle talk. Prostration.

But give, rather, the spirit of chastity, humility, patience and love to Thy servant. Prostration.

Yea, O Lord and King, grant me to see mine own faults, and not to judge my brother, for blessed art Thou unto the ages of ages. Amen. Prostration.

¶ Then twelve bows, saying the Prayer of the Publican, God be merciful to me a sinner, after which the entire Prayer of St. Ephraim is said again, with one prostration. Then we continue, as usual, with the prayer O greatly merciful and most merciful Lord.

GREATLY merciful and most merciful Lord, and Giver of all that is good, O Lover of mankind and King of the whole world, glorious Master and Lord: wretched and lowly am I, who dare to call upon Thy wonderful, and terrible, and holy Name, at which all the creation of the heavenly Powers doth tremble in fear. Thou didst, of Thine unutterable love for mankind, cause consternation by the sending of Thy beloved Son down to earth, Whom Thou didst from the beginningless bosom of Thy Fatherly glory utter forth without separation from the Godhead, that men might be joined into one body with the angels. Remember, O Lord, my abject humility: I, who am like dung and dirt, call upon Thee of the ineffable light, I who am clothed in the infirmity of the flesh which Thy Word did graciously take, and Who by His death hath freed our souls from slavery to the enemy, so that all who fell away by Satan's cunning might once again become partakers of Thy glory by taking upon themselves the yoke of Thy service. Have mercy upon me, who am darkened by sinful thoughts, and lift up my mind, which is choked by the thorns of laziness and the tares of recalcitrance. Set my heart aflame for Thee, send to mine eyes a fountain of tears and, before the departure of my soul, make me into someone that pleaseth Thee perfectly, guiding me to strive zealously after Thee. Remember, O Lord, in Thy mercy, my parents, and all my relatives, and brethren, and friends, and neighbors, and all Orthodox Christians, and by the prayers of all the saints do Thou save me. And favorably receive these psalms and prayers, which I have recited before Thee in their behalf, and may this petition with sighs be not abhorrent unto Thee, for merciful art Thou, and the Lover of mankind, and we glorify Thee, the Father without beginning, together with Thine only-begotten Son, and Thy Holy Spirit; now, and ever, and unto the ages of ages. Amen.

Then we say:

MORE honorable than the Cherubim, and incomparably more glorious than the Seraphim; who without corruption gavest birth to God the Word, the very Theotokos, thee do we magnify.

Glory be to the Father, and to the Son, and to the Holy Spirit; Both now, and ever, and unto the ages of ages. Amen.

Lord, have mercy [Thrice].

Bless, O Lord.

¶ If there is a priest, he concludes accordingly. If not, the ending is as follows:

O LORD Jesus Christ, Son of God, through the prayers of Thy most pure Mother, by the power of the precious and life-giving Cross, and of the holy bodiless Powers, and of our venerable and God-bearing Fathers, and of the holy Prophet David, and of all the Saints, have mercy upon me and save me a sinner, for Thou art good and lovest mankind. Amen.

The Rite Chanted Following the Departure of the Soul from the Body

¶ When the soul has parted from the body, straightway the priest begins, Blessed is our God . . . , and the reader says the Trisagion through to the Lord's Prayer. After For Thine is the kingdom . . . , together with those present, the priest sings or says these troparia, in Tone IV:

With the souls of the righteous that have finished their course, give rest, O Saviour, to the soul of Thy servant [handmaiden], keeping it in the blessed life which is with Thee, O Lover of mankind.

In the place of Thy rest, O Lord, where all Thy saints repose, give rest also to the soul of Thy servant [handmaiden], for Thou alone art the Lover of mankind.

Glory be to the Father, and to the Son, and to the Holy Spirit;

Thou art the God Who descended into hell and loosed the chains of the captives; do Thou Thyself give rest also to the soul of Thy servant [handmaiden].

Both now, and ever, and unto the ages of ages. Amen.

O only pure and immaculate Virgin, who

without seed gavest birth unto God, pray that his [her] soul be saved.

Then the priest says the following litany:

Priest: Have mercy upon us, O God, according to Thy great mercy, we pray Thee, hearken and have mercy.

Choir: Lord, have mercy. Thrice.

Priest: Again we pray for the repose of the soul of the departed servant [handmaiden] of God, [N.], and that he [she] may be forgiven every transgression, both voluntary and involuntary.

Choir: Lord, have mercy. Thrice.

Priest: That the Lord commit his [her] soul to where the righteous repose.

Choir: Lord, have mercy. Thrice.

Priest: The mercy of God, the kingdom of heaven, and the remission of his [her] sins, let us ask of Christ, the immortal King, and our God.

Choir: Grant this, O Lord.

Priest: Let us pray to the Lord.

Choir, slowly: Lord, have mercy.

And the priest says this prayer:

GOD of spirits and of all flesh, Who hast trampled down death, and overthrown the Devil, and given life to Thy world, Do Thou, the same Lord, give rest to the soul of Thy departed servant [handmaiden], [N.], in a place of light, in a place of green pasture, in a place of repose, whence all sickness, sorrow, and sighing are fled away. Pardon every sin committed by him [her] in word, or in deed, or in thought, for a good and philanthropic God art Thou; for there is no man that liveth and doth not sin, for Thou alone art without sin, Thy righteousness is an everlasting righteousness, and Thy word is truth.

Exclamation:

For Thou art the resurrection, and the life, and the repose of Thy departed servant [handmaiden], [N.], O Christ our God, and unto Thee do we send up glory, together with Thine unoriginate Father, and Thy most holy, and good, and life-creating Spirit; now, and ever, and unto the ages of ages.

Choir: Amen.

¶ Having finished the prayer, he says Psalm 90, Whoso dwelleth in the help of the Most High, and then at once sings or reads this canon for the departed one:

Tone VIII

Canticle I

Irmos: Crossing the water as though it were dry land, and escaping the evil of Egypt, the Israelites cried aloud, Let us sing unto our Deliverer and our God!

Refrain: Give rest, O Lord, to the soul of Thy departed servant [handmaiden]!

Opening my lips, O merciful Saviour, grant me utterance concerning him [her] that is now departed, I pray Thee, that Thou grant rest to his [her] soul, O Master.

O Saviour, as Thou wast mortal in Thy flesh and wast laid in a tomb with the dead, grant rest unto the soul of Thy servant [handmaiden] in a place of green pasture, for Thou art merciful.

Glory be to the Father, and to the Son, and to the Holy Spirit:

Hearken unto my voice of supplication, O God in three Persons, and commend Thou the soul of the departed one to the bosom of Abraham, O Deliverer.

Both now, and ever, and unto the ages of ages. Amen.

Thou, O most pure Theotokos, didst give birth unto thy Son, conceiving Him without experience of man. Entreat Him to grant rest to thy departed servant [handmaiden].

Canticle III

Irmos: O Lord, Fashioner of the vault of heaven and Creator of the Church, Do Thou, O Summit of desire, confirm me in Thy love, O Confirmation of the faithful, O Thou Who alone lovest mankind.

O Christ, Who alone art merciful, Grant rest to the soul of Thy departed servant [handmaiden] in a place of green pasture, a place of repose, where the choirs of the saints rejoice.

O Master, as Thou alone art the Master of life and earth, where the choirs of the saints are do Thou bring him [her] that obeyed Thee with all his [her] heart, and took Thy yoke upon his [her] shoulders.

Glory be to the Father, and to the Son, and to the Holy Spirit:

O Almighty, heavenly Father, only-begotten Son, and Holy Spirit, Who proceedest, overlook the transgressions of him [her] that hath departed, and cause him [her] to dwell in the Church of the Firstborn, that he [she] may glorify Thee with all who have been pleasing unto Thee.

Both now, and ever, and unto the ages of ages. Amen.

O Mary Theotokos, Mistress of all, as the holy Mother of the all-holy God, entreat Him, with all the saints, that He grant rest to thy servant [hand-maiden] in the mansions of heaven.

Canticle IV

Irmos: I have heard the mystery of Thy dispensation, O Lord; I have considered Thy works, and have glorified Thy divinity.

Descending into the nethermost parts of the earth, O Christ, Thou didst raise up all the dead. Grant rest also to him [her] that hath departed from us, O Saviour, in that Thou art compassionate.

No one is without sin, save Thou alone, O Master. Wherefore, forgive the sin of him [her] that hath departed, and cause him [her] to dwell in Paradise.

Glory be to the Father, and to the Son, and to the Holy Spirit:

Hearken unto the voices of supplication which are offered unto Thee in the Church for the departed one, O Holy Trinity, and with the light which belongeth to Thy Godhead illumine his [her] soul, which hath been darkened by vain attachments.

Both now, and ever, and unto the ages of ages. Amen.

O most pure Virgin, without the seed of a man didst thou give birth to the perfect God and perfect Man, Who taketh away our sins. Him do thou beseech, O Lady, to grant peace to thy departed servant [handmaiden].

Canticle V

Irmos: Illumine us with Thy commandments, O Lord, and by Thine uplifted arm grant us Thy peace, O Lover of mankind.

O Christ God, Who hast authority over life and death, Grant rest unto him [her] that hath departed from us, for Thou, O Saviour, art the life and repose of all.

Placing all his [her] hope on Thee, O Saviour, he [she] that hath died hath departed from us. Do Thou, O Lord, take pity on him [her], as Thou art the greatly merciful God.

Glory be to the Father, and to the Son, and to the Holy Spirit:

O thrice-holy and hymned Master, enlighten us that entreat Thee, that we may receive heavenly peace; and in peaceful abodes number the soul that hath departed from things temporal in the hope of unending life.

Both now, and ever, and unto the ages of ages. Amen.

As thou art the Mother of our Saviour and God, O most pure Virgin Lady, entreat thy Son to deliver him [her] that hath reposed from a place on His left hand.

Canticle VI

Irmos: I pour forth my prayer unto the Lord, and to Him do I declare my woes, for my soul hath been filled with evils and my life hath drawn nigh unto hell, and like Jonah do I pray, Lead me up from corruption, O God!

Having despoiled hell, Thou didst raise up them that died in ages past, O Master; and now do Thou, O God, cause him [her] that hath departed from us to dwell in the bosom of Abraham, forgiving all his [her] transgressions, as Thou art full of mercy.

"O God, the commandment which Thou gavest me I did break, and thus I became mortal. But, O God, Who went down into the grave and raised the souls of past ages, Do not raise me up to torment, but to rest, O Master," the departed one doth cry out unto Thee through us, O greatly merciful One.

Glory be to the Father, and to the Son, and to the Holy Spirit:

We entreat Thee, O unoriginate Father, Son, and Holy Spirit: O God my Saviour, cast Thou not down to the bottom of hell the soul which hath been afflicted with the malice of this soul-tormenting world, and hath now departed to Thee, its Creator.

Both now, and ever, and unto the ages of ages. Amen.

O most pure one, like the dew upon the fleece did Christ our God descend upon thee from Heaven, setting the whole world afire, drying up all the streams of ungodliness, and Him do Thou beseech, that He grant rest to Thy departed servant [handmaiden].

Kontakion, in Tone VIII

With the saints give rest, O Christ, to the soul of Thy servant [handmaiden], where there is neither sickness, nor sorrow, nor sighing, but life everlasting.

Ikos

Thou alone art immortal, Who didst create and fashion man; but we mortals were formed of earth, and unto earth shall we return, as Thou Who madest me didst command and say unto me, For dust thou art and unto dust thou shalt return, whither all we mortals are going, making as a funeral dirge the song, Alleluia, alleluia, alleluia.

Canticle VII

Irmos: The children that went down from Judah, in Babylon once trod down the flame of the furnace by their faith in the Trinity, singing, O God of our fathers, blessed art Thou!

O Master Christ our God, when Thou shalt judge the world, take pity on the soul of Thy servant [handmaiden], whom Thou hast taken from us, and who crieth out, O God of our fathers, blessed art Thou!

In the delight of Paradise, wherein the souls of the righteous that have served Thee rejoice, do Thou, O Christ, number with them the soul of Thy servant [handmaiden], who sang, O God of our fathers, blessed art Thou!

Glory be to the Father, and to the Son, and to the Holy Spirit:

O Thou that didst save the three children of Judah in the fire and art hymned in three Persons, Deliver from eternal fire him [her] that hath departed, and that sang unto Thee faithfully, O God of our fathers, blessed art Thou!

Both now, and ever, and unto the ages of ages. Amen.

Isaiah called thee a staff, O pure one; Daniel called thee an unquarried mountain; Ezekiel called thee the door through which Christ did pass; and we extol thee, calling thee the true Theotokos.

Canticle VIII

Irmos: Madly did the Chaldean tyrant kindle the fire sevenfold for the divinely pious ones; but, beholding them saved by a higher power, he cried out to the Creator and Deliverer, Bless Him, ye children; chant unto Him, ye priests; ye people, exalt Him above all for ever.

"Having run the course, I flee to Thee, O Lord," the departed one crieth now. "Forgive my transgressions, O Christ God, and condemn me not when Thou shalt judge all, for faithfully have I cried unto Thee, All ye works of the Lord, praise the Lord, and exalt Him above all for ever!"

Though he [she] bore Thy yoke and light burden upon his [her] shoulders, yet, not always; even so, do Thou cause his [her] soul to dwell in the abode of Thy saints, O Master, for he [she] sang unto Thee, O Saviour Christ: Ye children, bless; ye priests, chant; ye people, exalt Him above all for ever!

Glory be to the Father, and to the Son, and to the Holy Spirit:

O holy and unoriginate Trinity, God the Father, Son, and Holy Spirit, number Thou the soul of Thy departed servant [handmaiden] among the choirs of the saints, and deliver it from eternal fire, that it may praise Thee, chanting for ever, O ye children, bless; ye priests, chant; ye people, exalt Him above all for ever!

Both now, and ever, and unto the ages of ages. Amen.

The choirs of the prophets foretold thee, O Virgin; for, gazing upon thee with clairvoyant eyes, one called thee a staff; another, a gate which faceth east; and yet another, a mountain unquarried by man. And we confess thee to be the true Theotokos, who gavest birth unto the God of all. Him do thou entreat, that He grant rest for ever unto him [her] that hath departed.

Canticle IX

Irmos: Heaven was terrified by it, and the ends of the earth were amazed that God appeared to men in the flesh, and that thy womb became more spacious than the heavens. Wherefore, the ranks of angels and men magnify thee, the Theotokos.

O Jesus, my Saviour and God, Thou didst take away the offense of Adam and didst taste death, that Thou mightest free man therefrom, O Thou Who art merciful. Wherefore, we beseech Thee, O Merciful One, As Thou art good, grant rest in Thy holy courts unto him [her] that hath departed, O Thou Who alone art all-good and merciful.

There is no man that hath not sinned, save Thou alone, O merciful Jesus Christ, Who takest away the sins of all the world. Wherefore, having cleansed Thy servant [handmaiden] of transgressions, commend him [her] to Thy holy courts, for Thou art the life and repose, the light and gladness, of all that have been well-pleasing unto Thee.

Glory be to the Father, and to the Son, and to the Holy Spirit:

All human nature marveled at how Thou, being the only-begotten Son of the unoriginate Father, didst take flesh of the Virgin through the activity of the Holy Spirit, and didst suffer as a man, that Thou mightest give life unto the dead. Wherefore, as Thou art good, we earnestly entreat Thee, In the land of the living do Thou number the soul of him [her] that hath departed from us.

Both now, and ever, and unto the ages of ages. Amen.

O most pure one, we call thee the Bride of the invisible Father, the Mother of the Son Who was incarnate of thee by the Holy Spirit; and we set thee forth as intercessor for thy departed servant [handmaiden]. For thee do we on earth have as our helper, and we magnify thee, singing with love.

¶ Then, It is truly meet ... (p. 294), and the Trisagion through to the Lord's Prayer. After For Thine is the kingdom ..., these troparia, in Tone VI:

O Christ, Who alone art the Creator of life and a truly unfathomable Abyss of goodness, Do Thou now vouchsafe Thy kingdom unto Thy servant [handmaiden], [N.], who hath now departed, for Thou alone hast immortality and an abundance of compassion.

Glory be to the Father, and to the Son, and to the Holy Spirit; both now, and ever, and unto the ages of ages. Amen.

O Lady, who gavest birth unto Jesus Christ, the Source of life and Redeemer of the world, Him do thou entreat, that He vouchsafe everlasting life unto thy servant [handmaiden], [N.], who hath now departed, for thou alone art the most renowned helper of Christians.

Then, Lord, have mercy [12], and this prayer:

REMEMBER, O Lord our God, Thy servant [handmaiden] who hath departed in the faith and hope of eternal life, our brother [sister], [N.], and, as Thou art good and lovest mankind, pardon his [her] sins and consume his [her] unrighteousness; release, remit and forgive all his [her] sins, voluntary and involuntary. Deliver him [her] from eternal torment and from the fire of Gehenna, and grant unto him [her] participation and enjoyment of Thine eternal blessings, which have been prepared for them that love Thee. For if [s]he sinned, yet [s]he did not renounce Thee and believed undoubtingly in Thee as God: the Father, the Son, and the Holy Spirit, glorified in Trinity, and confessed the Unity in Trinity and the Trinity in Unity in Orthodox fashion, even until his [her] last breath. Therefore, be merciful unto him [her], and impute his [her] faith in Thee instead of deeds and, as One gracious, grant unto him [her] rest with Thy saints. For there is no man who liveth and sinneth not, and Thou only art without sin, and Thy righteousness is righteousness for ever. For Thou alone art a God of mercy, and compassion, and love for mankind, and unto Thee do we ascribe glory, to the Father, and to the Son, and to the Holy Spirit; now, and ever, and unto the ages of ages. Amen.

People: Amen.

Priest: Wisdom! Most holy Theotokos, save us!

People: More honorable than the Cherubim, and incomparably more glorious than the Seraphim, thee who without corruption gavest birth to God the Word, the very Theotokos, thee do we magnify.

Priest: Glory to Thee, O Christ, our hope, glory to Thee.

People: Glory be to the Father, and to the Son, and to the Holy Spirit; both now, and ever, and unto the ages of ages. Amen.

Lord, have mercy. Thrice. Father, bless.

Priest: O Christ our true God, Who didst rise from the dead, through the prayers of Thy most pure Mother, of the holy, glorious and all-praised apostles, of our venerable and God-bearing fathers, and of all the saints, commend Thou the soul of Thy servant [handmaiden], [N.], who hath departed from us, to the habitations of the righteous; grant him [her] rest in the bosom of Abraham, number him [her] with the righteous, and have mercy upon us, for Thou art good and lovest mankind.

People: Amen.

And the priest says:

In a blessed falling asleep, grant, O Lord, eternal rest unto Thy departed servant [handmaiden], [N.], and make his [her] memory to be eternal.

¶ And those present sing thrice in farewell, Memory eternal! and depart to their own homes.

Reading the Psalter for the Departed

¶ In the Orthodox Church there exists from of old the pious custom to read the Psalter over the body of a deceased deacon, monastic or lay person.[1] The psalms are read continuously (except during those times when a Pannyhida or Litia is being served), from the conclusion of the Rite Following the Departure of the Soul from the Body until the funeral of the reposed, and in his memory after burial. This reading serves as prayer to the Lord for the reposed, comforts those grieving for the deceased, and directs their prayers for him to God. Any pious Christian may read the Psalter for the reposed, and those who do so perform a good work. The Psalter is read, standing, from a lectern at the west end of the coffin, which is so placed that the feet of the deceased person are to the east. The order of the reading is as follows: After the usual beginning (pp. 51–53), we say the First Kathisma. At the end of the first stasis, we say the **Glory . . .** , as indicated, except that, instead of the second **Glory be**, we say this prayer, thrice:

[1] The Four Gospels are read over the bodies of deceased priests and bishops.

Remember, O Lord, the soul of Thy departed servant [handmaiden], [N.] Bow.

Have mercy upon him [her], for whatever sins [s]he hath humanly committed, as Thou art a God Who lovest mankind. Bow.

Deliver him [her] from eternal torment. Bow.

Make him [her] a sharer of the Kingdom of Heaven. Bow.

And do what is profitable for his [her] soul. Bow.

¶ After the second stasis, we do likewise. After the third stasis, we say the **Trisagion** through to the **Lord's Prayer**, as usual, but instead of the troparia and prayer printed in the Psalter, we sing these troparia, in Tone VI:

O Christ, Who alone art the Creator of life and a truly unfathomable Abyss of goodness, Do Thou now vouchsafe Thy kingdom unto Thy servant [handmaiden], [N.], who hath now departed, for Thou alone hast immortality and an abundance of compassion.

Glory be to the Father, and to the Son, and to the Holy Spirit; both now, and ever, and unto the ages of ages. Amen.

O Lady, who gavest birth unto Jesus Christ, the Source of life and Redeemer of the world, Him do thou entreat, that He vouchsafe everlasting life unto thy servant [handmaiden], [N.], who hath now departed, for thou alone art the most renowned helper of Christians.

¶ Then, Lord, have mercy [12], and this prayer:

REMEMBER, O Lord our God, Thy servant [handmaiden] who hath departed in the faith and hope of eternal life, our brother [sister], [N.], and, as Thou art good and lovest mankind, pardon his [her] sins and consume his [her] unrighteousness; release, remit and forgive all his [her] sins, voluntary and involuntary. Deliver him [her] from eternal torment and from the fire of Gehenna, and grant unto him [her] participation and enjoyment of Thine eternal blessings, which have been prepared for them that love Thee. For if [s]he sinned, yet [s]he did not renounce Thee and believed undoubtingly in Thee as God: the Father, the Son, and the Holy Spirit, glorified in Trinity, and confessed the Unity in Trinity and the Trinity in Unity in Orthodox fashion, even until his [her] last breath. Therefore, be merciful unto him [her], and impute his [her] faith in Thee instead of deeds and, as One gracious, grant unto him [her] rest with Thy saints. For there is no man who liveth and sinneth not, and Thou only art without sin, and Thy righteousness is righteousness for ever. For Thou alone art a God of mercy, and compassion, and love for mankind, and unto Thee do we ascribe glory, to the Father, and to the Son, and to the Holy Spirit; now, and ever, and unto the ages of ages. Amen.

¶ Then the reading of the Psalter continues with O come, let us worship . . . , and the next kathisma.

After completing the entire Psalter:

If there is a priest,

IT is truly meet to bless thee, O Theotokos, ever-blessed and most pure, and the Mother of our God. More honorable than the Cherubim, and incomparably more glorious than the Seraphim; who without corruption gavest birth to God the Word, the very Theotokos, thee do we magnify. Prostration.

Priest: Glory to Thee, O Christ God, our hope, glory to Thee.

Choir (or Reader): Glory to the Father, and to the Son, and to the Holy Spirit; both now, and ever, and unto the ages of ages. Amen.

Lord, have mercy. Thrice. Father, bless.

Priest: O Christ our true God, Who didst rise from the dead, through the prayers of Thy most pure Mother, of the holy, glorious, and all-praised apostles, of our venerable and God-bearing fathers, and of all the saints, commend Thou the soul of Thy servant [handmaiden], [N.], who hath departed from us, to the habitations of the righteous; grant him [her] rest in the bosom of Abraham, number him [her] with the righteous, and have mercy upon us, for Thou art good and lovest mankind.

Choir: Amen.

Deacon (or Priest): In a blessed falling asleep, grant, O Lord, eternal rest unto Thy departed servant [handmaiden], [N.], and make his [her] memory to be eternal.

Choir: Eternal memory! Thrice.

> But if it be a layman, he says,

IT is truly meet to bless thee, O Theotokos, ever-blessed and most pure, and the Mother of our God. More honorable than the Cherubim, and incomparably more glorious than the Seraphim; who without corruption gavest birth to God the Word, the very Theotokos, thee do we magnify. Prostration.

Glory to the Father, and to the Son, and to the Holy Spirit; both now, and ever, and unto the ages of ages. Amen.

Lord, have mercy. Thrice. Bless, O Lord.

O LORD Jesus Christ, through the prayers of Thy most pure Mother, of our holy, venerable, and God-bearing fathers, and of all the saints, have mercy and grant rest unto the soul of Thy departed servant [handmaiden], [N.], unto unceasing ages, for Thou art good and lovest mankind. *Amen.*

Then the following is proclaimed, thrice:

To the servant [handmaiden] of God, [N.], Eternal memory!

Choir (or reader): Eternal memory! Thrice.

The Rite for Singing the Twelve Psalms

Which the venerable fathers of the desert were wont to sing day and night; concerning which, account is found in the books of the fathers and in the lives and sufferings of many saints. This rite was brought to Russia from the Holy Mountain by Dositheus, Archimandrite of the Kiev Caves.

If there is a priest, he says:

Blessed is our God, always; now, and ever, and unto the ages of ages. Amen.

If not, say with compunction:

Through the prayers of our holy fathers, O Lord Jesus Christ our God, have mercy upon us. Amen.

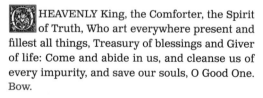

HEAVENLY King, the Comforter, the Spirit of Truth, Who art everywhere present and fillest all things, Treasury of blessings and Giver of life: Come and abide in us, and cleanse us of every impurity, and save our souls, O Good One. Bow.

¶ From Pascha until the Feast of the Ascension, instead of the prayer, **O heavenly King, the** troparion for Holy Pascha, **Christ is risen,** is

344

said, thrice. And from Ascension Day until Pentecost, begin with the Trisagion.

The Trisagion

Holy God, Holy Mighty, Holy Immortal, have mercy upon us. Thrice, with bows.

Glory be to the Father, and to the Son, and to the Holy Spirit; Both now, and ever, and unto the ages of ages. Amen. Bow.

O Most Holy Trinity, have mercy upon us. O Lord, wash away our sins. O Master, pardon our transgressions. O Holy One, visit and heal our infirmities for Thy Name's sake.

Lord, have mercy. Thrice.

Glory be to the Father, and to the Son, and to the Holy Spirit; Both now, and ever, and unto the ages of ages. Amen. Bow.

The Lord's Prayer

UR Father, Who art in heaven, hallowed be Thy Name. Thy kingdom come. Thy will be done, on earth as it is in heaven. Give us this day our daily bread. And forgive us our debts, as we forgive our debtors. And lead us not into temptation; but deliver us from the evil one.

If there is a priest, he says:

For Thine is the kingdom, the power, and the glory: of the Father, and of the Son, and of the Holy

Spirit; Now, and ever, and unto the ages of ages. *Amen.*

If not, say:

O Lord Jesus Christ, Son of God, have mercy upon us. Amen.

Then:

Glory be to the Father, and to the Son, and to the Holy Spirit; Both now, and ever, and unto the ages of ages. Amen.

Lord, have mercy. Thrice.

O come, let us worship God our King. Bow.

O come, let us worship and bow down before Christ, our King and God. Bow.

O come, let us worship and bow down before Christ Himself, our King and God. Bow.

Then, Psalm 26

THE Lord is my light, and my Saviour; whom then shall I fear? The Lord is the defender of my life; of whom then shall I be afraid? When they that had enmity against me, even mine enemies, and my foes, came nigh to eat up my flesh, they faltered and fell. Though a legion were laid against me, yet shall not my heart be afraid; and though there rise up war against me, yet will I put my trust in Him. One thing have I desired of the Lord, which I will require; even that I may dwell in the house of the Lord all the days of my life, to behold the fair beauty of the Lord, and to visit His holy temple. For in the day of my trouble He hath hidden me in His tabernacle; yea, in the secret place of His dwelling did He shelter me, and set me up upon a rock. And now, behold, He hath lifted up mine head above mine enemies; therefore have I gone round about and offered in His dwelling a sacrifice of praise and jubilation; I will sing and chant unto the Lord. Hearken, O Lord, unto my voice, with which I have cried, Have mercy upon me, and hear me. My heart hath said unto Thee, I will seek the Lord; my face hath sought Thee; Thy face, O Lord, will I seek. O turn not Thou Thy face from me, nor turn away from Thy servant in displeasure; be Thou my helper; reject me not, neither forsake me, O God, my Saviour. For my father and my mother have forsaken me, but the Lord taketh me up. Teach me a law, O Lord, in Thy way, and set me on the right path, because of mine enemies. Deliver me not over to the souls of them that afflict me, for false witnesses are risen up against me, and iniquity hath lied to itself. I believe that I shall see the goodness of the Lord in the land of the living. Wait thou on the Lord; be of good courage, and let thine heart stand firm, and wait thou on the Lord.

Psalm 31

LESSED are they whose iniquities are forgiven, and whose sins are covered. Blessed is the man unto whom the Lord imputeth no sin, and in whose lips there is no guile. Because I was silent, my bones consumed away, whereupon I called the whole day long. For Thy hand was heavy upon me day and night; I was brought to misery by a piercing thorn. I have acknowledged my transgression and my sin have I not hid; I said, Against myself will I confess my transgression unto the Lord, and so Thou forgavest the irreverence of my heart. For this shall everyone that is godly make his prayer unto Thee in a seasonable time; therefore in the great water-floods the waves shall not come nigh him. Thou art my refuge from the afflictions that overwhelm me; my Joy, deliver me from them that circle me round about. I will teach thee, and set thee on the way wherein thou shalt go; Mine eyes shall watch over thee. Be ye not like to horse and mule, which have no understanding, whose jaws must be bound with bit and bridle, if they be skittish unto thee. Many are the wounds of the sinful, but whoso putteth his trust in the Lord, mercy embraceth him on every side. Be glad in the Lord, and rejoice, O ye righteous, and sing praises, all ye that are true of heart.

Psalm 56

HAVE mercy upon me, O God, have mercy upon me, for in Thee hath my soul trusted, and in the shadow of Thy wings shall I hope, until wickedness be over-past. I will call unto the most high God, even unto the God that doeth good things for me. He sent from heaven and saved me, He hath given over to reproof them that trod me down; God hath sent forth His mercy, and His truth. And He hath delivered my soul from the midst of the lions' whelps; troubled, I slept my sleep. As for the children of men, their teeth are spears and arrows, and their tongue is a sharp sword. Be Thou exalted above the heavens, O God, and Thy glory above all the earth. They have laid a net for my feet, and pressed down my soul; they have digged a pit before me, and are fallen into it themselves. My heart is ready, O God, my heart is ready; I will chant and sing in my glory. Awake up, my glory; awake, psaltery and harp; I myself will awake right early. I will give thanks unto Thee among the people, O Lord; I will sing unto Thee among the nations. For the greatness of Thy mercy reacheth unto the heavens, and Thy truth even unto the clouds. Be Thou exalted above the heavens, O God, and Thy glory above all the earth.

¶ Then, the Trisagion through to the Lord's Prayer. And these troparia, in Tone I:

Make haste to open unto me Thy Fatherly embrace, for as the Prodigal I have wasted my life. In the unfailing wealth of Thy mercy, O Saviour, reject not my heart in its poverty, for with compunction I cry unto Thee, O Lord: Father, I have sinned against heaven and before Thee.

Glory be to the Father, and to the Son, and to the Holy Spirit:

When Thou shalt come to earth in glory, O God, all shall tremble; for a river of fire shall flow before the judgment seat, the books shall be opened, and secrets revealed. Then do Thou deliver me from the unquenchable fire, and vouchsafe me to stand at Thy right hand, O Judge most righteous.

Both now, and ever, and unto the ages of ages. Amen.

We all who in love have recourse to thy goodness know thee to be truly the Mother of God, who, even after having given birth, hath been shown to be Virgin; for thee do we sinners have as a protection, and thee have we obtained as salvation in the midst of temptations, who alone art most immaculate.

Then, Lord, have mercy [30], and O come, let us worship . . .

Psalm 33

I WILL bless the Lord at all times, His praise is ever in my mouth. In the Lord shall my soul be praised; let the meek hear, and be glad. O magnify the Lord with me, and we shall exalt His Name together. I sought the Lord and He heard me, yea, He delivered me out of all my troubles.

Come unto Him, and be enlightened, and your faces shall not be ashamed. This poor man cried and the Lord heard him, and saved him out of all his troubles. The angel of the Lord tarrieth round about them that fear Him, and delivereth them. O taste, and see, that the Lord is good; blessed is the man that trusteth in Him. O fear the Lord, all ye that are His saints, for they that fear Him lack nothing. The rich have lacked, and suffered hunger, but they that seek the Lord shall want no manner of thing that is good. Come, ye children, and hearken unto me; I will teach you the fear of the Lord. What man is he that lusteth to live, and would gladly see good days? Keep thy tongue from evil, and thy lips, that they speak no guile. Shun evil, and do good; seek peace, and pursue it. The eyes of the Lord are over the righteous, and His ears are open unto their prayers. But the countenance of the Lord is against them that do evil, to root out the remembrance of them from the earth. The righteous cried, and the Lord heard them, and delivered them out of all their troubles. The Lord is nigh unto them that are of a contrite heart, and will save such as be of an humble spirit. Many are the troubles of the righteous, but the Lord delivereth them out of all. The Lord keepeth all their bones; not one of them shall be broken. The death of sinners is evil, and they that hate the righteous shall sin greatly. The Lord will deliver the souls of His servants, and all they that put their trust in Him shall do no sin.

Psalm 38

I SAID, I will take heed to my ways, that I sin not with my tongue; I kept my mouth as it were with a bridle, when the sinner stood up against me. I was mute and held my peace; I kept silent, even from good words, and my sorrow was renewed. My heart grew hot within me, and while I was thus musing, the fire kindled; I spake with my tongue, O Lord, tell me mine end, and the number of my days, what it is, that I may know what is wanting to me. Behold, Thou hast made my days as it were a span long, and my existence is as nothing before Thee; verily, every man living is altogether vanity. Therefore man walketh as a shadow, and disquieteth himself in vain; he heapeth up riches, and knoweth not for whom he gathereth them. And now, who is my patient endurance? Is it not the Lord? Even my existence is from Thee. From all mine offenses deliver me; Thou hast made me a rebuke unto the foolish. I became dumb, and opened not my mouth, for it was Thy doing. Take Thy scourges from me, for I have fainted from the vehemence of Thy hand. With rebukes hast Thou chastened man for sin, and hast brushed his life away like a spider's web; yea, every man is but vanity. Hear my prayer, O Lord, and give ear unto my petition; hold not Thy peace at my tears. For I am a sojourner with Thee, and a pilgrim, as all my fathers were. O spare me, that I may recover my strength, before I go hence, and be no more.

Psalm 40

BLESSED is he that considereth the poor and needy; the Lord shall deliver him on the evil day. The Lord preserve him, and keep him alive, and bless him upon the earth, and deliver him not into the hands of his enemies. The Lord comfort him on his sickbed; Thou hast turned all his bed in his sickness. I said, Lord, have mercy on me; heal my soul; for I have sinned against Thee. Mine enemies spake evil of me, When shall he die, and his name perish? And if he came to see me, he spake vanity in his heart, he gathered iniquity to himself; he went forth and spake in like manner. All mine enemies whispered against me; even against me did they imagine this evil. They spread a slanderous word against me, Now that he sleepeth, he shall not rise up again. Yea, even mine own familiar friend, in whom I trusted, who did eat of my bread, hath lifted up his heel against me. But Thou, O Lord, have mercy upon me, and raise me up, and I shall pay them back. By this I know Thou favorest me, that mine enemy doth not triumph against me. But Thou hast taken my side by reason of my innocence, and hast established me before Thee for ever. Blessed be the Lord God of Israel from everlasting to everlasting. So be it. So be it.

¶ Then, the **Trisagion** through to the Lord's Prayer. And these troparia, in Tone IV:

Visit Thou my lowly soul, O Lord, which hath wasted all its life in sin. Receive and save me, as Thou didst the harlot.

Glory be to the Father, and to the Son, and to the Holy Spirit:

All my life have I shamefully squandered on harlots, wretch that I am, O Lord, and, like the Prodigal, I cry out in contrition: I have sinned, O heavenly Father, do Thou cleanse and save me! And disdain not me who have estranged myself from Thee, and who am now become a pauper because of my unfruitful works.

Both now, and ever, and unto the ages of ages. Amen.

Ye sinful and humble, let us now earnestly flee to the Theotokos, and let us fall down in repentance, crying out from the depths of our soul, O Lady, who hast had mercy upon us, make haste to help us, for we perish from the multitude of our transgressions. Turn not thy servants away empty, for thee do we have as our only hope.

Then, Lord, have mercy [30], and O come, let us worship . . .

Psalm 69

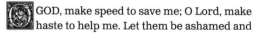GOD, make speed to save me; O Lord, make haste to help me. Let them be ashamed and

confounded that seek after my soul. Let them be turned backward and be ashamed that wish me evil. Let them for their reward be soon brought to shame that say over me, Well, well. Let all those that seek Thee be joyful and glad in Thee, O God, and let all such as delight in Thy salvation say always, The Lord be praised. But I am poor and needy, O God; help me! Thou art my helper and my redeemer, O Lord; make no long tarrying.

Psalm 70

IN Thee, O Lord, have I put my trust, let me never be confounded. Rescue me in Thy righteousness, and deliver me; incline Thine ear unto me, and save me. Be Thou unto me a defending God, and a strong-hold to save me, for Thou art my buttress and my safe haven. O my God, deliver me out of the hands of the sinner, out of the hands of the law-breaker and the offender. For Thou art the thing that I long for, O Lord; O Lord, Thou art my hope, even from my youth. Through Thee have I been holden up from the womb, from my mother's belly art Thou my protector; my praise shall be always of Thee. I am become as it were a spectacle unto many, but Thou art my strong helper. O let my mouth be filled with Thy praise, that I may sing unto Thy glory, and all day unto Thy majesty. Cast me not away in the time of old age; forsake me not when my strength faileth me. For mine enemies spake against me, and they that lay wait for my soul took their counsel together. They said, God hath forsaken him; persecute him, and take him, for there is none to deliver him. O my God, go not far from me; my God, haste Thee to help me. Let them be confounded and wiped out that are against my soul; let them be covered with shame and confusion that seek to do me evil. But I shall always hope in Thee, and will set myself to praise Thee more and more. My mouth shall speak of Thy righteousness, and all day of Thy salvation, because I have not learned to write. I will go forth in the strength of the Lord; O Lord, I will remember Thy righteousness only. O my God, which hath taught me from my youth up even until now, I will declare Thy wondrous works; yea, forsake me not, O my God, even unto mine old age, when I am gray-headed, until I have made known Thy strength unto every generation that is yet to come. Thy power and Thy righteousness, O God, are very high, for Thou hast done great things for me. O God, who is like unto Thee? O what great troubles and adversities hast Thou showed me! And yet didst Thou turn and revive me, and broughtest me up from the depths of the earth. Thou hast heaped Thy majesty upon me, and Thou hast returned to comfort me, and broughtest me up again from the depths of the earth. Therefore will I confess Thy truth to Thee among the people, O Lord, upon instruments of psalmody; I will sing unto Thee upon the harp, O God, Thou Holy One of Israel. My lips will be glad when I sing unto Thee, and so will my soul whom Thou hast delivered. My tongue also shall be occupied in Thy righteousness all the day long, when they are confounded and brought unto shame that seek to do me evil.

Psalm 76

WITH my voice I cried unto the Lord, even unto God with my voice, and He heard me. In the day of my trouble I reached out to God with my hands by night before Him, and I was not deceived; my soul refused to be comforted. I remembered God, and I was glad; I mused, and my spirit faltered. Mine eyes anticipated the morning watches; I was troubled and spake not. I considered the days of old, and remembered the years of ages past, and I pondered. By night I communed with mine own heart, and searched my soul. Will the Lord be contemptuous for ever, and will He be no more favorably disposed? Or will He cut off His mercy for ever, His word from generation to generation? Will God forget to be gracious, or will He withhold His loving-kindness in His displeasure? And I said, Now have I begun; this change is of the right hand of the Most High. I remembered the works of the Lord, for I will be mindful of Thy wonders from the beginning. And I will ponder all Thy works, and muse upon Thy undertakings. Thy way, O God, is in the sanctuary; who is so great a god as our God? Thou art the God that doest wonders; Thou hast declared Thy power among the people. With Thine arm hast Thou delivered Thy people, even the sons of Jacob and Joseph. The waters saw Thee, O God, the waters saw Thee, and were afraid; the depths were troubled. Great was the noise of the waters; the clouds gave voice, for Thine arrows shall pass. The voice of Thy thunder is in the wheel, Thy lightnings lit up the whole world; the earth trembled and shook. Thy ways are in the sea, and Thy paths in many waters, and Thy footsteps shall not be known. Thou leddest Thy people like sheep, by the hand of Moses and Aaron.

¶ Then, the Trisagion through to the Lord's Prayer. And these troparia, in Tone VI:

I think upon the dreadful day, and weep for my evil deeds. How shall I answer the immortal King? Or with what boldness shall I look upon the Judge, prodigal that I am? O compassionate Father, only-begotten Son and Holy Spirit, have mercy upon me!

Glory be to the Father, and to the Son, and to the Holy Spirit.

In the vale of tears, at the place which Thou hast appointed for when Thou shalt take Thy seat to render Thy righteous judgment, O Merciful One, condemn not my secret sins, nor put me to shame before the angels; but take pity on me, O God, and have mercy on me!

Both now, and ever, and unto the ages of ages. Amen.

The doors of compassion open unto us, O blessed Theotokos, for hoping in thee, let us not perish; but through thee may we be delivered from adversities, for thou art the salvation of the Christian race.

Then, Lord, have mercy [30], and O come, let us worship . . .

Then, the prayer of the poor man, when he is downcast, and poureth out his complaint before the Lord,

Psalm 101

HEAR my prayer, O Lord, and let my cry come unto Thee. Turn not Thy face from me; in the day of my trouble, incline Thine ear unto me; in the day when I call upon Thee, quickly hearken unto me. For my days have disappeared like smoke, and my bones are burnt up like kindling. My heart is smitten down, and withered, for I forgot to eat my bread. From the voice of my groaning hath my bone cleaved unto my flesh. I am become like a pelican in the wilderness, I was like an owl in the ruins. I have watched, and was even as it were a sparrow, that sitteth alone upon the house-top. Mine enemies reviled me all the day long, and they that praised me swore at me. For I have eaten ashes as it were bread, and mingled my drink with tears, Because of the face of Thine indignation and Thy wrath, for, having taken me up, Thou hast cast me down. My days are gone like a shadow, and I am withered like grass. But, Thou, O Lord, shalt endure for ever, and Thy remembrance is unto generation and generation. Thou shalt arise, and have mercy upon Zion, for it is time that Thou have mercy upon her, yea, the time is come. For Thy servants have been well pleased by the stones thereof, and they shall be merciful unto her dust. And the nations shall fear the Name of the Lord, and all the kings of the earth Thy glory. For the Lord shall build up Zion, and reveal Himself in His glory. He hath regarded the prayer of the humble, and hath not despised their petition. Let this be written for another generation, and a people yet to be born shall praise the Lord; for He hath looked down from the height of His sanctuary; out of heaven did the Lord behold the earth, to hear the moaning of such as are in shackles, to free the sons of the slain, to declare the Name of the Lord in Zion, and His praise in Jerusalem, when the people are gathered together, and the kings also, to serve the Lord. He answered Him in the way of his strength; the fewness of my days shalt Thou make known unto me. O take me not away in the midst of my days; as for Thy years, they endure throughout all generations. In the beginning, O Lord, hast Thou laid the foundation of the earth, and the heavens are the work of Thy hands.

They shall perish, but Thou shalt endure; yea, they all shall wax old as doth a garment, and as a vesture shalt Thou change them, and they shall be changed. But Thou art the same, and Thy years shall not fail. The sons of Thy servants shall abide, and their seed shall prosper for ever.

The Prayer of Manasseh, King of Judah

LORD Almighty, God of our fathers, Abraham, Isaac, and Jacob, and of their righteous seed; Who hast made heaven and earth, with all the ornament thereof; Who hast bound the sea by the Word of Thy commandment; Who hast shut up the deep, and sealed it by Thy terrible and glorious Name; Whom all men fear, and tremble before Thy power; for the majesty of Thy glory cannot be borne, and Thine angry threatening toward sinners is unbearable: but Thy merciful promise is immeasurable and unsearchable; for Thou art the most high Lord, of great compassion, long-suffering, very merciful, and repentest of the evils of men. Thou, O Lord, according to Thy great goodness hast promised repentance and forgiveness to them that have sinned against Thee: and of Thine infinite mercies hast appointed repentance unto sinners, that they may be saved. Thou therefore, O Lord, that art the God of the just, hast not appointed repentance to the just, as to Abraham, and Isaac, and Jacob, which have not sinned against Thee; but Thou hast appointed repentance unto me that am a sinner: for I have sinned above the number of the sands of the sea. My transgressions, O Lord, are multiplied: my transgressions are multiplied, and I am not worthy to behold and see the height of heaven for the multitude of mine iniquities. I am *so* bowed down with many iron bands, that I cannot lift up mine head, neither have any release: for I have provoked Thy wrath, and done evil before Thee: I did not Thy will, neither kept I Thy commandments: I have set up abominations, and have multiplied offences. Now therefore I bow the knee of mine heart, beseeching Thee of grace. I have sinned, O Lord, I have sinned, and I acknowledge mine iniquities: wherefore, I humbly beseech Thee, Forgive me, O Lord, forgive me, and destroy me not with mine iniquities. Be not angry with me for ever, by reserving evil for me; neither condemn me to the lower parts of the earth. For Thou art the God, even the God of them that repent; and in me Thou wilt show all Thy goodness: for Thou wilt save me, that am unworthy, according to Thy great mercy. Therefore I will praise Thee for ever all the days of my life: for all the hosts of the heavens do praise Thee, and Thine is the glory for ever and ever. Amen.

Then:

LORY to God in the highest, and on earth peace, good will among men. We praise Thee, we bless Thee, we worship Thee, we glorify

Thee, we give thanks unto Thee for Thy great glory. O Lord, heavenly King, God the Father Almighty; O Lord, the only-begotten Son, Jesus Christ; and O Holy Spirit. O Lord God, Lamb of God, Son of the Father, that takest away the sin of the world, have mercy upon us; Thou that takest away the sins of the world, receive our prayer; Thou that sittest at the right hand of the Father, have mercy upon us. For Thou only art Holy, Thou only art the Lord, Jesus Christ, to the glory of God the Father, Amen.

Every day will I bless Thee, and I will praise Thy Name for ever, yea, for ever and ever.

Vouchsafe, O Lord, to keep us this day without sin.

Blessed art Thou, O Lord, the God of our fathers, and praised and glorified is Thy Name for evermore. Amen.

Let Thy mercy, O Lord, be upon us, according as we have put our trust in Thee.

Blessed art Thou, O Lord; teach me Thy statutes.

Blessed art Thou, O Master; give me understanding of Thy statutes.

Blessed art Thou, O Holy One; enlighten me by Thy statutes.

O Lord, Thy mercy is for ever; despise not the works of Thy hands.

To Thee belongeth praise; to Thee belongeth song; to Thee belongeth glory, to the Father, and to the Son, and to the Holy Spirit; now, and ever, and unto the ages of ages. Amen.

Then,

The Prayer of St. Eustratius

EXULTING, I extol Thee, O Lord, for Thou hast regarded my lowliness and hast not left me fast in the hands of the enemy, but hast saved my soul from want. And now, O Master, let Thy hand cover me, and let Thy mercy come upon me, for my soul is troubled and pained over its departure from this, my wretched and defiled body, lest the wicked council of the adversary meet it and detain it in darkness, because of the many sins, known and unknown, which I have committed in this life. Be Thou merciful unto me, O Master, and let not my soul behold the dark visages of the evil demons, but let Thy radiant and most luminous angels receive it. Give glory to Thy holy Name, and by Thy might lead me up to Thy divine judgment seat. When my time cometh to be judged, let not the hand of the prince of this world seize me to drag me down to the abyss of hell, but stand Thou before me and be my Saviour and Helper, for these bodily torments are gladness for Thy servants. Have mercy, O Lord, upon my soul, which hath been defiled by the passions of this life, and receive it purified by repentance and confession, for blessed art Thou unto the ages of ages. Amen.

¶ Then, the Trisagion through to the Lord's Prayer. And these troparia, in Tone VIII:

With Thy compassionate gaze behold my low estate, O Lord, for I have gradually wasted my life and there is no salvation for me in my deeds. Wherefore, I pray Thee, With Thy compassionate gaze, O Lord, behold my low estate and save me.

Glory be to the Father, and to the Son, and to the Holy Spirit:

My time cometh to an end and Thy dread tribunal is made ready. My life passeth by; judgment awaiteth me. Fiery torment and the unquenchable flame are my lot. Extinguish its power and grant me a torrent of tears, O Thou that desirest that all men should be saved.

Both now, and ever, and unto the ages of ages. Amen.

O Thou, Who for our sakes wast born of the Virgin, and didst endure crucifixion, Who didst cast down death by death and, as God, hast shone forth the Resurrection, Disdain not them that Thou hast created with Thy hand; but show forth Thy love for mankind, O Merciful One; accept the Theotokos, who bore Thee and doth pray for us, and save Thou Thy despairing people, O our Saviour.

Lord, have mercy [30].

¶ Here, during the Great Fast, except on Saturdays and Sundays, as well as during the other fasts, and also during Cheesefare Week on Wednesday and Friday, we say:

The Prayer of Our Holy Venerable Father, Ephraim the Syrian

O Lord and Master of my life, take from me the spirit of sloth, despondency, avarice and idle talk. Prostration.

But give, rather, the spirit of chastity, humility, patience and love to Thy servant. Prostration.

Yea, O Lord and King, grant me to see mine own faults, and not to judge my brother, for blessed art Thou unto the ages of ages. Amen. Prostration.

¶ Then twelve bows, saying the Prayer of the Publican, God be merciful to me a sinner, after which the entire Prayer of St. Ephraim is said again, with one prostration. Then we continue, as usual, with More honorable than the Cherubim.

MORE honorable than the Cherubim, and incomparably more glorious than the Seraphim; who without corruption gavest birth to God the Word, the very Theotokos, thee do we magnify.

Glory . . . , Both now . . . , Lord, have mercy [Thrice]. Bless, O Lord.

¶ If there is a priest, he concludes accordingly. If not, the ending is as follows:

LORD Jesus Christ, Son of God, through the prayers of Thy most pure Mother, by the power of the precious and life-giving Cross, and of the holy bodiless Powers, and of our venerable and God-bearing Fathers, and of the holy Prophet David, and of all the Saints, have mercy upon me and save me a sinner, for Thou art good and lovest mankind. *Amen.*

Directions for Those Wishing to Read the Twelve Psalms in the Cell:

¶ During the Holy Quadragesima: In place of the Hours and Vespers, we sing nine psalms. In place of Great Compline, the remaining three. But at night, all 12 psalms, and the dismissal, as above.

¶ Outside of the Holy Quadragesima: In place of the Hours, we sing the first six psalms. In place of Vespers and Compline, the last six. But in the night (i.e., for Matins), we sing 12 psalms, and we perform the Lesser Dismissal,

LORD Jesus Christ, through the prayers of Thy most pure Mother, of our holy, venerable, and God-bearing fathers, and of all the saints, have mercy upon us and save us, for Thou art good and lovest mankind. Amen.

Appendix

The Numbering of the Psalms

Between the Septuagint numbering of the psalms and that given in the Hebrew there is usually a difference of one, the Hebrew figure normally being one greater. The Vulgate, Church Slavonic, and the Douay-Rheims use the Greek numbering; the Authorized (King James) and most modern English translations follow the Hebrew. Additionally, for those psalms which have a superscription in the Hebrew, the superscription is counted as Verse 1 in the Greek, Vulgate, and Church Slavonic.

Greek	Hebrew
1–8	1–8
9:2–21	9
9:22–39	10
10–112	Add one to the number of each psalm
113:1–8	114
113:9–26	115
114	116:1–9
115	116:10–19
116–145	Add one to the number of each psalm
146	147:1–11
147	147:12–20
148–150	148–150